Reclaiming Romanticism

Environmental Cultures Series

Series Editors:

Greg Garrard, University of British Columbia, Canada
Richard Kerridge, Bath Spa University

Editorial Board:

Frances Bellarsi, Université Libre de Bruxelles, Belgium
Mandy Bloomfield, Plymouth University, UK
Lily Chen, Shanghai Normal University, China
Christa Grewe-Volpp, University of Mannheim, Germany
Stephanie LeMenager, University of Oregon, USA
Timothy Morton, Rice University, USA
Pablo Mukherjee, University of Warwick, UK

Bloomsbury's *Environmental Cultures* series makes available to students and scholars at all levels the latest cutting-edge research on the diverse ways in which culture has responded to the age of environmental crisis. Publishing ambitious and innovative literary ecocriticism that crosses disciplines, national boundaries, and media, books in the series explore and test the challenges of ecocriticism to conventional forms of cultural study.

Titles available:
Bodies of Water, Astrida Neimanis
Cities and Wetlands, Rod Giblett
Civil Rights and the Environment in African-American Literature, 1895–1941, John Claborn
Climate Change Scepticism, Greg Garrard, George Handley, Axel Goodbody, Stephanie Posthumus
Climate Crisis and the 21st-Century British Novel, Astrid Bracke
Colonialism, Culture, Whales, Graham Huggan
Ecocriticism and Italy, Serenella Iovino
Fuel, Heidi C. M. Scott

Literature as Cultural Ecology, Hubert Zapf
Nerd Ecology, Anthony Lioi
The New Nature Writing, Jos Smith
The New Poetics of Climate Change, Matthew Griffiths
This Contentious Storm, Jennifer Mae Hamilton
Climate Change Scepticism, Greg Garrard, Axel Goodbody, George B. Handley and Stephanie Posthumus

Forthcoming Titles:
Ecospectrality, Laura White
Teaching Environmental Writing, Isabel Galleymore
Radical Animism, Jemma Deer
Cognitive Ecopoetics, Sharon Lattig
Eco-Digital Art, Lisa FitzGerald
Environmental Cultures in Soviet East Europe, Anna Barcz
Weathering Shakespeare, Evelyn O'Malley
Imagining the Plains of Latin America, Axel Pérez Trujillo Diniz
Ecocriticism and Turkey, Meliz Ergin

Reclaiming Romanticism

Towards an Ecopoetics of Decolonization

Kate Rigby

BLOOMSBURY ACADEMIC
LONDON • NEW YORK • OXFORD • NEW DELHI • SYDNEY

BLOOMSBURY ACADEMIC
Bloomsbury Publishing Plc
50 Bedford Square, London, WC1B 3DP, UK
1385 Broadway, New York, NY 10018, USA
29 Earlsfort Terrace, Dublin 2, Ireland

BLOOMSBURY, BLOOMSBURY ACADEMIC and the Diana logo
are trademarks of Bloomsbury Publishing Plc

First published in Great Britain 2020
This paperback edition published in 2021

Copyright © Kate Rigby, 2020

Kate Rigby has asserted her right under the Copyright, Designs
and Patents Act, 1988, to be identified as Author of this work.

For legal purposes the Acknowledgements on p. x–xiv constitute
an extension of this copyright page.

Cover design: Burge Agency
Cover image © Shutterstock

This work is published open access subject to a Creative Commons
Attribution-NonCommercial-NoDerivatives 4.0 International licence
(CC BY-NC-ND 4.0, https://creativecommons.org/licenses/by-nc-nd/4.0/).
You may re-use, distribute, and reproduce this work in any medium for
non-commercial purposes, provided you give attribution to the copyright
holder and the publisher and provide a link to the Creative Commons licence.

Bloomsbury Publishing Plc does not have any control over, or responsibility for,
any third-party websites referred to or in this book. All internet addresses given in
this book were correct at the time of going to press. The author and publisher
regret any inconvenience caused if addresses have changed or sites have
ceased to exist, but can accept no responsibility for any such changes.

A catalogue record for this book is available from the British Library.

A catalog record for this book is available from the Library of Congress.

ISBN: HB: 978-1-4742-9059-3
       PB: 978-1-3502-4326-2
     ePDF: 978-1-4742-9061-6
    eBook: 978-1-4742-9060-9

Series: Environmental Cultures

Typeset by Integra Software Services Pvt. Ltd.

To find out more about our authors and books visit www.bloomsbury.com
and sign up for our newsletters.

For

Robert Hartley

Contents

Acknowledgements	x
Introduction	1
1 'Come forth into the light of things': Contemplative ecopoetics	23
2 'Season of mists and mellow fruitfulness': Affective ecopoetics	53
3 'piping in their honey dreams': Creaturely ecopoetics	83
4 'the wrong dream': Prophetic ecopoetics	113
5 'Deeper tracks wind back': Decolonial ecopoetics	149
Postscript: Ecopoetics beyond the page	191
Notes	195
Works Cited	209
Index	231

Acknowledgements

Any work of scholarship based on long years of research, multiple presentations, sharing of drafts and seemingly endless rewriting surely deserves to be classified as 'sympoetical', to use a felicitous phrase coined by the early German Romantic Friedrich Schlegel. In the co-production of this book, I am indebted to many more people than I can name. Among them are the students with whom I have pondered some of the poems discussed here as well as participants in the research seminars and conferences where I have tried out my readings and reflections. Since 2015, these have taken place in the UK and elsewhere in Europe, notably at Cardiff University, Durham University, Warwick University, Augsburg University, Stavanger University and the Goethe University in Frankfurt, and at the 2016 ASLE-UK-I Postgraduate Conference, the 2016 international conference on Zoopoetics and Environmental Poetics and the 2017 and 2019 conferences of the British Association for Romanticism Studies. Thanks to my generous hosts, panel convenors and interlocutors on these occasions, especially Aidan Tynan, Jamie Castell, Kerstin Oloff, Daniel Finch-Race, Tom Bristow, Catriona Ní Dhúill, James Hodkinson, Hubert Zapf, Christopher Schliefake, Roman Bartosch, Dolly Jørggensen, Magne Drangeid, Claudia Lillge, Gisela Ecker, Michelle Poland, Adeline Johns-Putra, Frederike Middelhof, Sebastian Schönbeck, Mark Lussier, Susan Oliver, Jeremy Davies, Tess Somerville, Joanna Taylor, Erin Lafford, Amelia Dale, Tim Fulford, Simon Kövesi and John Goodridge.

Research towards this book was generously supported by a Marie S. Curie Co-fund Fellowship and by a grant from the Alexander von Humboldt Foundation, which enabled me to spend a glorious six months at the Freiburg Institute of Advanced Studies in the second half of 2015. For this, I am also indebted to the support of Evi Zemanek and Hubert Zapf.

The initial stimulus for this project arose from my participation in the Australian ecological humanities research network throughout the first decade of new millennium. Curating conversations among environmental historians, anthropologists, ecophilosophers, cultural geographers, social ethnographers and ecocritics, in pubs, galleries, museums and around the campfire, together with academic seminars and symposia, this network also created a space for dialogue and collaboration between eco-humanities researchers and natural scientists, especially conservation biologists, ecologists and climatologists (Rigby 2019b). Among those who contributed most significantly to the ideas that have made their meandering way into this book are Deborah Bird Rose, Val Plumwood, Freya Mathews, Libby Robin, Tom Griffiths and Christine Hansen. Climatologist Will Steffen, a strong supporter of the eco-humanities at the ANU, introduced many of us to the controversial concept of the Anthropocene, while Dave Griggs and Amanda Lynch at Monash helped me to understand more about the science of climate change and the difficulties of anticipating its impacts. For conversations about ecology and the arts, I am grateful to fellow members of the Kangaloon collective not already named, especially Jim Hatley and Linda Williams. Many thanks also to Anne Elvey, Norm Habel, Constant Mews, Kevin Hart, Janet Morgan and Deborah Guess, for inspiration and guidance in my engagement with biblical texts and traditions, and to Elyse Rider and Rabbi Jonathan Keren Black, for links to Australia's vibrant interfaith ecology scene. For conversations around ecopoetics, specifically in an Australian context, I am indebted to Martin Harrison, Stuart Cooke, Michael Farrell, Peter Boyle, Luke Fischer, Mark Tredinnick, Peter Minter, Philip Mead, Jennifer Coralie and (once again) Anne Elvey.

Since moving to Bath Spa University, I have been introduced to new dimensions of the environmental humanities, thanks to my colleagues Owain Jones, Sian Sullivan, Mike Hannis, Paul Reid-Bowen and Sam Walton. I have also valued opportunities for ongoing ecocritical conversations at closer quarters with Richard Kerridge, Terry Gifford, Sue Edney and Axel Goodbody, as well as with David Higgins, Pippa Marland, David Farrier and Julian Wolfreys (among others). Thanks, too, to John Strachan for conversations about William Wordsworth in those odd moments when he could be winkled away from his duties as Bath Spa's pro-vice-chancellor (Research and Enterprise) and also for his support for me in this role.

For invaluable comments on draft chapters, I am very grateful to Libby Robin, Anne Elvey, Kevin Hart and Philip Mead, and on the manuscript as a whole, to series editor Richard Kerridge. Many thanks also to Helen Goodman at BSU for research assistance in the final stages. Needless to say, any remaining errors are entirely my own. I am very grateful to Richard and Greg Garrard for the opportunity to publish in this series, and to David Avital, Lucy Brown and all the team at Bloomsbury for seeing the book into press.

Among the innumerable other-than-human entities that have contributed to the *sympoiesis* of this book, I would like to honour in particular the Merri Creek, which flows into the Yarra River in the heart of Melbourne. In the inaugural issue of the journal that I co-founded with Freya Mathews and Sharon Pfueller, *PAN* (*Philosophy Activism Nature*), we included an extract from John Anderson's book-length poem *the forest set out like the night* (1995), which celebrates this little waterway. With John, then, I join in praise of:

> the Merri Creek saying the right things
> over and over …
>
> (2000: 22)

At the same time, I am mindful that whatever the Merri has had to say over the millennia will have been received differently through the cultural prisms of diverse human listeners. Those who have had longest to learn her aqueous tongue are the Wurundjeri, whose Country the Merri helped to shape, and from whom nineteenth-century colonizers from far distant climes learnt to hail her as such: 'Merri Merri', 'many rocks'. In honouring the Merri, then, I would also like to pay my respects to Wurundjeri Elders, past, present and future.

I would also like to acknowledge all those who continue to care for the Merri and the multispecies communities she enlivens. Among them is Freya Mathews, an erstwhile pilgrim to her hidden source (2003), to whom I am indebted for the photo that graces the cover of the book. It was taken at the CERES urban environment park, to which I return in the second chapter. To me, it signals emerging possibilities, in the shadow of all that is summoned by the electrical power pylon in the background, of social and ecological healing as an ongoing praxis of decolonization. In that spirit, this book culminates with my own endeavour to attend to what contemporary Wiradjuri poet Jeanine Leane has to say about another waterway, the Molonglo at Gundagai, and I am profoundly grateful for her generous permission to cite and, however inadequately, to respond to her words here.

Over the past few years of seemingly endless writing and rewriting, walks with the gracefully ageing Laska have helped to keep me moderately sane.

The book is dedicated to my human partner of forty years, Robert Hartley, without whom none of this would have been possible.

Excerpts from the following publications have been incorporated into different chapters of this book in amended form, with kind permission from the publishers:

'Writing in the Anthropocene: Idle Chatter or Ecoprophetic Witness?' Ecological Humanities Corner, *Australian Humanities Review* Issue 47 (November 2009).

'Gernot Böhme's Ecological Aesthetics of Atmosphere', in A. Goodbody and K. Rigby (eds), *Ecocritical Theory: New European Approaches*, 139–52, Charlottesville: University of Virginia Press, 2011.

'"Come forth into the light of things": Material Spirit and Negative Ecopoetics', in G. C. Stallings, M. Asensi and C. Good (eds), *Material Spirit: Religion and Literature Intranscendent*, 111–28, New York: Fordham University Press, 2014.

'Literature, Ethics, and Bushfire in Australia', in J. Adamson and M. Davis (eds), *Humanities for the Environment: Integrated Knowledges and New Constellations of Practice*, 210–24, London: Routledge, 2016.

'"Piping in their honey dreams": Towards a Creaturely Ecopoetics', in F. Middelhof, S. Schönbeck, R. Borgards and C. Gersdorf (eds), *Texts, Animals, Environments: Zoopoetics and Ecopoetics*, 281–95, Freiburg i.B.: Rombach, 2019.

For poetry permissions I am grateful to the following authors and/or their publishers:

Jordie Albiston for 'Lamentations' from *XIII Poems* (2013).

Anne Elvey for 'Post(?)colonial' from *White on White* (2018), and, with 5 Islands Press, for 'Claimed by Country I, II and III' from *Kin* (2014).

Kevin Hart, with Notre Dame University Press, for 'That Bad Summer' from *Wild Track* (2015).

HarperCollins for 'Dust' by Judith Wright from *Collected Poems* (1994) and poems by David Campbell from *Collected Poems* (1989).

Jeanine Leane for 'Kumbilor, hill in my Country', 'Tracks Wind Back' and 'River Memory' from *Walk Back Over* (2018).

Tim Lilburn, with McClelland and Stewart, for 'End of August' from *The Names* (2016).

Curtis Brown for poems by John Clare from *John Clare: A Critical Edition of the Major Works* (1984).

Natasha Trethewey, with Greywolf Press, for 'Carpenter Bee' by Natasha Trethewey © 1998, 2000.

Norton & co. and the Audre Lorde Estate for 'The Bees' by Audre Lorde © 1997, 2000.

When this book was already in press, Australia began to burn as never before. As I write this final acknowledgement, the fires are burning still, currently covering an area almost the size of England. Thankfully, only a small number of human lives have been lost thus far, but thousands have been rendered homeless, and some billion animals have perished (infinitely more if insects are factored in), possibly propelling some species over the brink of extinction and further compromising damaged ecosystems. This is a particularly grim instance of those sentinel events, such as I discussed in my last book, *Dancing with Disaster*, that are proliferating worldwide, bearing witness to the ecocidal trajectory of today's fossil-fuelled industrial-capitalist societies. Parts of this book are bound to have come out differently had they been written in the still uncertain aftermath of this eco-catastrophe. As it is, I wish to remember the unhoused and injured, those who have died and those who mourn, and to acknowledge, with gratitude, the efforts of all who are endeavouring to protect, tend and support those, human and otherwise, most immediately afflicted. With this book, I join in solidarity with those who are seeking to voice and heed the call issuing from this truly apocalyptic conflagration: a call, that is, for a profound transformation, at once decolonial and ecological, in our relations with one another, other others, and the ravaged Earth in these ever-more perilous times.

Bath, January 2020

Introduction

> Only now is Antiquity arising. ... The remains of ancient times are but the specific stimuli for the formation of Antiquity. ... It is the same in the case of Classical literature as it is with Antiquity; it is not actually given to us – it is not at hand (*vorhanden*) – rather, it is yet to be engendered by us. Only through assiduous and inspired study of the Ancients might a Classical literature arise before us – one that the Ancients themselves did not have.
>
> (Novalis 1960: 640–42; my trans.)

Romanticism, decolonization and ecopoetics

The question of how to inherit the cultural legacies of former times comes into critical focus when continuity can no longer be taken for granted. This is undoubtedly the case for people today, who are struggling to orient themselves in the face of massive change and uncertainty on numerous fronts, as the weather grows weirder, wildlife dwindles and many places become strange or even unliveable. Yet it was also true for those Europeans in the late eighteenth century, whose inherited notions of 'nature', 'culture' and society were being challenged by new scientific discoveries, inventions and modes of production; encounters with so-called 'primitive' peoples, whose lifeways provided purchase for European self-critique (whilst also being massively disrupted as a consequence of colonization); and an efflorescence of emancipatory political movements of various stripes. The resultant sense of living at a time of rupture contributed to the emergence of the self-consciously modern hermeneutic sensibility exemplified in the above quotation from Novalis' 1798 essay on the neoclassical turn of his renowned older contemporary, F. W. Goethe. Novalis' insistence on the need for both 'assiduous' attention and 'inspired' interpretation in our reception of earlier literatures, recognizing that cultural legacies are always (co-)constructed after the event, is one of the many facets of European Romanticism that I seek to reclaim for the perilous present in this book. To begin with, it informs my approach to the very question of Romantic inheritances. If, for the generation that would subsequently become known as 'Romantic' (or 'Early Romantic', in the case of Novalis and friends in Jena in the 1790s), the 'study of the Ancients' was to give rise to a 'Classical literature... that the Ancients themselves did not have', then we must acknowledge in turn that our own study of Novalis and his contemporaries on both sides of the Channel (like that of previous generations of Romanticism scholars) will inevitably produce a 'Romantic literature' that the 'Romantics' (most of whom did not think of themselves as such) did not have.

This is not to say that the work of reclamation in which I am engaged here is intended to produce yet another account, however self-consciously qualified as an interpretive construct, of Romanticism *per se*. On the contrary: my starting point is that Romanticism, understood as a defined 'movement', does not exist outside of the pages of literary historiography. The flurry of exploration, experimentation, agitation, reflection and creation across diverse fields of activity that was going in northwestern Europe around 1800, fanning out to other parts of the world during the course of the nineteenth century and beyond, took diverse forms and had divergent tendencies. These have been variously identified and evaluated by successive ecocritics over the past thirty years or so.[1] In the landmark early ecocritical work of Jonathan Bate (1991), British Romanticism was hailed as the source of a distinctively left-green 'environmental tradition' extending from William Wordsworth to William Morris, whilst for Lawrence Buell (1995), Thoreau's writing was exemplary of a North American 'environmental imagination' of a more deep ecological hue. These were wholly affirmative accounts, and there were many more besides.[2] Unsurprisingly, more critical perspectives were soon being voiced, including in my own earlier work on European Romanticism (2004).[3] In the meantime, however, I have become troubled by the summary dismissal of Romanticism *per se* that has become commonplace among ecocritics and ecopoets, who are at pains to dissociate themselves from such allegedly 'romantic' misdemeanours as individualism, sentimentalism and an anachronistic hankering after either pastoral idylls or sublime wilderness. Such tendencies, I would agree, are problematic, and they can certainly be identified in some instances of Romantic thought and literature. As much recent Romanticist scholarship has amply demonstrated, however, there are also countervailing tendencies that were historically salient and remain of signal value from a contemporary perspective. These include, for example, the links with Buddhism traced by Mark Lussier (2011), the 'ecology of wonder' explored by Louise Economides (2016) and the emancipatory geopolitics that J. A. Hubbell (2018) identifies in the work of Byron.[4]

Reclaiming Romanticism extends this new phase of sympathetic re-evaluation of key aspects of the heterogeneous inheritance of European Romanticism with a view to delineating a decolonizing ecopoetics for our own time of multifaceted rupture. This entails a reconsideration not only of particular works of British Romantic verse, viewed within the wider frame of European Romantic thought and literature, but also of the significantly different afterlives of European Romanticism in the new worlds of North America and Australia. This is explored further by bringing Romantic ecopoetics into conversation with the verse of American and Australian writers from the mid-twentieth century to the present. Crucially, I also consider how the decolonizing ecopoetics that I trace in their work, and its Romantic antecedents, might be translated into forms of ecopolitical praxis beyond the page.

The concept of 'decolonization', upon which this discussion is premised, is bio-inclusive, in that it concerns relations of domination obtaining between humans and nonhumans, in addition to (and often in connection with) those that obtain among humans, especially on the basis of race, class and gender.[5] In this, I draw on Val Plumwood's ecopolitical analysis of what she termed the 'logic of colonisation' (1993), in conjunction with Deborah Bird Rose's proposals for an 'ethics of decolonization' (2004).[6] Integrating feminist, socialist and postcolonial critiques of hegemonic social relations with the radical ecological critique of human domination of 'nature', Plumwood argued that all these forms of frequently (albeit not necessarily or intrinsically) interlinked oppression were grounded in a conceptual structure of 'hierarchical dualism'. Key features of hierarchical dualism, in her analysis, include 'backgrounding' the independent interests and agency of the subordinate group and the denial of dependence upon their services on the part of the dominant one; the refusal to recognize any similarities between the dominant and subordinate groups in favour of a 'hyperseparated' construction of their differences ('radical exclusion'); the definition of the subordinate group in terms of lack vis-à-vis the valued traits of the dominant one ('incorporation'); a disregard for differences among members of the subordinate group ('homogenisation'); and the accordance of value to them primarily or exclusively as a means to an end ('instrumentalism') (41–59).[7] While Plumwood's own work was primarily ecofeminist in orientation, Rose's 'ethics for decolonisaton' arose from her work with First Nations Australians, especially with communities in and around Yarralin, Lingara, Pigeon Hole and Daguragu in the Northern Territory, and Wallaga Lake and Narooma in New South Wales. Rose's analysis of the entanglement of Aboriginal dispossession with environmental degradation brings Aboriginal ontologies into conversation with the philosophical ethics of Emmanuel Levinas (1996), especially as read though, and in conjunction with, the post-Holocaust philosophy of James Hatley (2000). For Rose,

> The ethical challenge of decolonization illuminates a ground for powerful presence. Against domination it asserts relationality, against control it asserts mutuality, against hyperseparation it asserts connectivity, and against claims that rely on an imagined future it asserts engaged responsiveness in the present.
> (2004: 213)

This perspective is avowedly countermodern, putting pressure on linear narratives of historical progress, whilst resisting the temptation to idealize the past. As such, it also highlights the difficulty and incompletion of decolonization as an ongoing process with uncertain outcomes. Acknowledging other-than-human agencies and interests operating across vast reaches of time and space, this approach affords a way of integrating the human-centred concerns with social justice animating postcolonial criticism with the 'dehumanizing' dimensions of the type of Anthropocene criticism adumbrated by Timothy Clark (2015: 115–38).[8]

In re-evaluating Romanticism through a decolonial lens, I draw also on a range of other approaches within the wider field of the environmental humanities, including ecoreligious studies, multispecies studies and biosemiotics, in order to identify within Romantic verse particular ecopoetic arts of resistance to hegemonic constructions of human subjectivity and instrumentalizing constructions of 'nature'. Such arts of resistance might be considered a mode of 'culture-critical metadiscourse', to recall Hubert Zapf's theory of 'cultural ecology', motivating 'a radical self-examination of prevailing cultural systems from an overarching ecological perspective of individual and collective survival and sustainability' (2016: 103). In this way, I argue, Romantic poetry harbours potentials for a decolonizing praxis, pitched against both human domination of nonhuman others and the domination of some humans by others, especially, in the case of settler nations, Indigenous and enslaved peoples by colonial powers. For that potential to be realized, however, it is also necessary to put pressure on the culturally specific and historically contingent assumptions about human relations with 'nature' that were exported to the colonies, including through the medium of Romantic verse: Romantic ecopoetics, in other words, must itself be decolonized. This in turn requires more inclusive conversations, a deepened dialogue between Indigenous and non-Indigenous writers, in order to discern alternative modes of perceiving, articulating and embodying our interrelationships with one another and other others, and with our ecologically imperilled earthly environs.

The decolonizing ecopoetics that I explore in this book is not tied to any particular form or style of poetic writing. I share with Stuart Cooke (2013) the view that what Philip Mead describes as the 'resistance to easily communicable "meanings" ' (Mead 2008: 6), the source of much of the pleasure of poetry for many readers, can also be ecopolitically salient. In particular, I argue in the first chapter that the propensity of poetry in its more-or-less unconventional uses of language to trip us up as we read along, demanding that we slow down and accept that not all it has to say to us is readily within our grasp, is crucial to its capacity to entrain a more contemplative way of being in the world. In my analysis, however, whatever ecopolitical efficacy might accrue to particular poetries beyond the confines of the literary sphere should be sought not primarily in their formal characteristics but rather in the wider networks in which they are received and through which their meanings are activated. The argument of, and for, form is overstated when, for instance, Angus Fletcher asserts, 'Underneath the bipolar structure of the couplet their always lurks a desire to define, to enclose, to delimit' (2004: 35). Heroic couplets might well have become rather hackneyed by the late eighteenth century (Blake, Wordsworth and Coleridge certainly thought so). But it is by no means self-evident that their deployment as a poetic device is necessarily politically suspect. More generally, I worry that much current discussion of ecopoetics remains beholden to the ideology of the avant-garde, according to which the rupturing of the aesthetic conventions of lyrical language and traditional forms of versification is an imperative of ecopolitical correctness.

While the advocacy for avant-garde ecopoetics generally takes its cue from the Modernists' self-professed break with Romanticism, a commitment to formal experimentation is itself part of the Romantic heritage: explicitly so, for example, in Wordsworth's 1798 Preface to the *Lyrical Ballads* (a title that was itself an affront to poetic convention), which explicitly recommends the poems included in this volume to their adventurous readers as 'experiments' (1974: vol. 1, 116). This is not to say that such experiments are not worthwhile or to deny that the formal properties of poetic texts carry their own semantic significance, as many contributors to the burgeoning field of ecopoetics have shown.[9] However, progressive perspectives can be mediated through a variety of poetic forms, and different kinds of poetry will resonate better with some readerships than others. As Jonathon Skinner observed in his contribution to the inaugural edition of his journal *ecopoetics*, any writer 'who wants to engage poetry with more-than-human life has no choice but to resist simply, and instrumentally, stepping over language' (Skinner 2001b: 105). In his editorial statement, Skinner nonetheless affirmed the diversity of ecopoetic writing in its capacity to 'subvert the endless debates about "language" vs. lyric, margin vs. mainstream, performed vs. written, innovative vs. academic, or, now, digitized vs. printed approaches to poetry' (2001a: 6). Skinner has recently reiterated this pluralistic approach to questions of poetic form, style and indeed medium, observing that 'ecopoetics may be more productively approached as a discursive site, to which many different kinds of poetry can contribute' (2017: 329): a view that is confirmed, in my analysis, by several other contributors to this ongoing discussion (e.g. Bristow 2015; Hume and Osborne 2018; Farrier 2019; and Bellarsi and Rauscher 2019).[10]

Poetry, as Mead puts it, is 'networked language' (2008), and what counts above all with respect to its ecopolitical salience are those social networks in and through which its aesthetic arts of resistance get translated into extra-literary practices of transformation. If the poetry of Romantic writers that I discuss here remains of more than merely historical or narrowly 'literary' interest, it is because of the ways in which it continues to be invoked in the public sphere: for example, when the poetry of Wordsworth and Keats becomes a springboard for public conversations around climate change[11]; when Blake is called upon to promote a 'radically expanded vision' in facing the challenges of the Anthropocene justly and nonviolently[12]; or when John Clare gets hailed by high-profile *Guardian* columnist and public intellectual George Monbiot as the 'poet of environmental crisis', who showed how the 'era of greed began with the enclosure of land'.[13] Rather than examining such translations in terms of the reception history of specific texts or writers, however, this book works with an extended concept of *oikopoiesis*, encompassing modes of crafting (which is to say, reclaiming, reconstructing, defending and decolonizing) collective living spaces that are modelled in the poetry under discussion, but put into action beyond the page. In the absence of such a move beyond the purely textual, as Aboriginal poet and scholar Evelyn Araluen has insisted, 'We run the risk of foreclosing decolonization to an academic elite by coding it purely within poetics and academic practice' (2017a: n.p.).[14]

From 'Anthropocene' to 'Ploutocene'?

As this book was nearing completion, two news items broke through the media clamour and commanded my full attention. The first was yet another in the rising tide of ecological bad news stories; and, once again, it was from Australia. What had long been predicted had now come to pass: for the first time, a fellow mammal had been declared extinct as a clear consequence of anthropogenic climate change. The critter in question was not charismatic: a nondescript rodent called the Bramble Cay melomys (*Melomys rubicale*), whose territory appears to have been confined to a small island in the Torres Strait off the northernmost tip of Queensland. The Bramble Cay melomys is believed to be the sole endemic mammal of the Great Barrier Reef, and their declining numbers had been noted by conservation biologists some years previously. A proposed protection plan was not put into action, however, and according to a scientific report for the Queensland government from 2016, the surviving population disappeared sometime between 2009 and 2014 (Gynther *et al.* 2016). Yet it was only when the federal minister for the environment relocated it from the ranks of the Endangered to the officially Extinct in her biodiversity update of 18 February 2019 that the national, and thence international, press sat up and took notice. For according to the conservation biologists who had been urging their protection, the vegetation that provided shelter and sustenance for the disregarded melomys had been declining for some time, probably as a consequence of growing storm surges, and it appears that the remaining population was simply washed away by rising waters of the Torres Strait.[15]

In the same press release that announced the extinction of the Bramble Cay melomys, the environment minister also commented on the re-categorization of the Spectacled Flying-fox from Vulnerable to Endangered in the wake of 'a recent heat stress event in north Queensland'.[16] In fact, some 23,000 individuals, representing almost a third of the remaining population of this species, which had already been halved over the previous decade, had fallen dead out of their arboreal roosting places over a deadly two-day period in November 2018.[17] I found this especially heartbreaking as it occurred only a month after the death of my friend and mentor Deborah Bird Rose, who had long been a champion of the flying-fox, along with those who care for them (e.g. Rose 2011a).[18] Among other things, Rose taught me that flying-foxes are an important pollinator species for Australian eucalypt forests. Few are likely to mourn the extinction of the Bramble Cay melomys in itself, but the plight of the Spectacled Flying-fox indicates that a great many more species are also experiencing immense suffering and mass mortality as a consequence of climate change. Among those who are likely to follow the fate of the Bramble Cay melomys, some will be keystone species; and as they disappear, entire ecosystems will begin to unravel. In this way, climate change is a harbinger of what Rose called 'double death': death, that is, that can no longer be folded back into life, because life can no longer keep pace with death; death that breeds yet more death, engendering 'cascades of death that curtail the future and unmake the living presence of the past'.[19]

Climate change is but one of several far-reaching alterations to Earth's biophysical systems that are taken to provide evidence for the by now all-too-familiar postulate that our planet has entered a new geological era driven by the largely unintended consequences of human activities. Another is the massive quantity of chicken bones that will be found in the future fossil record of those parts of the world where there were profits to be made from intensive farming and fast food. Others include the global distribution of nuclear radiation from the detonation of atomic weapons; dwindling populations and species of non-domesticated plants and animals vis-à-vis growing populations of humans and their domesticated species; changes in the phosphorus and nitrogen cycles; and large concentrations of novel materials, such as concrete, steel and plastics. Problematically dubbed the Anthropocene, this era might be described as one in which the endeavours of what was initially a very small and relatively privileged proportion of Earth's human population to make itself at home in the world in a new fashion – namely, by means of fossil-fuelled industrialization – has effectively unhoused countless others, human as well as nonhuman. If the elites of the older industrial heartlands are finally beginning to acknowledge that we are facing a 'climate' and 'environmental emergency', then it is surely at least in part because those who have hitherto benefitted disproportionately from this form of 'development' are starting to feel threatened by its adverse consequences. Yet the experience of becoming de-domiciled, of finding one's home territory rendered inaccessible or unrecognizable as a consequence of the home-making efforts of others, has long been familiar to colonized peoples. From the perspective of Potawatomi philosopher Kyle White and the Indigenous communities with whom he works, anthropogenic climate change is 'an intensification of environmental change imposed on Indigenous peoples by colonialism' (2017: 153; see also Davis and Todd 2017). In some parts of the world, moreover, notably in the Americas, colonization entailed the exploitation of the labour of enslaved peoples forcibly removed from elsewhere. There were, as Kathryn Yusoff puts it, 'a billion black Anthropocenes' (2019).

Yet in the penal colonies of New South Wales and Tasmania, white bodies too were bound, brutalized and set to work in the service of empire. Given the subaltern ranks from which these convicts were generally drawn, along with impact of the Highland clearances and parliamentary enclosures in propelling many 'free' settlers to the colonies, it becomes clear that the homogenizing term 'Anthropocene' masks differentials of class as well as race.

In Australia, as in parts of North America, colonization also brought a raft of new species, along with a very different set of ideas about, and practices of, land use. And there too, the invaders' claim to possession of the colonial earth was frequently asserted by force of arms. The extent of frontier violence in Australia is only now beginning to come to light; and, as in the case of climate change, many are still in denial. This was brought home to me by the second news story that erupted into my workaday world in the week following the reported extinction of the Bramble Cay melomys: a special report in the *Guardian Australia* on the University of Newcastle's interactive map charting the spread of massacre sites across the country between 1794 and 1928 – sites, that is, where six or more Aboriginal people are known to have been murdered in frontier violence. For me, as a descendant of settler Australians, watching those red dots, some small, some large, proliferating like the pox across the face of the continent was a chilling experience. It was made all the more so by the rider at the top of the map: 'Data is incomplete with more sites still to be added, particularly in WA.'[20] The First Nations Australians who were variously shot, poisoned and run off cliffs are now thought to total at least 100,000 – as many as all of the Australians (some of whom were Aboriginal) who died in all foreign military engagements put together, and around 12 per cent of the estimated pre-contact population of 850,000 (representing some 700 language groups). Many more died as a result of introduced diseases and reduced food sources: by the time of Federation in 1901, the Aboriginal and Torres Strait Island population is thought to have diminished to around 117,000.[21] Genocide, like ecocide, perpetrates double death; and in colonial Australia, as in some other settler nations, genocide and ecocide were interconnected (Rose 2004: 34–36). Today, moreover, too many Aboriginal people's lives are still blighted by maladies linked with the continuing trauma of displacement, disadvantage and discrimination. The life expectancy of non-Indigenous Australians is about eight years longer than that of Aboriginal and Torres Strait Islanders, who are also more than twice as likely to die at their own hands.[22] The causes for this discrepancy are complex, but redressing it will certainly require proper acknowledgement of the extent of the violence perpetrated against Aboriginal people in the frontier wars and the unjustifiability of the suffering they have endured and continue to experience. As Rose stresses in her 'ethics for decolonization', suffering is exacerbated when it goes unacknowledged, and, as Levinas argues, the 'justification of the neighbor's pain is certainly the source of all immorality' (qtd. Rose 2004: 7).

These two news items, one highlighting how anthropogenic global heating is set to ramp up an already disastrously high extinction rate, the other pointing to the still inadequately acknowledged extent of frontier violence in Australia, are indicative of the hermeneutic horizon within which my re-consideration of Romantic legacies is located. But they also point back to the historical conjunction within which European Romanticism emerged, when both of these trajectories were set in train: the former, in 1784, with the invention of James Watt's steam engine, and its subsequent deployment in the expansion of fossil-fuelled capitalist industrialization; and the latter, in 1788, when the First Fleet hove into Botany Bay to establish a penal colony on the continent that the British had dubbed Australia and claimed for the Crown. It was the first of these that provided Paul Crutzen and Eugene Stoermer with their proposed dating of the onset of the Anthropocene. Yet, as I have already indicated, their coinage is problematic. For in attributing those Earth system changes to which it refers to an amorphous *Anthropos*, it veils the uneven distribution of culpability and vulnerability among different sectors of the human population (both within and between nations). Among the alternatives that have been proposed, 'Capitolocene' (Moore 2015) has considerable diagnostic value, to the extent that turbo-charged capitalism has been, and remains, a driving force in the production, perpetuation and exacerbation of these Earth system changes, along with their inequitable impacts. However, it risks overlooking the appalling environmental record of the non-capitalist regimes of Maoist China and the Soviet Union; and it is worth noting that the shift to renewable energy production is currently being undertaken by some corporations regardless of government policies, or, in the case of the USA under Donald Trump, even in spite of them. Anna Tsing's and Donna Haraway's term 'Plantationocene' helpfully highlights another salient dimension of the socioecological crisis that continues to unfold around the world: namely, 'the devastating transformation of diverse kinds of human-tended farms, pastures, and forests into extractive and enclosed plantations, relying on slave labor and other forms of exploited, alienated, and usually spatially transported labor' (Haraway 2015: 162). This is a term that I take up in my third chapter, in order to explore the entanglement of industrialized farming not only with colonization (internal, in the form of enclosure, as well as external) but also with slavery. It seems unlikely, however, that these practices would have left a significant trace in the future geological record in the absence of the widespread combustion of fossil fuels. Haraway's other coinage 'Chthulucene' is too much of a mouthful, but I appreciate the way that she deploys it to designate a 'timeplace for learning to stay with the trouble of living and dying in response-ability on a damaged earth' (2016: 2). By contrast with H. P. Lovecraft's 'misogynist racial-nightmare monster Cthulhu' (2016: 101), Haraway's Chthulucene envisages the formation and proliferation of inclusive alliances among the 'earthbound', human and otherwise. This coinage, then, is not so much diagnostic as aspirational, signaling an ecopolitical commitment to act in ways that might render the Anthropocene not an era in its own right but merely a transitional period. Even more aspirational is Glenn Albrecht's use of the term 'Symbiocene' to designate not where we are and how we might 'stay with the trouble' in more life-affirming ways but rather a utopian horizon towards which we might move: an era in which 'human action, culture and enterprise will be exemplified by those cumulative types of relationships and attributes nurtured by humans that enhance mutual interdependence and mutual benefit for *all* living beings (desirable), all species (essential) and the health of all ecosystems (mandatory)' – an era characterized by the deployment of technologies of biomimicry within an ecosocial polity of 'sumbiocracy', nourishing the human impulse towards 'sumbiophilia', the love of living together in multi-species communities (2015). This is, to be sure, an appealing (if at this stage rather vague and decidedly remote) prospect. But it leaves open the question of how best to designate the new geological era in which 'we' (which is to say, diverse collectives in differing ways) currently find ourselves.

The time frame that is gaining acceptance among geologists for the onset of the Anthropocene is the mid-twentieth century, coinciding with the Great Acceleration of industrial modernity. All that, however, was contingent upon the development of fossil-fuelled manufacturing and transportation, as noted by Crutzen and Stoermer in their original proposal of a late eighteenth-century dating: the point at which glacial ice began to accumulate evidence of growing carbon dioxide emissions.[23] Around a year after James Watt patented his steam engine, the English poet Anna Seward composed a poem that conveys something of the shock of the immediate environmental impact of industrialization, as well as suggesting another way in which our current era might be framed. Lamenting the violation of 'sylvan Colebrook' by the air, water and noise pollution from Britain's first coal-fired iron foundry, Seward imagines the 'Genius' of the place having been 'by Plutus brib'd', such that this once-beautiful valley on the verdant surface of the Earth had fallen under the sway of Erebus, the Greek god of deep darkness associated with the passage into Hades (1810: 314–19). Plutus is the Romanized form of Ploutos, the Greek god of wealth, traditionally associated with agricultural bounty. In 'Colebrook Dale', however, the wealth generated by the iron foundry was not agricultural but rather dependent upon the exploitation of mineral riches extracted from Earth's dark depths. This kind of wealth was associated in Greek literature with another deity, Plouton, who also ruled the realm of the dead. In the case of the extraction of fossil fuels, moreover, it is the dead who are themselves being exhumed and exploited: the remains, that is, of ancient forests and sea creatures. In this way, one might say that, with fossil-fuelled industrialization (along with its by-products, including plastics), the realm of the dead has invaded the lifeworld of Gaia's 'Critical Zone': Earth's permeable boundary layer, extending from groundwaters to treetops, where life is generated and sustained by means of complex interactions among rock, water, soil and living organisms (Arènes, Latour and Giallardet, 2018). This colonization of the Critical Zone is propelling those processes of ecological unravelling that are tipping the dance of lifedeath (life understood as encompassing death, and *vice versa*) towards the terminus of double death. Perhaps, then, a fitting alternative to Anthropocene might be 'Ploutocene', understood as the era in which the inequitably distributed wealth pursued by Ploutocrats (beginning with those who ensured the ascendency of steam over water power in the late eighteenth century [Malm 2016]) is garnered at an increasingly unbearable cost to, and unimaginably long-term consequences for, the wider collective, human as well as nonhuman, of the living Earth.

Capitolocene, Plantationocene, Chthulucene, Symbiocene … Ploutocene: all of these alternatives (and others) are valuable for illuminating particular dimensions of the genesis and character of our current situation, along with our potential future prospects. They seem unlikely to dislodge the geologists' favoured terminology of the Anthropocene, not least because it is gaining traction for socioecological discussions in the public arena beyond the bounds of the terminologically obsessed academy. It is nonetheless crucial to be mindful of the implications of the divergent narratives within which it is being deployed, with their differing accounts of 'how we got here', where we should be heading, who should get us there and how (Bonneuil 2015). While I agree that 'Anthropocene' falls short as a diagnostic term, I share David Farrier's view that it is proving useful as a 'provocation' (Yusoff 2013: 781): namely, to reconsider 'what it means to be human in a time of political, ethical, and ecological crisis' (Farrier 2019: 17).[24] In this way, Anthropocene discourse, whilst risking the effacement of salient social differences with respect to both responsibility and vulnerability, nonetheless opens the possibility of putting pressure on the *anthropos*. And it is not least for its probing of the category of the human, and of humankind's relations with otherkinds and our shared earthly environs, that Romanticism has long been of interest to ecocritics. This questioning was prompted in large part by those technoscientific and socioeconomic developments that launched the perilous Ploutocene, but it was also profoundly informed by colonial encounters with other peoples, lifeways and landscapes.[25]

Romantic inheritances revisited

The charge most commonly laid against Romanticism by postcolonial ecocritics is that raised by William Cronon in his highly influential essay 'The Trouble with Wilderness; or, Getting Back to the Wrong Nature' (1996). In Johnson's Dictionary of 1755, the definition of 'wilderness' carries a distinctly negative connotation as a 'tract of solitude and savageness'. Yet, as I discuss in the first chapter, such places had long been sought out by monks and mystics as places of contemplative retreat. Towards the end of the seventeenth century, this Christian religious tradition, which has counterparts in other faiths and philosophies, was brought into conversation with the classical concept of the 'sublime', following Nicolas Boileau's French translation of Longinus' essay 'On the Sublime' in 1674. In Lord Shaftesbury's *The Moralists, A Philosophical Rhapsody* (1709), for example, those wild regions that were once reviled as desolate and god-forsaken are revalued as more truly theophanic (revelatory of the divine) than places which had been made over by humans:

> I shall no longer resist the passion in me for things of a natural kind; where neither Art, nor the Conceit or Caprice of Man has spoil'd their genuine order, by breaking in upon that primitive state. Even the rude Rocks, the mossy Caverns, the irregular unwrought Grotto's, and broken Falls of Waters, with all the horrid Graces of the Wilderness itself, as representing NATURE more, will be the more engaging, and appear with the Magnificence beyond the formal Mockery of princely Gardens.
>
> (Pevsner 1968: 82–83)

Subsequently, Edmund Burke and Emmanuel Kant formulated differing accounts of the sublime as an aesthetic phenomenon. Whereas Burke follows Shaftesbury in associating the sublime with an attitude of respect for that which transcends the merely human, Kant's aesthetic theory is supremely logocentric. Although

Kant's examples are similar, including the contemplation of awe-inspiring natural phenomena that threaten to overwhelm the human spectator through their magnitude or incomprehensibility, he argues that the sublime moment only arrives when we realize 'the supremacy of our cognitive faculties on the rational side over the greatest faculty of sensibility' (1892: 106): for there is in Nature no power greater than our own exclusively human capacity of reason.

The Burkean and Kantian versions of the sublime undoubtedly informed Romantic aesthetics in certain ways and to varying degrees. In my assessment, however, Cronon misconstrues the significance of the aesthetics of the sublime with respect to European Romanticism, projecting back onto British writers a predilection for 'pristine wilderness' that really only gained prominence in North America. To claim that Wordsworth, Thoreau and Muir 'agree completely about the church in which they prefer to worship' (Cronon 1996: 75) is to overlook crucial differences between European and North American Romanticisms. The Wordsworth passage Cronon cites in support of this claim comes from Book 6 of *The Prelude*, where the speaker reads into the sublime landscape of the Alps 'Characters of the great Apocalypse,/The types and symbols of Eternity,/Of first, and last, and midst, and without end' (qtd. Cronon 1996: 74). Cronon admits that Wordsworth's experience of the 'Black drizzling crags', 'stationary blasts of waterfalls', 'bewildered winds' and 'giddy prospect of the raving stream' that he records encountering on the Simplon Pass 'inspired more awe and dismay than joy or pleasure' (74). But what also needs to be noted is how atypical is this passage in Wordsworth's writing around 1800, which, as Louise Economides (2016) has shown, is more concerned with experiences of 'wonder' than with the sublime. Such experiences can just as readily be come by on an evening stroll at home in Grasmere, along the river Wye or even in view of London at dawn; they certainly do not require you to go traipsing around in rugged foreign climes. Moreover, in previous passages in Book 6, it becomes apparent that what the speaker values most about this alpine region is not only, or even primarily, its sublime landscape, which, as he notes wryly with respect to Mont Blanc, sometimes falls short of the expectations aroused by earlier literary representations, but rather the mode of human dwelling that he believed ('romantically', to be sure) was to be found in its pastoral vales: egalitarian, democratic and attuned to the natural environment.

Nor does 'pristine wilderness' hold much appeal for other European Romantics. Blake's concern was precisely to unmask unconscious human assumptions about 'Nature', as a precursor to beneficially (re-)humanizing the world (were he alive today, Blake might well find himself among the ranks of those who embrace an egalitarian and bio-inclusive variant of the 'good Anthropocene'). From this perspective, entirely unpeopled places constituted a dismal, even meaningless, prospect. For Blake, all living things were imbued with an immanent holiness. But the recognition of this indwelling holiness was a human accomplishment to be cultivated on city streets no less than in any 'lonely dell', such as that in which the 'little girl found' came to live among the wild beasts in his 'Songs of Experience' (1794). Shelley, contemplating the unquestionably sublime vista of Mont Blanc in his 1817 poem of that name, also highlights the very different meanings that humans might derive from the 'mysterious tongue' of this dynamic landscape, whether 'awful doubt' or a 'faith so mild,/So solemn, so serene, that man may be,/But for such faith, with nature reconciled' (l.77–79).[26] Viewing with horror the destruction of human and nonhuman habitations alike by the ineluctable force of the expanding glacier that he witnessed there in the 'year without a summer', it is evident that he inclines to the former interpretation. And when Keats, uncharacteristically, ventured into the celebrated wilds of Scotland, what he experienced 'at the top of Ben Nevis', as he recorded in the sonnet occasioned by this jaunt, was not a rapturous encounter with the divine but rather the discovery, in the mist veiling his view, of an apt figure for the narrow limits of human knowledge. This is, to be sure, an epiphany of sorts, but one keyed to privation and negativity, rather than rapturous union with the divine. The landscape of German Romantic 'nature poetry' (*Naturlyrik*), such as that of Joseph von Eichendorff or Clemens Brentano, might have had its wild edges; but, like that of the Wordsworth, Coleridge, Keats and John Clare, it was predominantly rural. And when the late Romantic German Jewish writer Heine joined other seekers of the fashionably sublime on the summit of the Brocken in the Harz Mountains in the 1820s, he was moved, not to awe or even wonder, but rather to satirize his fellow bourgeois tourists' by now highly conventionalized expressions of appreciation for 'how beautiful nature is, by and large!' (1993: 69).

In this connection, it is crucial to distinguish between 'wildness' and 'wilderness'. The experience of wonder is contingent upon an encounter with the self-disclosure of things 'doing their own thing', as it were, pursuing their own way in the world: as if they were in some sense, if not necessarily consciously so, agentic or 'self-willed', and hence 'wild' in the root meaning of the word, rather than pinned down as the passive object of human knowledge and power. It is along these lines that I read Thoreau's famous pronouncement: 'In wildness is the preservation of the World' (qtd. Cronon 1996: 69). As Cronon admits, Thoreau's description of his experience in the sublime 'wilderness' of

Mt. Katahdin is closer to Wordsworth's on the Simplon Pass than it is to the 'domesticated sublime' that he traces in John Muir's 'late romantic' descriptions of Yosemite and the Sierra Nevada, which 'reflect none of the terror or anxiety one finds in earlier writers' (75). The crucial point to add here, though, is that the work for which Thoreau is rightly most famous, *Walden Pond*, is precisely not concerned with wilderness but with the author's experiment in becoming a good 'neighbour' (a key word in this text, carrying a profound resonance in a largely Christian culture) to more-than-human others in a peopled place, close to Boston and in earshot of the railway.[27] In this respect, Thoreau remains far truer to the European Romantic legacy than does Muir, an émigré Scot who made his way to North America from Victorian-era Britain. For far from endorsing the separation of a domain demarcated as wholly 'natural', let alone as 'wilderness', from one cast as 'cultural', European romantic ecopoetics is tilted towards an ecoprophetic call for the (re-)creation of forms of collective flourishing in places that are inextricably naturalcultural.

Closely allied to the charge of wilderness fetishism is the critique of the allegedly 'egotistical sublime' commonly attributed to the Romantic poetics of solitary rambling. The primary whipping boy here is Wordsworth, the original target of Keats' unkind comment, and it is also this accusation that I set out to challenge in the first chapter. Solitude, I argue here, is integral to the contemplative practice that is at once advocated and modelled in Wordsworth's early verse. While the particular tradition of contemplation that Wordsworth had to draw on was Christian, it has counterparts in many other cultural and religious traditions, including Buddhism, the Romantic resonance of which has been highlighted by Mark Lussier (2011), and other Eastern traditions, as well as in Native American and Australian Aboriginal cultures.[28] In my opening chapter, I read Wordsworth's contemplative ecopoetics through the lens of Douglas Christie's 'contemplative ecology' (2013) as an art of resistance to the reductively instrumental rationality that was then threatening to sacrifice the 'poetry of nature' to the artifices of industry. Drawing also on speculative realist and new materialist accounts of the 'dazzlement of things' (Shaviro 2011: n.p.), I show how the wonder afforded by Wordsworthian wandering, far from comprising an 'egotistical sublime', was affectionately fraternal, radicalizing the 'brotherliness' that was to have been brought about, but which was ultimately betrayed, by the French Revolution, by extending it democratically to places, animals and indeed all manner of 'things', including other people. The text that exhorts its readers to 'come forth into the light of things', moreover, invites its readers to view it too in a contemplative mode. At the same time, it is only by drawing attention to its own inadequacy as a purely verbal response to the radiant realities to which it gestures that the poem might succeed in luring its recipients to experience them through their own contemplative practice. For the contemporary Canadian poet Tim Lilburn, the retrieval of the Western variant of the transcultural practice of contemplation is intrinsic to the process of decolonization, in so far as this can be approached from the side of the colonizers. Leading on from my discussion of Lilburn's contribution to a decolonial contemplative ecopoetics, I conclude the first chapter by considering how contemplative practices are currently being incorporated into the vital work of 'inner transition' to ways of living that promise to be more conducive to collective flourishing.

In the second chapter, I consider how contemplative praxis can also engender a deeper appreciation of the bodily dimensions of human existence, and thereby also of our environmental affectivity, pushing back against ratiocentric constructions of the human subject as a quasi-disembodied mind, immune to environmental influences. This pertains to a somewhat different kind of 'trans-corporeality' from that proposed by Stacy Alaimo (2010). Alaimo's coinage highlights the inequitable distribution of environmental harms arising from the passage of toxic chemicals through the semi-permeable membrane of human skin and gastro-intestinal tracts. Here, I explore the affective aspect of trans-corporeality: namely, how the physical qualities of things, spaces, times of day and times of year, as perceived through the sensate human body, impinge upon our sensibility, mood and state of mind, as seen through the lens of Gernot Böhme's 'ecological aesthetics'. Focusing this discussion around a reading of John Keats' 'To Autumn', I counterpose the comforting seasonal affects invoked in this ode to the uncanny Anthropocene affects evoked in Kevin Hart's surreal 'That Bad Summer', which imagines downtown Melbourne in the grip of anthropogenic global heating. This too has implications for environmental justice. In urban, industrialized societies, the well-heeled generally have greater opportunity to protect themselves from the adverse consequences of industrial pollution and to reside and ramble in the kinds of environments that are increasingly recognized as conducive to a heightened sense of well-being (environments, that is, that are also conducive to the flourishing of other life forms). The ecopoetic cultivation of an increased awareness of the affective powers of place, then, finds a necessary ecopolitical counterpart in the democratization of what ecocritic Samantha Walton has termed the 'cultures of nature and wellbeing'.[29] As I show with respect to CERES Community Environment Park in inner Melbourne, inclusive practices of ecological flourishing and human well-being can well be cultivated in urban spaces and in ways that interlink the local and the global.

If contemplative ecopoetics entrains a praxis of non-appropriative attentiveness to things beyond the text, while affective ecopoetics turns that attention back upon the self in its trans-corporeal responsiveness to its environs, the creaturely ecopoetics, with which I am concerned in Chapter 3, highlights human entanglements, at once material and moral, with other living beings. These entanglements entail shared, if unevenly distributed, vulnerabilities as well as shared, if variegated, communicative capacities. They harbour the ever-present risk of conflict and harm but also opportunities to co-create emergent multi-species worlds no longer constrained by the colonizing logic of human-nonhuman hyperseparation, and hence conducive to more felicitous forms of coexistence and 'sympoiesis' (a term coined by Friedrich Schlegel) in our own perilous times. Here, I turn my attention specifically to the potentially risky co-becoming of humans and bees, along with the plants they pollinate, in the poetry of John Clare, viewed against the horizon of the Plantationocene, within which the loss of the commons, both in England and the Americas, was integrally bound up with the history of transatlantic slavery. In this context, I examine two very different bee poems by African American writers Audre Lorde and Natasha Trethewey, both of which contemplate the rupturing of human-bee coexistence, whilst raising tricky questions regarding the intersection of racist, sexist and speciesist oppression and violence. I conclude this chapter with a discussion of a conservation initiative among largely African American and Hispanic American churchgoers in Chicago, in which the entangled histories of human and other-than-human displacement and disadvantage have given rise to a hopeful multispecies praxis of social and ecological healing.

In the fourth chapter, I consider how the ecopoetic arts of contemplation, affective attunement and creaturely *sympoiesis* open onto a call for radical ecopolitical transformation, above all in the work of William Blake: one that took inspiration from biblical prophetic and apocalyptic writing. For Blake and other Romantic writers, a creative engagement with biblical texts, no longer bound by doctrinal strictures, was facilitated by the historical and aesthetic reframing of the scriptures as historically situated, culturally contingent and poetically crafted works of literature. Among the biblical prophets who ghost Blake's work was Jeremiah, hailed by environmental and climate ethicist Michael Northcott as 'the first ecological prophet in literary and religious history' (2007: 12). In the latter part of the chapter, I discern an echo of Jeremiah's ecoprophetic call to heed the cry of the Earth, as manifest in the drying out of soil and dying out of plants and animals, in a poem by the Australian author and activist Judith Wright. It is from Wright's poem 'Dust' (1945), composed on the cusp of the Great Acceleration, that this chapter takes its title. The socioecological ills and deceptive cultural imaginary that Wright targets here pre-dated current concerns about climate change. This poem acquires a new salience in our own context, however, in that it queries the construction of the dust storm to which it responds as a 'natural disaster', highlighting the role of ecologically inappropriate settler Australian agricultural practices in its hybrid naturalcultural causation. Similarly, Jordie Albiston's poetic sequence 'Lamentations' (2013) returns to the biblical 'Lamentations of Jeremiah' to find a prophetic mode of response to the Victorian 'Black Saturday' firestorm of January 2009, in which the dire implications of anthropogenic global heating for this part of Australia became horrifically legible.

For the Romantics, prophetic language was held to be performative: its value lay in the change that it effected, both in individuals and in the wider society. Among twentieth-century Australian poets, Wright was undoubtedly the most (poetically and politically) significant inheritor of this Romantic conception of the poet as prophet. Towards the end of her life, though, she despaired of the political efficacy of the poetic word: the idealist project of engendering a new imaginary, a better dream, by purely literary means had begun to look like another 'wrong dream'. Throughout this book, I too have stressed the insufficiency of poetry in the face of the complex socioecological challenges of the Anthropocene. Following Wright, then, this chapter concludes with a consideration of a contemporary example of scientifically-informed, faith-based ecopolitical activism in Australia, which takes prophetic ecopoetics well beyond the page.

If Australia looms large in this monograph, it is in part because the violent colonial history of that nation is one with which I continue to grapple on a personal level as an Anglo-Celtic Australian. Among my nineteenth-century forbears were impoverished rural labourers from Wiltshire, who took a supported passage to work on a pastoral property in South Australia. They ended up doing pretty well for themselves and their descendants out of wheat farming on land that had been stolen from the Yorta Yorta people of Northern Victoria, where some of my relatives remain to this day. The Australian story is of wider interest, however, since as Timothy Clark observes, it 'provides a particularly stark example of the challenges of the Anthropocene' (2015: 116), with a highly urbanized society living at some remove from the impacts of the agricultural and mining industries upon which their prosperity depend, the negative consequences of which have largely been borne by Australia's First Nations and the indigenous plants and animals of their ancestral lands. As Tom

Griffiths observed in a talk first presented in 2003, 'Australian history is like a giant experiment in ecological crisis and management', in which the impact of culturally inflected and historically contingent differences of perception and practice has been starkly evident in the treatment of the land (2007: n.p.). Partly for this reason, Australia also offers a rather different perspective on the question of Romanticism and Empire from the by now far more familiar one that has been told with respect to North America by ecocritics such as Kevin Hutchings (2009) and William Cronon. Romanticism looks different from 'down under': not least because during the time of its European efflorescence, the British colonization of Australia was just getting underway. In the rough and ready penal settlements of New South Wales and 'Van Diemen's Land' (Tasmania), the shear 'physical battle for survival', as Wright observed in 'Romanticism and the Last Frontier' (1958), left little time or energy for 'the life of the mind, education and culture' (1975: 61). The first British people to wind up in Australia (most of them unwillingly) viewed their strange new place of sojourn or stay through a pre-Romantic lens; and by the time a self-consciously Australian settler literary culture began to emerge in the 1830s, Romanticism was already on the wane in Britain and Germany. Nor was there anything comparable to the delayed Romanticism propagated by the New England Transcendentalists from the 1830s through to the 1850s. It would appear that in Australia, 'romanticism simply did not happen' (Kane 1996: 10). Between 1800 and 1850, works by British Romantic poets, notably Byron, Southey, Shelley and Wordsworth, were nonetheless among the most frequently advertised literature in the Australian colonies; but so too were works by Pope, Thompson, Cowper and Burns, among other earlier writers, along with those by newer ones, especially Browning, Tennyson and Longfellow (Kane 1996: 212).

Though Romanticism is absent as a discrete 'movement', Romantic inheritances do nonetheless surface in various guises in Australian literature from the 1830s onwards (Lansdown 2009).[30] Literary historians have perused these Romantic traces in many different ways, depending, in large part, on their literary critical and cultural historical assumptions regarding the character of European (or more commonly, only British) Romanticism. To provide a full account of Romanticism in Australia from an ecocritical perspective would require a monograph in its own right. Within the limits of my final chapter, however, I delineate some of the ways in which the afterlives of Romanticism have played out differently there from in North America.

For one thing, wilderness neo-romanticism arrived only very late in Australia, largely via the influence of US environmentalism from the late 1970s, and it swiftly came under fire in the contemporaneous context of the Aboriginal land rights movement and its champions (which included Judith Wright).[31] It does not appear to have played a significant role in the settler Australian reception and reworking of European Romantic ecopoetics in the nineteenth century. In this context, it was not so much the valorization of 'wilderness' as nostalgia for England's 'green and pleasant land', nourished by European pastoral and georgic imaginaries, together with a linear view of historical development, which became entangled with the economic imperative of making a living from stolen land, and hence complicit with the violence of colonial expansion. Here, I explore this 'pastoral imposition' (Kinsella 2007a: xii) in relation to the work of a lesser-known contemporary of Judith Wright, David Campbell, who, like Wright, was a descendant of pioneering pastoralists. In my reading, Campbell's incomplete journey towards a decolonizing ecopoetics during the 1970s underscores the impossibility of succeeding in such an undertaking in the absence of Indigenous interlocutors. To the extent that Wright arguably advanced further along this path, her friendship with Oodgeroo Noonuccal (formerly known as Kath Walker) was a crucial enabling factor. In their affection for one another, and through their literary interchange and political alliance, they contributed to the emergence of a distinctively Australian transcultural decolonial ecopoetics, or rather, *ecopoethics*, which, as Peter Minter has shown, was at once 'radically ecocentric and variously anti-hegemonic' (Minter 2015: 74).[32] The further development of such an ecopoethics along genuinely *trans*cultural (rather than, more modestly, *inter*-cultural) lines will require the participation of multiple voices, including, in a contemporary Australian context, those of non-Indigenous people belonging to diverse minority ethnic groups. Those who inherit the dominant colonial culture, however, are faced with particular challenges and responsibilities with respect to past wrongs and ongoing injustices. Here, then, I bring the work of one such contemporary Anglo-Australian poet, Anne Elvey, into conversation with that of the Wiradjuri writer Jeanine Leane. In so doing, I discern the lineaments of a decolonial renegotiation of the relationship between Indigenous and non-Indigenous Australians and a vision of how they might 'walk back over' their fraught histories and work together in pursuit of justice, reconciliation and renewed care for country, amidst the ramifying damage of the Anthropo(and other)cene(s).

1

'Come forth into the light of things': Contemplative ecopoetics

'Romantic poesy', according to one of its most ardent early advocates, Friedrich Schlegel, combines 'inspiration and criticism, the poetry of art and the poetry of nature', reflecting self-consciously on its own creative purposes, processes and open-ended potential for interpretation. This is not to say that many works of pre-Romantic literature might not also have done this. Indeed, in Schlegel's aphorism on 'romantic poesy', first published anonymously in his co-edited journal, *Athenäum*, 'romantic' does not designate a historically new type of literature so much as the essence of the literary. By this account, 'all poetry is, or should be romantic', that is, a mode of writing that can

> make poetry lively and sociable, and life and society poetical; poeticize wit and fill and saturate the forms of art with every kind of good, solid matter for instruction, and animate them with the pulsations of humor... [and] can hover at the midpoint, between the portrayed and the portrayer, free of all real and ideal self-interest, on the wings of poetic reflection, and can raise that reflection again and again to a higher power, can multiply it in an endless succession of mirrors.
> (Simpson 1988: 192–93)

In hindsight it is clear that this was a characteristically Romantic construction of what poetic literature *per se* should be and do. Not all literature of the Romantic period, to be sure, fulfilled Schlegel's criteria (which, by his own account, were most fully realized in the endlessly malleable, forever hybridizing and gloriously polylogic form of the novel). Yet much of the writing that was later taken to comprise the Romantic canon certainly does manifest a high degree of often ironic self-reflexivity, frequently conjoined with a consciously modernizing mission. In the Advertisement for *Lyrical Ballads, with a Few Other Poems* (1798), for example, Wordsworth averred that most of the poems in this collaborative collection were 'to be considered experiments' (1974: vol. I.117). This implied, as he observed in 1815 (and with a degree of frustration regarding the generally poor reception of his earlier work), that 'every author, so far as he is great and at the same time *original*, had had the task of *creating* the taste by which he is to be enjoyed' (1974: vol. III.80).

Installing innovation at the heart of artistic creativity, early Romanticism was the first avant-garde movement in European cultural history. This has already been argued persuasively with respect to what Schlegel termed the 'symphilosophical' and 'sympoetic'[1] collaboration that gave rise to the *Athenäum* in 1798 (Lacoue-Labarthe and Nancy 1988: 8). Yet it is no less true of Wordsworth's and Coleridge's expressly 'experimental' collaboration on the *Lyrical Ballads*, which came out that very same year. Among the poems included in this volume are a pair penned by Wordsworth that constitutes a lyrical counterpart to Schlegel's fragment on 'romantic poesy'. Titled 'Expostulation and Reply' and 'The Tables Turned: An Evening Scene on the Same Subject', these deceptively simple verses set forth a literary project that promised to 'make poetry lively and sociable, and life and society poetical' in a very specific way: namely, by means of a contemplative ecopoetics that is explicitly cast as countering the reductively instrumental rationality that was then threatening to sacrifice the 'poetry of nature' to the artifices of industry.

Contemplative practices can be found throughout the world and are embedded in diverse religious and philosophical traditions. Wordsworth inherits the Christian variant, the renewed salience of which has been elaborated by Douglas E. Christie in the face of ramifying socioecological crisis in *The Blue Sapphire of the Mind* (2013). Whilst I draw on Christie's 'contemplative ecology' in this chapter, I also show how Wordsworth loosens contemplative experience away from any narrowly Christian or theistic frameworks of belief and weds it to a *poethics* of non-appropriative encounter with all manner of 'things forever speaking', as he puts it 'Expostulation and Reply': things, that is, which I interpret through a new materialist lens as at once utterly singular and dynamically intra-active. The ecopoetic art of contemplation is currently enjoying a renaissance not only in contemporary verse, such as that of the Canadian poet Tim Lilburn, for whom it offers critical decolonizing potentials, but also in the praxis of those engaged in the vital work of 'inner transition' to ways of living that promise to be more conducive to collective flourishing.

Into the 'light of things': Wordsworth's contemplative ecopoetics

'Expostulation and Reply', like it's counterpart, is a conversation poem, staging a dialogue between two speakers, in which 'Matthew' (who turns out to be the fall guy) upbraids 'William' for sitting around idly daydreaming when he should be improving his mind by imbibing 'the spirit/breathed/From dead men to their kind' (l. 7–8) in the medium of the written word.[2] William, who, in the fourth stanza, is revealed as the lyrical 'I' and, therefore, in control of how this conversation comes across, counters with a philosophical defence of contemplation, arguing that the cultivation of a 'wise passiveness' (l.24) provides a different kind of mental nourishment: namely, one that is afforded by a heightened receptivity to those other-than-human utterances that arrive unbidden from 'the mighty sum/Of things forever speaking' (l.25–26).

Ghosting the opposition between book learning and contemplating nature that Wordsworth sets up in this dialogue is the long-standing theological distinction between scripture and creation as sources of divine revelation. That the Book of Nature, as it became known, could be theophanic, affording intimations of its heavenly author, had biblical warrant. Nowhere is this view advanced more startlingly than in the book of Job. Speaking from the whirlwind, the voice of the Lord exhorts the titular hard-pressed man-of-faith to look up from his merely personal woes, grievous and undeserved as they were, in order to behold the vastly more-than-human world that everywhere bore the trace of its attentive creator. This is disclosed as a world in which a myriad of creatures – the lion and the raven, mountain goat and deer, wild ass and oxen, ostrich and eagle – were busy going about their own lives, facing their own challenges, independently from human interests and oversight (Job 38.39–39.18); a world where even domesticated animals, such as the undaunted horse, retain their own agency and seek their own satisfaction (39:19–25); a world in which the Lord causes it to rain in the 'desert, which is empty of human life' (38:26), extending provision to all creatures equally and taking particular delight in those that elude human control: the hippo-like Behemoth, hailed as 'the first of the great acts of God' (Job 40.19), and the crocodilian Leviathan, 'king over all that are proud' (41:34). This rambunctiously biodiverse world is said to display the heavenly 'wisdom' that is woven into its 'inward parts' (38:36), together with the divine care with which it is sustained, regardless of narrowly human concerns and ultimately beyond human ken.[3]

The lesson learnt by Job has generally been backgrounded within Western European Christianity, but certainly not forgotten. Here, for example, is a restatement of it by the highly influential thirteenth-century philosopher, and early proponent of 'natural theology', Thomas Aquinas:

> God brought things into being in order that God's goodness might be communicated to creatures, and be represented by them; and because God's goodness could not be adequately represented by one creature alone, God produced many and diverse creatures, that what was wanting to one in the representation of the divine goodness might be supplied by another. For goodness, which in God is simple and uniform, in creatures is manifold and divided.
>
> (Part 1, Qu. 47, Article 1; 1917)

Still, you will look in vain in the Christian New Testament for anything resembling the marvellous Hebrew hymn to the heterogeneous collective of creatures that thrive as best they can amidst the elemental forces of earth and sky in Job. There is a faint echo of the Lord's exhortation to Job to lift his gaze from his human-all-too-human self-preoccupation in those Gospel passages where Jesus observes that not one sparrow 'will fall to the ground without the Father's care' (Mt. 10.29) and invites his followers to 'consider the lilies, how they grow: they neither toil nor spin; yet I tell you, even Solomon in all his glory was not clothed like one of these' (Lk. 12.27; see also Mt. 6.28). Here, though, in contrast to the bio-inclusive vision disclosed to Job, the point of the exercise is to reassure the faithful of God's special care and provision for them as privileged members of the created order, notwithstanding their current oppressed condition as Jewish subjects of the Roman Empire ('you are of more value than many sparrows' Mt. 10.31; 'how much more will he clothe you?' Lk. 12.28). The theophanic character of creation as a whole is nonetheless stunningly restated in the opening of John's gospel, which declares that the divine Word/Logos, which was incarnate in human guise in Jesus of Nazareth, had been inscribed into all things from the beginning of time:

> In the beginning was the Word, and the Word was with God, and the Word was God. He was in the beginning with God. All things came into being through him, and without him not one thing came into being. What has come into being in him was life, and the life was the light of all people.
>
> (Jn. 1.1–4)

This passage, beloved of ecotheologians, has given rise to the panentheistic doctrine of the Cosmic Christ, which proclaims, with Paul, that the divine is at once 'above all and through all and in all' (Eph. 4:6).[4]

Yet long before there were ecotheologians, there were any number of misfit mystics, for some of whom the contemplation of creation was also a primary source of religious experience, and a vehicle for communing with the divine. Among these were many of the Desert Fathers and Mothers of the late third and fourth centuries, whose counter-cultural experiments laid the foundation for the development of monasticism, in which Wordsworth developed a keen interest, closely linked with his advocacy of contemplative practice (Fay 2018). Although this movement began at a time when Christians were still suffering violent persecution at the hands of Roman authorities, it expanded in the years following Constantine's Edict of Milan (313), which, in decriminalizing Christianity, initiated the process whereby a socially critical grassroots insurgency eventually became the official religion of the troubled late Roman Empire. Turning aside from the newly tolerated imperial church, these spiritual seekers followed Jesus in his forty-day sojourn among the wild beasts by withdrawing from mainstream Roman society in favour of living an ascetic life of prayerful quietude and service to others as hermits, or in small communities, in the deserts of Egypt, Syria, Asia Minor and Judaea. In the midst of our own troubled times, the spiritual practice inaugurated by the Desert Fathers and Mothers is being critically reclaimed in the guise of what Douglas E. Christie has termed a 'contemplative ecology'.[5] And it is in the horizon of the contemporary theorization and instantiation of contemplative ecology that I want to resituate Wordsworth's ecopoetic project.

Returning to 'Expostulation and Reply', we might begin by noting the physical location and somatic comportment attributed to the speaker named 'William':

Why, William, on that old grey stone,
Thus for the length of half a day,
Why, William, sit you thus alone,
And dream your time away?

(l.1–4)

Viewed through the lens of the Christian contemplative tradition, William's solitary reverie on an 'old grey stone' – one that William later informs us looks out over Esthwaite Lake – accords with the praxis of *anachoresis*, withdrawal, in order to cultivate an inner stillness (*heschia*) conducive to silent prayer. For the Desert Fathers and Mothers, this meant putting considerable physical distance between themselves and the centres of Roman civilization over long periods of time. But *anachoresis* can be undertaken anywhere, anytime, if you can find a place of quietude that affords a degree of distance from mainstream society and the general busy-ness of everyday life. That this is the case with William's sojourn on the stone is suggested by Matthew when he observes in the third stanza:

> You look round on your Mother Earth,
> As if she for no purpose bore you;
> As if you were her first-born birth
> And none had lived before you!
>
> (l.9–12)

William's purposelessness is precisely the point: contemplative practice entails the relinquishment of goal-directed activity in order to simply be present to each passing moment. As you allow yourself to surrender to the here and now, you are loosened away from your fixed social identity, with its heavy weight of memory and expectation, and freed up to become otherwise, as if, in this moment, you were indeed Earth's 'first-born birth'. Traditionally, *anachoresis* was associated with varying degrees of *apotaxis*, or renunciation, embodied in a range of sometimes extreme and, as Virginia Burrus (2019) has shown, decidedly 'queer' ascetic practices.[6] Wordsworth was not one for hairshirts and self-flagellation (although his household was a necessarily frugal one at this time). There is nonetheless an element of *apotaxis* and, its companion, *apophasis* (self-emptying) here, to the extent that William has explicitly disavowed active 'seeking' – specifically, after knowledge – in favour of a 'wise passiveness'. The discipline of renunciation and self-emptying has a liberating aspect, entailing a freedom from worry or striving (*atoraxia*), which in turn enables a heightened attention to whatever is making itself manifest in the here and now (*prosoche*).

As Kevin Hart has observed with respect to the medieval Scottish mystical theologian Richard of St. Victor (1096–1141), the inheritors of the contemplative practices of the Desert Fathers and Mothers shared with later phenomenologists a concern with the 'conversion of the gaze from the natural attitude to another attitude', akin to what Edmund Husserl termed *epoché* and 'bracketing': the practice of bringing to mind and then setting aside unconscious biases or assumptions in order to attend more fully to the way in which the phenomenon being contemplated discloses itself to the perceiver in the given situation (Hart 2018: 2). This self-reflective modification of consciousness is implicit in William's assertion:

> The eye – it cannot chose but see;
> We cannot bid the ear be still;
> Our bodies feel, where'er they be,
> Against or with our will.

> Nor less I deem that there are Powers
> Which of themselves our minds impress.
>
> (l.17–22)

Attending to these mental impressions, which William speculatively attributes to the agency of unspecified Powers (and to which I will return anon), while bracketing what we think we know and seek to discover, is a source of intellectual nourishment of an entirely different sort from that 'spirit breathed/ From dead men to their kind' afforded by book learning. In the Christian contemplative tradition, benefiting from such nourishment is understood to entail discernment (*diakrisis*), leading to a glimpse of, or even participation in, the divine *Logos* woven in and through all things. While drawing on this tradition, Wordsworth is nonetheless taking it off in a new direction: one that is compatible with a panentheistic form of Christianity but also conducive to a modern, secular, or at least non-doctrinal, ecopoetics.[7] In order to bring this into view, it is helpful to compare this Wordsworthian take on contemplation with that of some of his contemporaries.

In the 'Advertisement' for the *Lyrical Ballads*, Wordsworth explains that the lines entitled 'Expostulation and Reply', and those that follow, 'arose out of a conversation with a friend who was somewhat unreasonably attached to modern books of moral philosophy' (Wu 2006: 332). The friend in question was William Hazlitt, who subsequently observed of their 'metaphysical argument' in his 1823 essay on 'My First Acquaintance with Poets' that 'neither of us succeeded in making ourselves perfectly clear and intelligible' (Wu 2006: 781). By relocating the conversation to Esthwaite Water, where Wordsworth had attended school at Hawkshead, he loosens the identity of the speaker's interlocutor away from that of Hazlitt. Moreover, given that he has bestowed his own moniker on one of the speakers in this conversation poem, it is tempting to read 'Matthew' as a cypher for the author's own friend, with whom he had co-produced the volume in which 'Expostulation and Reply' was published: a possibility that might well have occasioned Coleridge a wry smile, if not a little irritation (and by no means for the only time in their oftentimes fractious friendship). Yet that would be decidedly unfair. Indeed, according to Hazlitt, whilst he and Wordsworth were engaged in metaphysical disputation, Coleridge 'was explaining the different notes of the nightingale to his sister' (Wu 2006: 781). Keen though he undoubtedly was on book learning, Coleridge was at least as interested in the thought of living, as distinct from dead, men: above all, that of certain contemporary German philosophers, in pursuit of which he had recently been studying at Göttingen University, infamously leaving William and his sister

Dorothy holed up in the small town of Goslar, without German – or much in the way of heating – over the long cold winter of 1798–9. Moreover, the author of 'Frost at Midnight' was clearly also a poet of contemplation. Here, Coleridge's speaker experiences a temporary *anachoresis* in his solitary nocturnal vigil in a cottage, whose other inmates were 'all at rest' (l.4). Yet, contrary to his expectation that this quietude would suit 'abstruser musings' (l.6), this very calm 'disturbs/ And vexes meditation with its strange/And extreme silentness' (l.8–9). While *heschia* eludes him, he does achieve a heightened level of self-awareness as he is prompted to reflect upon his own restless state of mind, and propensity for projection, by attending to a fluttering film of soot on the grate:

> Whose puny flaps and freaks the idling Spirit
> By its own moods interpret, everywhere
> Echo or mirror seeking of itself,
> And makes a toy of Thought.
>
> (l.20–24)[8]

Even as the speaker finds a queer companionship by sharing in the 'unquiet' of this strange 'stranger', as such sooty films were known at the time, he fails to achieve that ecstatic communion with the living Word made manifest in the natural world, which he wishes for his sleeping son:

> … so shalt thou see and hear
> The lovely shapes and sounds intelligible
> Of that eternal language, which thy God
> Utters, who from eternity doth teach
> Himself in all, and all things in himself,
> Great universal Teacher! He shall mould
> Thy spirit, and by giving make it ask.
>
> (l.58–64)

Contemplative experience can just as readily open onto absence as onto presence, unknowing as illumination: indeed, there is an entire variant of Christian mysticism dedicated to this *via negativa* (also referred to as *apophatic* as distinct from *kataphatic* spirituality). Entering into communion with creation, moreover, can also deepen your anguished awareness of suffering and wrong: contemplation is by no means a wholly joyous experience. Yet, while the speaker of 'Frost at Midnight' was evidently unable to find his way onto the *via positiva*, this was not always so for Coleridge himself. In his later *Lectures on the History of Philosophy*, and specifically on the relationship between philosophy and religion from Thales to Kant (1818–19), Coleridge speaks of the 'joy' that he had experienced in those moments of 'reverie' afforded by aimless rambling, when 'individuality is lost' and the self no longer experiences itself as entirely separate from 'the flowers, the trees, the beasts, yea from the very surface of the [waters and the] sands of the desert' (qtd. Cooper 2017: 41).

Coleridge's reference to the desert sands recalls the specifically Christian tradition of contemplation inaugurated by the Desert Fathers and Mothers, within which communion with creation is commonly not an end in itself but rather motived by a desire for union with the divine: a longing, never to be fully requited in this life, which lends to much Christian mysticism a decidedly erotic bent, inspired by the profoundly sensual (if to modern ears, also somewhat peculiar) poetic discourse of the biblical Song of Songs. Yet in the very same year in which the *Lyrical Ballads* appeared, a young German clergyman and theologian published a slender volume of essays that identified contemplative experience as the transhistorical and transcultural core or 'essence' of religion *per se*. Friedrich Schleiermacher's *On Religion* is subtitled 'Talks to Its Cultured Despisers', among whom were several of the author's own close friends, including Friedrich Schlegel, who could not fathom why Schleiermacher could have any truck with religion in their enlightened age. Extensively researched, and acutely aware of contemporary debates concerning epistemology, ontology and ethics, as well as literature and aesthetics, these 'Talks' paved the way for modern post-dogmatic theology, historical-critical biblical scholarship and comparative religious studies (Crouter 1988).[9]

Schleiermacher argued that what his friends, who had all been raised in either Christian or Jewish households, rightly objected to in the inherited religious beliefs and practices of their day were the moribund rituals, outdated metaphysical assumptions and repressive moral codes, which had historically become attached to these, and other religious traditions, over time. But these cultural-historical accretions were by no means definitive of religion. Religion *per se*, he argued, had to be distinguished from metaphysics and morals. It did not necessarily entail belief in any kind of supernatural deities or an immaterial afterlife. Nor was revelation to be found in literalistic readings of holy scriptures, all of which were written by one, or usually several, human-all-too-human authors, however inspired, in potentially very different contexts from those in which they were read, and they were inevitably open to a wide range of interpretations. The world's diverse religious traditions, in his view, had nonetheless grown out of what Schleiermacher took to be a common human experience of an essentially contemplative kind: 'Religion's essence is neither thinking nor acting but intuition and feeling. It wishes to intuit the universe, wishes devoutly to overhear the universe's own manifestations and actions, longs to be grasped and filled by the universe's immediate influences in childlike passivity' (1988: 102).

It becomes apparent here that Schleiermacher has not been able to dispense with metaphysics entirely, for he has smuggled a rather big metaphysical concept into his definition of religious experience in the guise of 'the universe' (*Universum*, a term that he changes to *Weltall*, literally, the world as a whole, i.e. cosmos, or simply *Welt*, world, in the revised edition of 1806). I will return to this later, but for now, let me simply note that Schleiermacher's 'universe' is evidently inflected by the new philosophy of nature currently being developed by another associate of the Jena Romantics, namely F. J. Schelling. In his *Ideas for a Philosophy of Nature* (*Ideen zu einer Philosophie der Natur*, 1797), Schelling drew on the heterodox seventeenth-century Jewish philosopher Benedict de Spinoza in conceptualizing Nature as twofold, manifesting in one dimension as a plurality of discrete entities (*natura naturans*, 'nature natured') and in another as a generative process of co-becoming (*natura naturata*, 'nature naturing', which Spinoza, scandalously equated with God). Similarly, Schleiermacher's dynamic Universe appears both in its multitudinous products and in its underlying productivity:

> The universe exists in uninterrupted activity and reveals itself to us in every moment. Every form that it brings forth, every being to which it gives a separate existence according to the fullness of life, every occurrence that spills forth from its rich, ever-fruitful womb, is an action of the same upon us. Thus to accept everything individual as a part of the whole and everything limited as a representation of the infinite is religion.
>
> (1988: 105)

Recalling Aquinas, notice this shift: for the former, 'The whole universe in its wholeness more perfectly shares in and represents the divine goodness than any one creature by itself.' In Schleiermacher's transcultural take on religious experience, by contrast, any finite entity might be seen to open onto the infinite, if, to the contemplative gaze, it is beheld as a *holon*: a part in which the whole is inherent.

To become aware of oneself as participating in the infinite as 'part of the whole', and hence, as having a 'world', requires, minimally, a relationship with another being, who is recognized as such in their alterity: hence, in Schleiermacher's reading of Genesis 2 (the truth value of which, needless to say, he assumes to be poetic rather than literal), it was through the creation of Eve as a separate being that

Adam 'discovered humanity, and in humanity the world'. Only then, moreover, did he become capable of 'hearing the voice of the deity and answering it' (1988: 119). Grounded in relationality, religion is also generative of sociability, in that those who have experienced religious intuitions and feelings typically desire to communicate such experiences to others: 'Once there is religion, it must necessarily be also be social' (163). But once it becomes social, it inevitably also acquires all those dubious ritualistic, metaphysical and moralistic accretions, which need to be subjected to constant critical review, if the religion is to remain alive.

Religious experience, while cultivated through shared practices, is nonetheless an intimately personal affair, albeit one that entails surrendering the illusion of isolated and sovereign selfhood in recognition of your profound interconnectedness with myriad others, and ultimate 'dependence' (a keyword of his mature theology[10]) upon the sacred 'whole':

> when we have intuited the universe and, looking back from that perspective upon our self, see how, in comparison with the universe, it disappears into infinite smallness, what can then be more appropriate for mortals than true unaffected humility?
>
> (1988: 129)

Emphatically rejecting the metaphysical 'distinction between this world and the world beyond' (94), Schleiermacher recasts 'immortality' in terms of an innerworldly and embodied experience of self-transcendence: 'Strive here already to annihilate your individuality and to live in the one and all', he exhorts his readers, for, '[t]o be one with the infinite in the midst of the finite and to be eternal in a moment, that is the immortality of religion' (139–40).

Schleiermacher insists that 'religion maintains its own sphere and its own character only by completely removing itself from the sphere of speculation as well as from that of praxis' (102). This implies, among other things, that the natural sciences should be absolutely free from religious dogma in their pursuit of empirical knowledge of the natural world: understanding how physical things function should be left to physicists and is not the job of religion. Nor should our moral precepts and principles be shackled to the mores of past times and distant places. This does not mean that religion, as Schleiermacher understood it, should be considered a purely personal, optional extra, however. Far from it: for him, religion is the 'indispensable third next to these two', disclosing the 'common ground' between them (102). Religious experience, that is to say, provides the necessary underpinning for both metaphysics and morals, without which the former is likely to become hubristic and the latter formulaic:

> To want to have speculation and praxis without religion is rash arrogance. It is insolent enmity against the gods; it is the unholy sense of Prometheus, who cowardly stole what in calm certainty he would have been able to ask for and expect. Man has merely stolen the feeling of his infinity and godlikeness, and as an unjust possession it cannot thrive for him if he is not also conscious of his limitedness, the contingency of his whole form, the silent disappearance of his whole existence in the immeasurable.
>
> (1988: 102–03)

Along with an intimation of one's own dependence upon the infinite, religious experience engenders a sense of the inherent holiness of all finite others: religion, Schleiermacher avers, 'considers everything holy' (94). The radical ethical implications of this religious attitude are suggested nowhere more powerfully than by another highly unorthodox Protestant of Schleiermacher's day, namely William Blake. In his 'Auguries of Innocence' (c. 1803), what follows from the perception of the inherence of the infinite in the finite, the heavenly in the earthly, is a call for the liberation of more-than-human life from all forms of human exploitation and cruelty. I am going to return to this poem in my discussion of Blake's 'prophetic ecopoetics' in Chapter 4. For now, I want to highlight a potential tension between the opening stanza, with its talk of the eternal, and what follows, namely a long list of particular instances of human cruelty to specific groups (mainly animals, but also marginalized humans, such as prostitutes and orphans). In Kevin Hutchings' analysis, Blake held that

> a 'holism' giving primacy to the whole over the part is potentially tyrannous, for when parts of a system are considered primarily in terms of their relationship to the greater system or whole, they are necessarily instrumentalized, as their perceived function in the grand scheme of things becomes their most important defining attribute.
>
> (2002: 34–35)

This returns us to the question I raised earlier regarding Schleiermacher's implicit reliance on a metaphysical premise, namely that of 'the universe', in his purportedly non-metaphysical conceptualization of religion. In view of the potential for the metaphysics of totality to become complicit with the politics of totalitarianism, we might want to diverge from Schleiermacher's terminology on this point. To be fair, Schleiermacher highlights connectedness, or communion, over unity and identity. In this respect, his account of religious experience differs from Deep Ecological ecospiritualities of self-identification with the Earth, which, as Plumwood observed, effectively obliterate alterity and elide the complexity of socioecological relations (2002: 196–217). But do we even need some version of the One (whether parsed as

God, Universe, World or Earth), as Schleiermacher evidently believed, in order to cultivate ethical relations with the Many? Here, I am inclined to agree with Timothy Morton in his advocacy of an ethics of co-existence, not in the closed compass of a 'world' but in an open 'mesh' without a centre or an edge (2010 and 2011). From this perspective, religious experience might be redescribed as affording the feeling not of 'oneness' with the 'universe' but of intimate enmeshment, which is to say also, enfleshment, with infinite others, human and otherwise, living and dead, 'animate' and 'inanimate', from whom you receive your existence, from moment to moment, as a gift, and to whom therefore you are, in a very profound sense, beholden.

Although he was an ordained minister, the young Schleiermacher vested his hopes for the renewal of religion in literature and the arts, hailing poets and seers, orators and artists as a 'higher priesthood', whose creative endeavours were able to 'bring deity closer to those who normally grasp only the finite and the trivial' by disclosing the inherence of 'the heavenly' in the earthly (1988: 83). His erstwhile irreligious friends were duly flattered and inspired to find their creative labours hailed as paving the way for those 'new formations of religion' that, he proclaims at the end of the last address, 'must appear and soon' (223).[11]

Across the Channel, the renewal of religion through art and literature was also very much on the agenda at this time, and nowhere more emphatically so than in the case of Blake. Wordsworth might not have conceived of his project in quite these terms, but in another of the *Lyrical ballads*, 'Composed a Few Miles above Tintern Abbey', his speaker too assumes the guise of poet-priest in inducting his sister into the holy mystery that had been disclosed to him on the banks of the River Wye: not, that is to say, within the institutional framework of the old religion represented metonymically by the ruined abbey, which is mentioned in the title, only to be bracketed out of the poem itself, but in the more-than-human world that he hails under the name of 'nature':

> And I have felt
> A presence that disturbs me with the joy
> Of elevated thoughts; a sense sublime
> Of something far more deeply interfused,
> Whose dwelling is the light of setting suns,
> And the round ocean and the living air,
> And the blue sky, and in the mind of man;
> A motion and a spirit, that impels
> All thinking things, all objects of all thought,
> And rolls through all things.
>
> (l.96–105)

It seems likely that the emphatically immanental sense of the sacred articulated here and elsewhere in early Wordsworth was at least partially Spinozan in orientation and indebted not only to the premise that the divine inhered in the physical world, the One in the Many, (*deus sive natura*, 'God or Nature' being two sides, as it were, of the same coin), but also to Spinoza's notion of *conatus*, the inherent impulse or drive within all things, human and non-human, animate and inanimate, to maintain and extend themselves, to and through, their dynamic interrelations with others in an open-ended process of mutual becoming.[12] It is this non-doctrinal sense of immanent holiness, I would suggest, that informs the poetic project announced in 'Expostulation and Reply' and its companion piece, 'The Tables Turned'.

What is particularly noteworthy in Wordsworth's take on contemplation in the first of these is the subtle swerve away from divine singularity to earthly multiplicity in the penultimate stanza:

> Think you, 'mid all this mighty sum
> Of things forever speaking,
> That nothing of itself will come,
> But we must still be seeking?'
>
> (l.25–29)

Here, it becomes apparent that the 'wise passiveness', which William is advocating, is not conventionally Christian. It is not being conducted with God in creation, nor even with the mighty '*soul* of the *world*', which would have been the slightly risqué, but nonetheless acceptably, even fashionably, Neoplatonist phrasing that Wordsworth possibly anticipated his readers might expect. This Neoplatonic formulation is invoked, for example, by Coleridge in his 'Effusion XXXV' of 1795. Best known in its revised form as 'The Aeolian Harp' (1834), Coleridge's speaker shares with his beloved interlocutor his philosophical speculation that 'all of animated nature/Be but organic harps diversely framed/ That tremble into thought, as o'er them sweeps,/Plastic and vast, one intellectual breeze,/At once the soul of each, and God of all' (l. 36–40). Wordworth's William, by contrast, is laying himself open to an address from within the '*sum/Of things, forever speaking*'. Interrupted, and hence highlighted, by the line-break, this phrase is also decidedly ambiguous. Does it imply that all things together, whether cumulatively – or, more likely, given the Romantic fascination with mutually constitutive influences (*Wechselwirkung*, as the Germans termed it), 'intra-actively', as the (not entirely) 'new' materialists of our own day have it (Barad 2007: 353–96) – are 'forever speaking'? Or are we to understand that every single thing, human or otherwise, 'animate' or 'inanimate', tangible or intangible – including, for instance, the old grey stone that William has claimed as a seat, or the lake beside which he is sitting, or those mysterious 'Powers' that bring food for thought – has something to say, and is therefore liable to address itself to the contemplative, or, as the speaker puts it in the last line, 'dreaming', mind in potentially surprising ways?

In the following poem, in which William 'turns the tables' on his studious friend, berating him for poring over his books when he should be heading outside for an evening stroll, this ambiguity is ultimately resolved on the side of 'things'. This is how it begins:

> Up! up! my Friend, and quit your books;
> Or surely you'll grow double:
> Up! up! my Friend, and clear your looks;
> Why all this toil and trouble?
>
> The sun, above the mountain's head,
> A freshening lustre mellow
> Through all the long green fields has spread,
> His first sweet evening yellow.
>
> Books! tis a dull and endless strife;
> Come, hear the woodland linnet,
> How sweet his music! On my life,
> There's more of wisdom in it.
>
> And hark! How blithe the throstle sings!
> He, too, is no mean preacher;
> Come forth into the light of things,
> Let Nature be your Teacher.
>
> (l. 1–16)

Now, it must be admitted that it is hard to recite this poem without an ironic smirk. The corniness of the imagery (replete with a 'mellow' 'yellow' sunset, the obligatory Lakeland mountain, 'green fields', and 'sweet' birdsong issuing from 'vernal woods') is compounded by the jaunty verse form, with its regular iambic metre and a-b-a-b rhyme scheme, which is liable to put one in mind of the kind of doggerel famously parodied by the urbane Dr. Johnson:

> As with my hat upon my head
> I walked along the Strand
> I there did meet another man
> With his hat in his hand.
>
> (Preminger and Brogan 1993: 301)

Add to this the heavy-handed didacticism of the Rousseauian exclamation, 'Let Nature be your Teacher', which was already looking somewhat jaded by the late eighteenth century, and it is seriously hard-going trying to convince your wired-up twenty-first-century students that this poem was penned by one of the greatest lyricists in the English language. It is, of course, Wordsworth's 'greatness', that is to say, his profound influence on many generations of later writers, that is part of the problem: if the imagery looks corny, it is because we have encountered it *ad nauseam* in the verse of so many of the Lakeland poet's epigones. Moreover, that seemingly saccharine neo-pastoral imagery, together with the sing-song simplicity of the verse form, were integral to the demotic ambition of the *Lyrical Ballads* in its emphatic rejection of the erudite diction and highly wrought prosodic structures of Neoclassicism. What interests me here, though, is not so much Wordsworth's literary innovation (although I will return to that too), but, rather, what I take to be the ontological and ethical implications of its poetic argument. This turns upon an arresting line, which occurs in the fourth stanza, immediately preceding, and thereby reconfiguring, the perhaps not so Rousseauian image of Nature as Teacher: 'Come forth into the light of things'.

Let me repeat that: Come forth into the light of things.

Up to this point, we have been bouncing along merrily with Wordsworth's folksy metre and conventional lexicon, when suddenly, in classic Wordsworthian manner, we are tripped up by an expression that is, on reflection, very queer indeed. The thing is, you see, that the preceding verses have primed you to expect another cliché, the waning 'light of day' being the most likely candidate. But the speaker suddenly takes another of those slight swerves away from the expected – so slight that you could easily miss it unless you are paying very close attention – and that subtle deviation, a single word in this case, changes everything. 'Come forth into the light of *things*'? What on earth is that supposed to mean? In what sense are we to conceive of things as having their own light, as distinct from being illuminated from the outside? What would it mean to expose ourselves to this light, that is not the light of the setting sun, or of moon, candle, light bulb or iPhone, although all those things too must be assumed to also manifest this peculiar other light? And how might we appear to ourselves in this strange other light, the light of things, of which we too perhaps are such: things, that is, with our own light?

The reason why this line has got me hooked is that I cannot quite get my head around it. But I think that is precisely the point: as a work of what I have elsewhere termed 'negative ecopoetics' (Rigby 2004a: 119–27; Rigby 2004b), this text turns on something you cannot grasp; something that dissolves the Rousseauian reification of Nature-as-a-whole into a plurality of entities that have the capacity to instruct precisely by escaping our hold on them; something that gets named, midway through the poem, 'the light of things'. Once we have got up and brushed ourselves down after being tripped up by this line, we discover, reading on, that what William wants his friend to lay aside, at least for a spell, is not only – perhaps not even primarily – his books, but rather, a mode of cognitive comportment. Because what gets in the way of apprehending 'the light of things' is not so much being indoors: it is, as we are told in the second-last stanza, our 'meddling intellect', which, 'Mis-shapes the beauteous forms of things: –/We murder to dissect' (l.28).

This reference to dissection, at a time when anti-vivisectionism was on the rise among early animal rights and animal welfare campaigners (Perkins 2003), suggests that Wordsworth's target is that mode of cognitive comportment most closely associated with Francis Bacon's *novum organum*, that is, the experimental method of modern empirical science. This reading is invited also by the preceding line, 'Sweet is the lore which Nature brings', if *lore* is taken to cut its figure against the *Laws* of Nature, as disclosed by Sir Isaac Newton *et al*. Now, this should not be assumed to imply a hostile attitude to the emerging natural sciences *per se*. Wordsworth was among those Romantic writers who were 'fascinated by the discoveries of their age' and had personal relationships with natural philosophers (Hall 2016: 4). At this time he was especially enamoured of Erasmus Darwin's work on the 'loves of plants' in *The Botanic Garden* (1791), and he later developed a friendship with the geologist (and priest) Adam Sedgwick (Reno 2016). The lexicon of 'Expostulation and Reply' is also suggestive of the vitalist physics of this period. Specifically, those peculiar 'Powers' could well refer to the 'powers' or 'potencies', dynamic forces in nature, postulated by contemporary natural philosophers. In Schelling's view, these 'potencies' underlay the inherent 'productivity' of nature, giving rise to its evidently self-transformative and evolutionary character through the intra-action of opposing forces, which perpetually generated novels entities. Such 'powers' were also postulated by Coleridge's acquaintance, the renowned chemist, Humphry Davy, whom Wordsworth later enlisted to edit the second edition of *Lyrical Ballads* (including correcting his punctuation), and for whom the primary 'power' of nature was light (Rigby 2004a: 26–28).[13]

And yet, to behold the peculiar light of things, as distinct from the physical light in which things appear, the light that Newton had famously refracted into its component colours, is to view them from a different perspective from that of the empirical scientist, who approaches the object under investigation with a pre-conceived hypothesis to be either proven or disproven. This approach can be extremely useful if you want to understand how physical entities function, and therefore also how they might be manipulated or replicated to suit human purposes. As Schelling observed, however:

> Every experiment is a question addressed to nature that nature is forced to answer. But every question contains a hidden *a priori* judgement: every experiment *qua* experiment is prophecy; experimentation in itself is a production of the phenomenon.
>
> (Schelling 1858: 276)

It is, of course, entirely possible to study natural phenomena empirically in a different manner, and this was precisely what Schelling's friend, the amateur scientist, and philosopher of science, J. G. Goethe attempted with his own counter-Newtonian studies of colour (and much else besides), which entailed the bracketing of prior assumptions in favour of paying attention to the way in which phenomena disclose themselves under a range of conditions, and in relation to one another and the observer. This participatory and contemplative mode of investigation Goethe termed a 'gentle empiricism': one that accords well with the phenomenological practice of transcendental reflection that represented for Husserl the '*theoria* of genuine science' (Seamon and Zajonc 1998). But this is still not quite the attitude that Wordsworth wants to privilege. The point seems to be that neither empirical investigation nor rational reflection, as purveyed, perhaps, by the books that the speaker wishes his friend to quit, should comprise the only and certainly not the primary way in which we relate to what he once again simply – and marvellously – calls 'things'.

How else, then, might we relate to them? This is suggested in the last two lines, where we are given a positive hint as to how we might put ourselves in the way of that strange other light: 'Come forth', the speaker once again exhorts his friend, but now he adds, 'and bring with you a heart/That watches and receives'. This is not, I would suggest, the coolly disinterested stance intended by Goethean 'gentle empiricism' or Husserlian phenomenology, but something closer to the original Greek understanding of *theoria*, which was derived from *thaumázō*, to wonder or revere. And it also carries more than a trace of the Christian tradition of contemplation, which, as Hart has stressed, 'is practiced in love, not scholarly disinterest' (forthcoming),[14] recalling in particular Duns Scotus' teaching that every creature is endowed with its own 'inner light', which we can perceive only if we recognize it as 'gifted by the loving Creator with a sanctity beyond our ability to understand, towards which we are in turn called to act as *imago Christi*, as images of Christ who embodied divine love' (Ingham 2003: 53, 54–56, 66). Wordsworth's contemplative ecopoetics, then, is perhaps better termed a 'poethics' (Retallack 2003). For it at once constitutes and enjoins a form of 'acknowledgement', as Harrison has it, which foregrounds 'the responsibility of the self in the presence of the "strange stranger," recognising the presences of things, whether sentient or not, and extending to them a sense of agency, autonomy, and moral personhood even as they recognise and respect their mystery and difference' (2016: 189).

The affectionate attention that Wordsworth is advocating here can be practiced anywhere, anytime. Going out of doors is not a prerequisite. And yet, as Coleridge discovered, and as Rousseau had described in his influential *Reveries of a Solitary Walker* (*Reveries d'un Promineur solitaire*, 1780) – an intertext that Wordsworth's readers would have readily recognized in 'The Tables Turned' – rambling can be highly conducive to reverie, wandering to wondering. David E. Cooper (2017), in his discussion of Coleridge and contemplation, describes this as 'meditation on the move', and notes that it is also cultivated in non-Western contemplative traditions, especially Daoism and Buddhism. The seventeenth-century Japanese poet Matsuo Bashŏ, whose walking poetry has been compared with Wordsworth's,[15] was a master of meditation on the move in the Zen Buddhist tradition; a tradition that continues to inspire contemporary ecopoets, such as Gary Snyder and Robert Gray. But whether or not we don our hiking boots, and regardless of whether, if we do step 'outside', we are heading out onto a rural lane or a city street, the key thing is that we seek to still ourselves sufficiently to allow things to disclose themselves to us in their own way and their own time, being mindful that in so doing they are always also withdrawing from us: nothing is ever fully revealed. In order to allow yourself to be illuminated by the light of things you are going to need to surrender for the moment your perhaps perfectly legitimate desire to objectively know and instrumentally use them, and position yourself instead as the recipient of whatever it is that they might have to reveal to you, in ways that forever exceed your expectations, comprehension, and capacity adequately to respond to their appeal.

Wordsworth, it turns out, was seriously into things. In this, he was far from alone. Indeed, in the eighteenth century, several writers, including Defoe, Pope, Swift, Gay and Sterne, took to writing narratives told by such things as coins, coaches, clothes, animals and insects (Lamb 2011). But Wordsworth's things are not fantasized as speaking English: they are, so to speak, doing their own thing, in excess of whatever we might have to say about them. According to Adam Potkay (2008), 'thing' or 'things' occur no less than 439 times in Wordsworth's corpus.

Moreover, Wordsworth deploys this term in a markedly different manner both from Samuel Johnson's authoritative *Dictionary* definition of 1755, according to which 'thing' designates 'Whatever is; not a person', and from William Blackstone's prototypically modern usage in his *Commentaries on the Laws of England* (1765–9) as 'a being without life or consciousness; an inanimate object, as distinguished from a person or living creature' (Potkay 2008: 394). By contrast, 'Wordsworth uses *things* in a way that blurs distinctions between persons and nonpersons, between entities and events' (395). In so doing, he 'borrowed from but gestured beyond Shaftesburian natural religion and Spinozan pantheism in imagining a joyous affection and non-appropriative stance towards natural things' (392). Potkay frames this radically democratic stance through Silvia Benso's philosophy of ethical responsiveness to the 'facialities' of material entities. Bringing Heidegger's thinking of the thing as a 'gathering' of earth, sky, gods and mortals into a mutually corrective conversation with Levinas' thinking of ethics as the 'dimension within which a nonviolating encounter with the other can come to pass' (2000: xxxii), Benso passes beyond both Heidegger and Levinas in proposing an ethics of things, whether manufactured, crafted or naturally occurring, including those that commonly get classified as 'inanimate' objects.[16]

Yet Wordsworth's contemplative ecopoetics also lends itself to a speculative realist interpretation, namely as entailing that fundamentally aesthetic mode of encounter in which, as Steven Shaviro (2011) puts it, the thing 'bursts forth in a splendour that dazzles and blinds me'. Shaviro explains,

> In these cases the understanding is frustrated, and the will reaches the limits of its power. It is only aesthetically, beyond understanding and will, that I can appreciate the *actus* of the thing being what it is, in what Harman calls 'the sheer sincerity of existence'. The dazzlement of things bursting forth is what Harman calls *allure*: the sense of an object's existence apart from, and over and above, its own qualities. Allure has to do with the showing-forth of that which is, strictly speaking, inaccessible; it 'invites us toward another level of reality'. In the event of allure, I encounter the very *being* of a thing, beyond all definition or correlation. I am forced to acknowledge its integrity, entirely apart from me. Such an encounter alters the parameters of the world, tearing apart 'the contexture of meaning', and rupturing every consensus.
>
> (Shaviro 2011: n.p.)[17]

In keeping with Harman's Object Oriented Ontology (OOO), Shaviro uses the terms 'thing' and 'object' interchangeably in this article. It is worth noting, though, that this substitution would be ruinous for Wordsworth's poem, and not only because it would wreck the phonetic patterning: 'things', at the end of the third line, rhymes with 'sings' in the first, and provides the metrically necessary stress. The problem is also semantic: 'Come forth into the light of *objects*' would set up dissonant connotations, inevitably summoning that hierarchical dualism of subject and object, whereby the privileged place of the former is to claim to know and command the latter: this is precisely the attitude that Wordsworth attributes to the 'meddling intellect' and its murderous dissections. Like Jane Bennett, then, I prefer to join Wordsworth in 'siding with things' (to recall Francis Ponge [1942], another notable poet of things). As Bennett observes,

> 'Thing' or 'body' has advantages over 'object', I think, if one's task is to disrupt the political parsing that yields only active (American, manly) subjects and passive objects. Why try to disrupt this parsing? Because we are daily confronted with evidence of nonhuman vitalities actively at work around and within us. I also do so because the frame of subjects and objects is unfriendly to the intensified ecological awareness that we need if we are to respond intelligently to signs of the breakdown of the earth's carrying capacity for human [and, I would add, diverse nonhuman] life.
>
> (2012: 231)

The other thing about 'things' is that they are both singular and interrelational: the etymology (much loved by Heidegger, of course, although that is not necessarily a recommendation) of 'thing' (Old High German *Ding*) is assembly, or meeting-place. In this connection, I also share Bennett's concern regarding 'the purity of Harman's commitment to the aloof object' (2012: 228), ontologically isolated from all assemblages, systems and processes.[18]

Shaviro provides a helpful correction on this point, namely in his pairing of allure with 'metamorphosis', understood as 'a kind of wayward attraction, a movement of withdrawal and substitution, a continual play of becoming. In the movement of allure', he suggests, 'the web of meaning is ruptured, as the thing emerges violently from its context; but in the movement of metamorphosis, the web of meaning is multiplied and extended, echoed and distorted, propagated to infinity, as the thing loses itself in the network of its own ramifying traces' (2011: n.p.). This take on 'metamorphosis' has a Whiteheadian orientation (in turn derived from Whitehead's reception of Goethe's philosophy of nature as metamorphic process), and his article concludes with a discussion of Whitehead's reading of Shelley's 'Mont Blanc' in *Science and the Modern World* (1967: 75–94), which demonstrates that 'the separation of entities, and their "cumulation" [Whitehead] or interpenetration, are two sides of the same coin; they are alike irreducible to subjectivism, sensationalism, and simple presence' (Shaviro 2011: n.p.).

From this perspective, then, to enter into the 'light of things' is not only to lay oneself open to an encounter with particular entities in their alluring singularity; it is also to find oneself caught up in dynamic processes of interconnectivity, 'conversing' with 'the mighty sum/Of things, forever speaking'. What matters, then, is *both* those radiantly alluring things that address us, and one another, as unique co-existents, as Morton puts it, discrete entities that the poet singles out by name – 'my friend', the sun, that mountain head, those green fields, that linnet, that throstle and that vernal wood – *and* the dynamic interrelations with one another (and an innumerable diversity of other others) through which they are forever being intra-actively (re- and de-)composed.

I have stressed that the contemplative attitude can be assumed anywhere, anytime. Yet, from a historical perspective, it is not irrelevant that the kinds of entities and processes that Wordsworth's speaker wants his friend to engage with are other-than-human. This is not a matter of fetishizing 'Nature' but of recognizing that industrial modernity, which was beginning to get a fossil-fuelled boost during Wordsworth's day, produces forms of human self-enclosure that are liable to render the privileged in particular at risk of a potentially hazardous disregard for other-than-human beings and processes (Plumwood 2002: 97–122). In this historical horizon, it does matter, after all, that 'William' should exhort his friend to 'close up those barren leaves', the human-all-too-human books he is perusing, and head out of doors. But note the catch here: it is only by means of such 'barren leaves', a metaphor which, in foregrounding the materiality of the text, deftly undercuts the dubious opposition between Nature and Culture that the poem might mistakenly be assumed to buy into, that the author, Wordsworth, issues his call to us, distant as we are to him in time as well as space, to 'come forth into the light of things'. Reading books and contemplating nature, it turns out, are complementary rather than opposed activities. In a classic instance of romantic irony, the very text, whose primary speaker seeks to lure his scholarly interlocutor out on an evening stroll, is pitching a poetic project: namely that of recalling and revaluing those contemplative encounters with beyond-human others that open us up to a bio-inclusive ethics of co-existence and collective flourishing. Moreover, the poetic text itself, in tripping the reader up from time to time, as Wordsworth does with that weird phrase 'the light of things', resisting our desire for a quick fix of meaning, asks to be approached contemplatively as an elusive thing in its own right, at once alluringly singular and metamorphically interrelational, its meaning infinitely deferred to Derrida's 'future future' (Morton 2012: 221). It is just such a mode of meditative perusal that Wordsworth recommends to his readers in the Preface to 'The Excursion', where he likens his poems to the 'cells, Oratories, and sepulchral Recesses' of a 'gothic Church' (Fay 2018: 27).

While it might draw on prior texts and traditions, this Romantic poetic project is self-consciously modern, deploying an innovative poetic language, which invites its readers to slow down and tarry with uncertainty, in contrast with the textual fast food proffered by the growing capitalist literary market. And while the contemplative comportment that this entrains is informed by Christian practices, which, as Schleiermacher recognized, were a local articulation of a perennial religious experience, the non-doctrinal mode of transcendence advanced by Wordsworth was lateral rather than vertical: across to all manner of earthly things, rather than up to a heavenly Other. The wonder afforded by Wordsworthian wandering, far from comprising an 'egotistical sublime', as Keats unkindly claimed, was affectionately fraternal, radicalizing the brotherliness that was to have been brought about, but which was ultimately betrayed, by the French Revolution, by extending it democratically to places, animals and things, as well as people. This radically democratic ethos is also in play in Wordsworth's formal experimentation: by creating a space within literate culture for the demotic forms of folksong, the *Lyrical Ballads* sought to open poetry to a wider readership. At the same time, though – and here I return to the necessarily 'negative' moment of ecopoetics – it is only by owning up to its inadequacy in mediating the inextricably material and moral encounters, which the poetic text recalls, that it might succeed in luring its readers to explore them for themselves, in the flesh, rather than (only) on the page.

Doing this, as William insists in 'The Tables Turned', not only affords mental nourishment; it also provides emotional and physical benefits. Nature's 'teachings', or at least, those that arrive in moments of reverential reverie, do not consist in moral codes or theoretical postulates but rather are sensed in the flesh in the revitalization that we experience in the midst of other things that are flourishing after their own lights:

> She has a world of ready wealth,
> Our minds and hearts to bless –
> Spontaneous wisdom breathed by health,
> Truth breathed by cheerfulness.

>   One impulse from a vernal wood
>   May teach you more of man,
>   Of moral evil and of good,
>   Than all the sages can.
>
>   (l. 17–24)

By casting contemplative practice as affording 'ready wealth' of a non-pecuniary kind, Wordsworth implicitly counter-poses this mode of relating to the world not only to that afforded by philosophical reflection and scientific investigation but also to that which sets upon the Earth as a source of financial gain: at this time of the dawning Ploutocene, that meant in particular the exploitation of ever deeper coal seams to fuel the growing manufactories and associated transportation systems of the Industrial Revolution. In addition to enhancing your own well-being, William maintains that this non-acquisitive approach to living things in particular (such as the interconnected collective of the 'vernal woods') can be a source of ethical guidance. This does not mean that it is possible to read off a moral code from 'nature'. Rather, if 'impulse' is taken to connote *conatus*, then these promised benefits, at once personal and ethical, are consistent with Wordsworth's neo-Spinozan ethic of collective flourishing.

'There is no presence': Tim Lilburn's contemplative ecopoetics of the *via negativa*

Within the horizon of Wordsworthian contemplative ecopoetics, the connection between contemplative encounters with natural phenomena and an enhanced sense of well-being – one that had been postulated by Rousseau, and is now recognized by the UK's National Health Service (as will be discussed further in the following chapter) – is experienced in quotidian contexts in more-or-less anthropogenic environments, potentially including urban ones, as Wordsworth indicated in his sonnet 'Composed on London Bridge'. Moreover, it was contingent on decolonizing human relations with the 'mighty sum/Of things, forever speaking'. Subsequently, however, the quest for spiritual experience (and/or physical adventure) 'in nature' became caught up with other kinds of colonial practice: notably in North America, where it was associated with the appropriation of indigenous homelands to create national parks framed as 'wilderness'. In such contexts, an ecopoetics of presence penned by non-Indigenous writers, celebrating their experiences of communing with Nature in the 'wild', risks perpetuating this colonizing gesture of erasing Indigenous place-making. Contemporary Canadian poet Tim Lilburn has responded to this dilemma by departing from the Wordsworthian *via positiva* to pursue a rigorously apophatic contemplative ecopoetics.

In his 2017 essay collection *The Larger Conversation: Contemplation and Place* (2017), informed by his conversations with First Nations Canadians, including the Saanich poet Kevin Paul, his instructor in the indigenous SENĆOŦEN language, Lilburn observes that 'Europe came maimed to North America' (236), beholden to 'a sort of reasoning that Val Plumwood called hyper-rationality, the cognitive lymph of turbo capitalism' (237). For this reason, he maintains that the work of decolonization, from the side of the colonizer, entails both the recognition of past wrongs and continuing social injustice and ecological damage *and* the recovery of the Western countertradition of contemplation:

> The renovation of Western philosophy required to imagine a post-imperial world…cannot be achieved by invention, but only by a retrieval…of lost cultural parts. It will entail the resuscitation of a larger version of the self, deepened interiority that is sustained by conversation with a range of interlocutors, not all of them human…what does justice now ask of us? an ascesis of contemplative acts…which offers no strategic efficiency, yet nevertheless contains within itself the germ of the sole durable politics.
> (Lilburn 2017: 230–31)

As a writer, Lilburn has long practiced a form of 'poetic attention' that, as Alison Calder observes, 'seeks not to appropriate the world, but to stand alongside it' (Introduction to Lilburn 2007: ix).[19] As Lilburn puts it in his essay collection *Living in the World As If It Were Home*, this 'involves submitting to be disarmed and taking on the silence of things, the marginality and anonymity of grass, sage, lichen, things never properly seen' (22). Far from offering a 'world of ready wealth', things are disclosed by Lilburn precisely as withholding whatever meaning and order that they might have in themselves (or for others) from the poet, who is, after all, only human, and a newcomer at that, and constantly at risk of seeing only himself in the other: 'The grass is a mirror that clouds as the bright look goes in', concedes the speaker in Lilburn's 'In the Hills, Watching' (2007: 18). This does not mean, though, that the things to which Lilburn's verse bears witness, however inadequately, are devoid of their own radiance. On the contrary: as he writes in a poem entitled, axiomatically, 'There Is No presence', 'What glitters in things is a mountain, it can't be held in the mouth' (2007: 25). Nor can this glittering even be glimpsed if you believe that the world 'is there to do with as you will' (1999: 35). What the glittering signifies is that while there is 'no presence' in the guise of an object to be possessed, there is what Silvia Benso terms 'presencing', namely in the event, or perhaps even the trace of the event, whereby something is glimpsed precisely as ungraspable.

In Lilburn's 1999 collection, *Desire Never Leaves*, the desire in question is twofold: to fully know the other from the inside out, as it were, to get inside them or become one with them, and then to render in words what you have experienced with them. There is no end to this desire, for it can never be fulfilled:

> Contemplative knowing is not a feeling, a rest, a peace that sweeps over one, reward for the ferocity of one's romantic yearnings, one's energetic Wordsworthian peerings. Contemplative knowing of the deer and the hill must gather about the conviction that neither can be known.
>
> (1999: 18)

And that each of them 'exceeds its name' (1999: 61). Lilburn's theologically informed post-romantic ecopoetics of the *via negativa* effects an implicit critique of the narcissism of consumer culture precisely by bespeaking the resistance of things to our desire for revelation, entailing the adoption of 'a stance of quiet before things in which your various acquisitivenesses – for knowledge, supremacy, consolation – are stilled, exhausted before the remoteness, the militant individuality of what is there' (1999: 21). Here is another stanza from 'There Is No Presence':

> You are good but no blond disc in the grass for you, none, no bone
> of light, no little palate or gland of stupid but shining
> intelligibility, the pure bride, none, none for you, in the grass prong.
> A glacier of night
> shoved through the centre of things. Juniper hard with absence.
> You are alone in the world: the flab of the river
> is anarchic, the water is feathered with ignorance,
> a dangerous mirror that makes your face darkness throwing its hair.
>
> (2007: 27)

'You are alone in the world': does this not risk reinstating human apartness, the toxic legacy of that dreaded reason-nature hierarchal dualism, which ecophilosophers such as Plumwood have held in large part responsible for our ecosocial woes? Potentially, but not necessarily. Lilburn is not denying mind to matter unequivocally but rather accepting the limits of human consciousness and facing up to radical non-identity. Nor does this insistence on the non-identity of self and other, word and thing necessarily set us apart from the world: other things too communicate in their own ways, such as the pumpkins, which, in Lilburn's poem of that name, 'sing, in the panic of September/sun' (2007: 5). In *The Larger Conversation*, moreover, he writes of how his relationship with the land shifted as he began to be invited into the world as spoken in SENĆOŦEN. While Lilburn found it particularly difficult to articulate its 'under the tongue' sounds, which, as Kevin Paul explained to him, echo 'the sound of rocks loosened and played by the tidal ebb and flow', learning the Indigenous names for things brought him into conversation with them in a new way: 'the trees, birds, plants "opened their eyes," or so it seemed. This animation was a reduction of distance between object in the land and me, as well as an apparent shuffling aside on the part of oaks, stones, salal, which permitted space for me in the forest' (2017: 232). By making the effort to learn an Indigenous language, one understood by its Saanich speakers as continuous with the more-than-human languages of the land, the non-Indigenous poet, it seems, no longer feels entirely 'alone in the world'.

In keeping with his new sense of the significance of different cultural traditions of naming and conceptions of language, Lilburn's most recent poetry collection is called *The Names* (2016). In 'The End of August', 'thinking' is not hoarded by the human speaker but rather distributed amongst any number of things:

> Queen Anne's lace, lurk
> of vetch in forests, white
> clover shaken in a fist of final bees,
> dust chalks everywhere.
> And the gloom of fireweed
> in abandoned quarries,
> autumn's vampiric looks;
> a leaf falls from oceanspray,
> this is thinking.
> A dog barks,
> cold pours its slag
>   in a scoop through sky.
>
> The hoard of neglect
> is in the beauty-vault of things.
> Fewer than eight red pear leaves
> among sodden pine needles on my low shed roof.
>
> (2016: 23)

Moving from forests through an abandoned industrial site to his own home, the contemplative gaze of Lilburn's speaker calls us to attend to commonly neglected things, upholding the lowly – plants lurking on the forest floor and others recolonizing a quarry, 'last bees' and a barking dog, chalk dust and cold air, fallen pear leaves and pine needles on his 'low shed roof' – as if to say, as did William Carlos Williams (whose 'Queen-Anne's Lace' is recalled in the opening line) of that red wheelbarrow in the rain, on the least of these too, 'it all depends'. Naming in this way affirms the mattering of things, even though their meaning, like Lilburn's verse itself, with its strange locutions ('hoard of neglect', 'beauty-vault of things') exceeds our grasp. In this way, the poetic work of human words, shaped so as to draw attention to the sonorous materiality of speech, becomes a mode of singing along with more-than-human others among the 'mighty sum/Of things, forever speaking'. As such, it might also afford a form of training in the art of co-existence on a planet in crisis, where the sum of living kinds is daily dwindling.

'Towards a contemplative commons': Contemplative *ecopoiesis*

The ecopoetics of contemplation, as Fay says of Wordsworth's 'monastic inheritance', is a device to 'convey and induce quietness' (Fay 2018: 27). This quietude, however, should not be confused with quietism. 'Disaster', as Lilburn notes, 'is often the precursor of great contemplative ages' (2017: 239). In the face of unfolding ecocide, contemplative praxis is increasingly emerging not only, as Lilburn sees it, as a response to grief but also as facilitating a successful transition to a post-capitalist, commons-based political economy. As the organizers of a workshop 'Toward a Contemplative Commons', held in August 2017 at the Potsdam Institute for Advanced Sustainability Studies observe, this 'will not only depend on the capacity for new technologies and social relations to alter the balance of political and economic power; it will also depend on developing social practices that underlie a broader cultural shift'.[20] Contemplative practices, drawn from different cultural traditions (often Eastern ones), are now seen as intrinsic to what is being termed the 'inner transition' to sustainability, notably in the context of the Transition Town movement, which began in Totnes in England in 2006, and has since spread to many other countries, including Canada.[21] Such practices 'allow us to expand [our] sense of self to become-with the world-in-becoming, while allowing us to cultivate a moment-to-moment familiarity with one's intimate relations to human and non-human others'.[22] The deep enjoyment this affords can help wean participants away from the pseudo-satisfactions of consumerism, as well as enhancing their awareness of the ways in which their (in)actions affect others, human and otherwise, potentially over great distances of time and space, sensitizing them to others' suffering, as well as potentially helping them to admit to their own. Opening a space in which guilt, grief and anger can be at once acknowledged and (for a time at least) set to one side, contemplative practices can also assist in the cultivation of collaborative capacities, respect for perceived opponents and non-violent modes of resistance. Undertaken out-of-doors in the context of ecopolitical activism, they can also help to remind protesters of 'what it is we are trying to protect', as one of the Quaker participants in the (currently ongoing) campaign against the enlargement of Kinder Morgan's Trans Mountain pipeline (bringing oil from the Alberta tar sands to the port at Burnaby in British Columbia), told Victor Lam: this is, she said, 'about really trying to get totally grounded and getting out of the us and them mentality and really wanting to be coming from a place of love' (Qtd Lam 2019).

Whether of the *via positiva* or *negativa*, contemplative ecopoetics has much to offer to the 'inner transition' advanced here. This kind of writing, an enduring legacy of the Romantic project to 'make poetry lively and sociable, and life and society poetical', provides training in a non-appropriative mode of being-toward and becoming-with more-than-human others, which is not exhausted by reading but persists in prodding us to 'lift our eyes from the page' (Bonnefoy 1990) and make our way back into the 'light of things'.

2

'Season of mists and mellow fruitfulness': Affective ecopoetics

Sometime towards the end of the last millennium, I started having global warming nightmares. I am sure I was not alone. For the most part, these dreams have entailed a sudden change in the sky, an overwhelming sense of foreboding, swiftly followed by the onset of a terrifying 'weather surprise' to which I find myself perilously exposed, and from which I invariably awaken in heart-thumping terror. The first one, though, was different. I was walking down an eerily derelict city street, such as might be familiar from any number of apocalyptic sci-fi movies; a few isolated others were also abroad, all wearing sunglasses and reeling in the shimmering heat. As I too staggered on, it dawned on me that this was it: this unbearable heat was here to stay, and there was no refuge from it any more. Heat. Thirst. Past the point of no return. An atmosphere of unspeakable dread.

So far, no heatwave has come to stay; but they are increasing in frequency and intensity around the world, with deadly consequences (Mora *et al*. 2017). Atmosphere: no longer something, well, air-fairy, this invisible, yet entirely material, dimension of our earthly environs has become an all-pervasive locus of human entanglement with other-than-human entities and processes. As a property of Earth, the atmosphere bears witness in its altered concentrations of greenhouse gases to those human activities (which is to say, particular activities of some humans in the fossil-fuelled Ploutocene) that will leave a trace in the geological record for millennia into the future. Humans, as Jonathan Bate reminds us in his prescient playdoyer for a 'global warming criticism' (1996), have always 'lived with the weather'. Now, though, the weather is not simply something in which we either rejoice, about which we grumble, or from which we seek refuge. It has become something uncanny, which we scrutinize anxiously for signs of our own misdeeds: we are not at home, it seems, with the weird weather that we (well, some of us) have inadvertently engendered. The atmosphere that co-determines Earth's climate has entered the sphere of human responsibility, and yet the weather, in which we must learn to recognize the signs of human agency, is no more at our command than it ever was (at least, not yet).

Atmosphere, in its meteorological manifestations and their poetic articulations, comes into play in this chapter.[1] But the affective ecopoetics that I am exploring here also concerns atmosphere in another sense: that which features in Gernot Böhme's ecological aesthetics as a mood-altering ambience that is felt in the flesh. This kind of atmosphere comes to light as a further consequence of the contemplative praxis discussed in the previous chapter. Contemplative ecopoetics, as I argued there, invites the reader into a non-appropriative and non-instrumental mode of encounter with things in both their ungraspable singularity and their unfathomable interconnectivities. Countering the objectifying and instrumentalizing logic of colonization, contemplative praxis fosters an ethos of being-towards, and becoming-with, more-than-human others. In this, it provides an aesthetic education conducive to contemporary efforts to reconstitute the commons in the ruins of the capitalist Anthropocene through a bio-inclusive political ecology of collective flourishing. This is a project to which I will return in later chapters. Here, though, I want to consider how contemplative praxis can also engender a deeper appreciation of the bodily dimensions of human existence, and thereby also of our own environmental affectivity, pushing back against ratiocentric constructions of the subject as a quasi-disembodied mind, immune to environmental influences. This praxis discloses a further dimension of 'trans-corporeality', as first proposed by Stacy Alaimo (2010). Alaimo's coinage highlights the inequitable distribution of environmental harms pertaining to the passage of toxic chemicals through the semi-permeable membrane of human skin and gastro-intestinal tracts. Here, I want to explore the affective aspect of trans-corporeality that was of particular interest to Romantic-era writers, philosophers and physicians: namely, how the physical qualities of things, spaces, times of day and times of year, as perceived through the sensate human body, impinge upon our sensibility, mood and state of mind.

In this chapter, I bring Gernot Böhme's ecological aesthetics to bear in a reading of the affective ecopoetics of Keats' ode 'To Autumn'. In the experience of weather, the meteorological and phenomenological meanings of atmosphere meet. What happens, though, if the inherited language of seasonal affects is no longer aligned with lived experience? This was the case for Australian colonial poets, such as Charles Harpur, whose 'Midsummer Noon in the Australian Forest' discloses the disjunction between Antipodean environs and European pastoral imaginaries. In the work of contemporary poet Kevin Hart, that disjunction is deepened in a wry evocation of Anthropocene affects occasioned by Australia's increasingly, and nightmarishly, anthropogenic summers-in-the-making. As well as highlighting human susceptibility to prevailing weather conditions, and their growing divergence from seasonal expectations, on the level of affect, Böhme's ecological aesthetics has implications for environmental justice. In urban industrialized societies, the well-heeled are generally less exposed to adverse weather conditions, whilst also enjoying greater opportunities to reside and ramble in the kinds of environments that are increasingly recognized as conducive to a heightened sense of well-being (environments, that is, that are also conducive to the flourishing of other lifeforms). The ecopoetic cultivation of an increased awareness of the affective force of our physical environs, then, finds a necessary ecopolitical counterpart in the democratization of what ecocritic Samantha Walton has termed the 'cultures of nature and wellbeing'.[2] As I show at the end of this chapter with respect to CERES Community Environment Park in inner Melbourne, inclusive practices of ecological flourishing and human well-being can well be cultivated in urban spaces, and in ways that interlink the local and the global.

Affect, atmosphere, and ecological aesthetics

The link between contemplative and affective ecopoetics can be traced in a poem that responds to precisely the kind of unbiddable encounter with 'things', glimpsed doing their own thing, recommended by Wordsworth's 'William' to his bookish friend. For the speaker of Wordsworth's 'I wandered lonely as a cloud', his happening upon that startling 'host of golden daffodils' was mood altering, their radiant colour and dancing motion eliciting in him a corresponding emotion: an enlivening sense of joyous participation in the vibrant materiality of the living Earth. As well as instantiating the psycho-spiritual nourishment that might be found by stepping 'forth into the light of things', this poem draws attention to what Wordsworth refers to in the 1850 edition of *The Prelude* as 'the moods/Of time and season,/to the moral power/The affections and the spirit of the place' (XII, 117–21). As with the assertion in 'The Tables Turned' that 'One impulse from a vernal wood/Can teach you more/Of moral evil and of good/ Than all the sages can', the 'moral power ... of the place' referred to here should not be mistaken for a code of do's and don'ts that can be directly discerned in nature. But nor is this later formulation as implicitly Spinozan in orientation as was the emphasis on 'impulse' (if parsed as *conatus*) in the lyrical ballad. Rather, in combination with 'affections', the 'moral power' referred to here is more suggestive of Lord Shaftesbury's concept of an indwelling 'moral sentiment', informed by 'affections', arising in turn from sensory perception ([1714] 1999). This is not to say that the place itself has moral sentiments, but that places have the power to elicit and entrain human affections, informing our disposition and shaping our moral sentiments, just as times of day and times of year can inflect our mood. Thinking along similar lines, Goethe coined the term *sinnlich-sittlich* (sensual-ethical) to describe the mood-altering properties of different colours on human observers in the proto-phenomenological section of his *Theory of Colour* (1810). As it happens, Goethe's identification of the effect of bright yellow as 'pleasurable and cheering, with an element of vivacity and nobility in the force with which it works' (1988: 497) accords well with Wordsworth's rendering of the emotional impact of encountering a moving mass of wild daffodils. Here, the mythic notion of 'spirit of place', *genius loci*, is ecopoetically repurposed to invoke the affective force of physical places as disclosed through the sensual-ethical experience of the trans-corporeal self. Within the terms of the ecological aesthetics explored in this chapter, *genius loci* manifests as 'atmosphere'.

'Atmosphere', in this sense, is the central concept of the aesthetic theory developed by the contemporary German environmental philosopher, Gernot Böhme. Rejecting the modern Western constriction of aesthetics to a discourse on the work of art, Böhme returns to its original meaning as a branch of philosophy, as framed by Alexander Gottlieb Baumgarten, initially in his 1735 Master's thesis for the University of Halle, and subsequently in his two part treatise *Aesthetica*, of 1750–8: namely, as 'the science of sensory cognition', a necessary counterpart or 'analogue' of, and hence counterweight to, reason (Baumgarten 2007: 11–19). For Terry Eagleton, Baumgarten's aesthetics signalled 'the first stirrings of a primitive materialism – of the body's long inarticulate rebellion against the tyranny of the theoretical' (Eagleton 1990: 13). In fact, it was part of a wider trend to rethink the relationship between mind and body that followed the discovery of the central nervous system by the physician and natural philosopher Thomas Willis in the 1660s, leading to a growing recognition of 'the central role of the senses and sensation in giving content to the mind and its creation' (Jackson 2018: 328). Many Romantic writers took an enthusiastic interest in these developments, not only helping to popularize the new science of sensation but, in some cases, also contributing to it. It is, for example, from Coleridge that we get the term 'psycho-somatic' (Jackson 2018: 329).[3] However, while Baumgarten is widely acknowledged as a founding figure in modern philosophical aesthetics, the counter-ideological potential that Eagleton and Böhme locate in the eighteenth-century philosopher's revalorization of corporeality – a revalorization to which much Romantic literature was also dedicated – failed to be fully realized. For the discipline of aesthetics, as it took shape in the following century, fled once more from the flesh, restricting itself instead to a consideration of the formal properties and moral-intellectual significance of the work of art. This forgetting of the body, moreover, was linked with a growing disassociation of 'art' from 'nature'.

One modern European philosopher who sought to overturn the dualism of art and nature was Theodor Adorno, who viewed natural beauty as the locus of a radical alterity that resisted assimilation into the prevailing social order of domination: as such, it retained the 'residue of non-identity in things, in an age when they are otherwise spellbound by universal identity' (Adorno 1997, 108). Adorno's rehabilitation of natural beauty constitutes another important point of departure for Böhme's ecological aesthetics: one that is at once profoundly phenomenological and thoroughly historical, scientifically literate and socially critical. Here, nature no longer figures primarily, as it did for Adorno, as the locus of a *promesse de bonheur* situated beyond the realm of social oppression and suffering but rather as itself a site of oppression and suffering, which we can now recognize as such because we are beginning to experience in our own bodies what industrial society has done to the living earth (Böhme 1989: 66).[4]

Böhme's work on aesthetics is part of a wider project entailing the rehabilitation of the German tradition of *Naturphilosophie* (natural philosophy) in the guise of a new Critical Theory of social-natural relations, interweaving (post-)Marxist social theory and the 'new phenomenology' of Hermann Schmitz. This project is underwritten by a sober recognition that 'we no longer stand on the brink of environmental catastrophe: we are in the midst of it' (Böhme 2002: 261). Under these circumstances Böhme calls for a pragmatically oriented *Naturphilosophie*, which, like the older Critical Theory as defined by Max Horkheimer, would be 'driven by the interest in reasonable conditions' (Böhme 2005: 80). However, it is premised also on the recognition that what constitutes 'reasonableness' with regard to socioecological relations cannot be presupposed but must be communicatively elucidated in the public sphere, and oriented towards safeguarding more-than-human life as the necessary precondition for collective ecological flourishing. The urgent need for such a critical theory of social-natural relations arises, in Böhme's analysis, from the increasingly anthropogenic character of our earthly environs, or 'the nature that we are not', coupled with the growing technologization of the human body, or 'the nature that we ourselves are'. This implies that at least on the scale that is most relevant for human life, the nature/culture binary that has for so long structured Western understanding, while always partially illusory and certainly culturally contingent, has now become highly problematic. In this context, the modern division of the natural and human sciences must also be challenged: what is required is a new 'social-natural science', which acknowledges both the social production of other-than-human nature and the bodily dimension of human subjectivity.

Perilous though our current situation might be, this is not something simply to be lamented, in Böhme's view. If the impact of industrial societies on other-than-human nature is rendering our planetary home increasingly uncongenial to life, human and otherwise, while the encroachment of technology on our own nature as bodily beings challenges our very sense of what it is to be human, he argues, then the onus is on us to figure out what kind of 'nature' (or 'naturecultures') we actually want to inhabit collectively and to embody individually. Under these historically unprecedented circumstances, the perennial question of how humans are to live well on this Earth and under this sky acquires a whole new dimension. Enlisting a resonant expression from Ernst Bloch's *The Principle of Hope (Das Prinzip Hoffnung* [1959] 1995) as the title of his book, *Die Natur vor uns* (2002), Böhme insists that while Earth might everywhere bear traces of human impact, that does not mean that we should simply consign 'nature' to the past, as pro-modernists (including many of those who today style themselves as 'postmodern') would have us do: on the contrary, for Böhme, 'nature' represents an undertaking that as yet lies 'before us' (Böhme 2002). This he identifies as the transformation of our industrially degraded earthly environs into a humane living space, in which a decent life might be enjoyed by all, together with the limitation of the technologization of the body to levels that we, individually, deem compatible with our human dignity: with that dignity, that is to say, which is proper to humans, not so much in contradistinction from animals, on the one side, and God, on the other, as in the past, but rather from machines. This is not to say that we are not, to a greater or lesser extent, all 'cyborgs' of sorts, as Haraway has long since argued (1991: 149–82): it is nonetheless to lend significance to the question of the degree to which we are happy to allow ourselves, and potentially our children, to become artefacts of intentional human design.

To construe 'nature' as a cultural project might well seem overweeningly anthropocentric. Böhme's philosophy is nonetheless far from endorsing any kind of human supremacism. To begin with, he assumes an understanding of natural phenomena as autopoietic, interdependent and communicative, and he follows Bloch in advocating a technology of 'alliance' rather than domination.

Moreover, in his work on ethics, understood as 'the art of dealing with serious questions' (Böhme 2001a) – that is to say, with those questions in our response to which will be decided what kind of a person I am or what kind of a society we constitute – he argues that the imperilment of the natural foundations of human life obliges us to consider anew the ethical dimension of our relations with non-human others. In becoming more respectful of our earth others and of the network of interrelationships that facilitate our collective flourishing, we also secure a practical advantage: rather than burdening ourselves with the impossible task of global environmental management, as some ecomodernists seem keen to do,[5] the ethos of alliance could enable us to create largely self-regulating socioecological complexes, which would be more conducive to human well-being than are the degraded environments produced by capitalist industrialism with its inequitable distribution of harms and benefits.

In order to know how to create humane living spaces within which non-human beings might also thrive, we are bound to need the guidance of the natural and technical sciences. Scientific and technical knowledge is nonetheless insufficient to the task of grounding an ethical relationship with other-than-human nature, let alone an ecological aesthetics: science might be able to define certain limit conditions for healthy environments, but it cannot tell us why we might desire to share our living space with a diversity of plants and animals or why we should treat them with respect in their own right. If we are to reposition ourselves as allies rather than conquerors of nature in the production of a newly 'habitable earth' (to recall the romantic utopianism of Shelley's *Queen Mab*[6]), we are therefore going to need an alternative form of knowledge: one premised not on objectification but on recognition. This would be a carnal kind of knowing, in Böhme's analysis, whereby we come to understand the other, if never fully, on the basis of a relationality that is given in and through our shared physical existence, however variously we might be embodied. In this way, the discovery of other-than-human natures is necessarily conjoined with the recovery of our own naturality. And that, according to Böhme, is where aesthetics comes in.

In order to answer the question as to what kind of nature we wish to inhabit and embody, we need to begin by ascertaining what 'nature' means to us from a non-instrumental perspective. On one level, as Simon Schama has demonstrated in *Landscape and Memory* (1995), this is a question for the cultural historian who traces the ways in which such things as oral narratives, books and paintings invest certain entities and places, whether near or far, with meaning and inscribe them in our affections. What is it, though, Böhme asks, about, say, roses, that have invited the kinds of symbolic significance that European culture, for one, has ascribed to them? This he construes as a question for the ecophenomenologist, for it concerns the way in which things physically manifest themselves to human perception in potentially mood-altering ways. Somatics, in other words, precedes semantics: in order to discover what other-than-human nature means to us, we need first to recover our own corporeality.

With regard to all this talk about 'the body', though, a bit more semantic precision is called for. German makes this easier than English, since in Böhme's mother tongue the body is doubled, appearing as *Leib* in one aspect and *Körper* in another. The latter is used by Böhme to refer to the body as a physical object: this is the body that you say you 'have'; the body that you 'use' to type or dig with, for instance; the body that contains the kind of heart that you 'take' to the cardiologist when it is ailing. The former is something altogether different, however: it is the body that, ineluctably, you 'are'; the body that aches when you have typed or dug too long; the body that includes the kind of heart that 'skips a beat' when you catch sight of your lover across a crowded room. Unlike your *Körper*, your *Leib* lacks clear physical boundaries, expanding and contracting by turns, flowing out into the circumambient space, mingling with other entities, such as the stick that becomes an extension of your arm when you walk with it, or recoiling in the face of something that strikes you as frightening or revolting. In the body qua *Leib*, the affective body, as Australian poet and ecocritic Mark Tredinnick so eloquently puts it, 'we are not finished at the skin' (2007).

It is this semi-porous body with its amorphous and shifting contours that figures in the phenomenology of both Maurice Merleau-Ponty and (of particular relevance for Böhme) Hermann Schmitz. However, the trouble with such purely phenomenological accounts of corporeality qua *Leiblichkeit*, in Böhme's view, is that they pay insufficient attention to the historicity of the body. The phenomenality of bodily existence, the particular ways in which people in different times, places and social situations experience their own corporeality, is profoundly informed by the kinds of bodily praxis, incorporating modes of thinking as well as acting, into which they have been socialized. Human bodies are never purely natural but always also inscribed with the sociocultural markers of gender, sexuality, race and class, from the inside out: qua *Leib* as well as qua *Körper*. Moreover, within that characteristically modern Western way of thinking and being, commonly referred to as Cartesian, which infamously sunders mind from body while privileging the former, the *Leib* is effectively colonized in its construction as an inferior externality vis-à-vis the mind, and thereby reduced to no more than *Körper*. Such mind-body dualism is no mere illusion that can be dispelled by means of a more 'holistic' account of human subjectivity, an ideology that the enlightened can discard at will. For the experience of the body as something external to the self, and the objectification and instrumentalization that this facilitates, has become a more-or-less habitual state of being for most moderns (Böhme 2003a: 48–52). This can readily be seen in the way that consumer culture construes the body primarily as a flat surface to be inscribed with social significance by means of clothing, cosmetics, coiffure, depilation and surgical intervention. Costuming and performance have probably always played a role in human culture to a greater or lesser extent and in a variety of ways. Within contemporary Western societies, however, the growth of such practices as genital surgery among young women concerned that their vulvas do not have the 'right' look is symptomatic of a particularly insidious version of the dualistic view of the body as property, something that you *have*, and to which you can do what you like, over the experience of the body as something that you *are*, and of which you would do well to be mindful.

Ethical questions, and the answers we give them, are always to some extent historically contingent, and for Böhme, it is precisely in the context of technological civilization that the regeneration of a corporeal sense of self, the reconciliation of *Körper* and *Leib*, assumes the status of an ethical imperative. If, in the past, it was commonly considered virtuous to exercise control over one's bodily impulses, today, he maintains, we need to make a virtue out of paying greater heed to our bodily sensations (2001a: 91–94). This is no easy matter, though, not only in view of our contemporary socialization into having a *Körper*, rather than existing as *Leib*, but also because bodily being is intrinsically trying. Let's face it: our bodies are forever slowing us down and tripping us up, limiting what we can do and where we can be; in the body, we are vulnerable to illness and injury, along with sundry oft troublesome appetites; in the body, we grow old, if we are lucky, and sooner or later, we die. For Schmitz, it is precisely out of negative experiences of fear and pain that the realization that we exist as a bodily being, bound ineluctably to a particular here and now, is borne (Böhme 2003a: 24): small wonder, then, that numerous cultures have come up with an array of strategies for variously denying, dominating or transcending this pesky mortal frame of ours. Consciously incorporating the body qua *Leib*, with its attendant messiness, discomfort, limitations, peculiarities and vulnerabilities into our sense of self, far from promising the alleged hedonistic delights of 'letting it all hang out', therefore entails conscious commitment: this is, in other words, an ethical choice, and, potentially, a mode of ecopolitical praxis.

Corresponding to the project of the transformation of the 'nature that we ourselves are not' into a humane living space, Böhme identifies the cultivation of the 'nature that we ourselves are', as a 'task' (2003a). Among other things, it might motivate the decision to resist certain forms or degrees of technologization of the body, such as cosmetic surgery, genetic engineering or life-support machinery. More pleasurably, it might mean cultivating a heightened sense of corporeal being-with-another in the experience of erotic encounter. For all of us, it implies enduring the tension between being a *Leib*, and this particular one at that, and having projects. Rather than assuming that this tension implies an irreconcilable opposition, however, Böhme recommends that we seek instead to mediate it through the practice of care for the self, incorporating a new dietetics oriented towards the acceptance, rather than the domination, of our own bodily being (2003a: 368–70). The cultivation of bodily existence begins with the daily discipline of paying attention to how you feel in the flesh, which is to say, necessarily, your flesh, in the presence of one or more others, human or otherwise, here and now. The articulation and theorization of this attentive sensing of one's own bodily existence in the presence of other people, things and places constitutes the core concern of Böhme's ecological aesthetics: one that opens onto the affective ecopoetics I am advancing here.

The key concept of his new aesthetics Böhme takes from Schmitz: namely, 'atmosphere'. Schmitz's project is centrally concerned with redressing the scandalous banishment of the body qua *Leib* from European philosophies of the subject since Plato. In particular, Schmitz seeks to undo what he terms the 'introjection of feeling' that is characteristic of modern psychologism. In Schmitz's analysis, feelings do not originate 'inside' the self; rather, they are given phenomenally in the guise of '"unlocalized, poured forth atmospheres... which visit (haunt) the body which receives them... affectively, which takes the form of... emotion"'. For Schmitz, then, atmospheres are '"affective powers of feeling, spatial bearers of moods"' that constitute what he terms a *Gefühlsraum* ('space of feeling' or 'mood') (cit. Böhme 1993: 119). As Böhme explains, the 'space of feeling is the space which, in a sense, attunes my mood, but at the same time it is the extendedness of my mood itself' (2003b: 5).

While Schmitz discusses aesthetics, he does not do so explicitly in relation to the phenomenon of atmosphere. In order to make this connection, Böhme modifies Schmitz's view of atmosphere as a phenomenon that is uncoupled from things and unlocalizable in space. In so doing, he turns back to Aristotle's notion of *ekstasis*, that is, the manner in which things go forth from themselves, manifesting themselves as possessed of particular qualities, for instance, size, shape or colour, in giving themselves to the perception of another. Needless to say, self-disclosure always also involves an element of self-concealment: no other is ever fully present to us, and we wrong the other that we take to be so. Being, according to Böhme's neo-Aristotelian ontology, is nonetheless always being-for-another, which is to say also being-in-communication (1995: 183–86) (something that is becoming increasingly apparent through research in the burgeoning field of biosemotics, to which I turn in the following chapter). In their ecstasies, people, things and places 'tincture' the environment in which they are perceived. It is by means of this tincturing of the environment by those ecstatic others in whose presence we find ourselves as corporeally affective beings that atmospheres are generated:

> Conceived in this fashion, atmospheres are neither something objective, that is, qualities possessed by things, and yet they are something thinglike, belonging to the thing in that things articulate their presence through qualities– conceived as ecstasies. Nor are atmospheres something subjective, for example, determinations of a psychic state. And yet they are subjectlike, belonging to subjects in that they are sensed in bodily presence by human beings and this sensing is at the same time a bodily state of being of subjects in space.
>
> (1993: 122)

The atmospheres that we encounter in such instances are initially experienced 'synaesthetically', as Böhme puts it, as 'poured-forth indeterminately into the distance' (1995: 85–98).

The atmospheres generated by other people, things and places in their ecstatic being-for-others can acquire the force of what Böhme terms an *Anmutung*, a highly multivalent term that is perhaps most readily, if inadequately, translated as 'impression' or 'appeal': this is how things 'strike us', as we say in English, potentially 'getting under our skin' and altering our current disposition (*Befindlichkeit*), filling us, for example, with desire or distaste, joy or sadness, cheerfulness or melancholy. Recognizing our somatic susceptibility to the impressions that something, someone or someplace make on us, our own emotional affectedness by the atmospheres they generate, we recognize ourselves also as sharing with them a material existence as a bodily being. Recovering a sense of our own corporeality, we discover also that we are ineluctably, for better or for worse, ecological selves, existing in environments and with others, by whom, like it or not, our psycho-physical state of being is inflected. Sometimes the impression made by another in whose atmosphere we have been caught up can also acquire a moral force: 'An aesthetic relation to nature', Böhme argues, 'consists in allowing oneself to be spoken to by it. Sensual perception means participating in the articulate presence of things' (1995: 187) – even, and perhaps especially, if what they have to say to us, we do not wish to hear.

Turning to Schmitz's materialist New Phenomenology, then, and drawing it into conversation with the social critique of the earlier Frankfurt School, Böhme returns aesthetics to its eighteenth-century origins as a general theory of sensual cognition, thereby overturning its post-Hegelian restriction to the highly specialized task of making judgements regarding those privileged human artefacts defined as works of art. Böhme delineates three domains in which this expanded aesthetics might usefully be deployed. Firstly, an enhanced understanding of the connexion between the physical properties of things, people and places, and the atmospheres that they radiate, is pertinent to a range of activities where a tacit (and sometimes explicit) knowledge regarding the production and manipulation of atmospheres has long been practiced by a diversity of 'aesthetic workers': for example, in cosmetics, make-up and fashion design; costume and set design; architecture and interior decorating; 'acoustic' and other kinds of furnishing; town planning and landscape architecture. Secondly, ecological aesthetics provides a vantage point from which to critique what Böhme terms the ever-increasing 'aestheticization of reality', and above all, the 'aesthetic economy' of capitalist consumerism, in which particular atmospheric effects are strategically deployed, for instance in advertising, supermarkets, shopping malls, product design and packaging, in order to engender desires that are guaranteed never to be sated with their fulfilment (2003c), exploiting our affective susceptibilities, whilst simultaneously entrenching the construction of the body as something to be made over as fashion dictates. Thirdly, Böhme accords an important function to the arts within the wider spectrum of the aesthetic perception, construction and critique of atmospheres. It is in this regard that his work becomes particularly interesting for ecocritics. Contemporary environmental artists, Böhme suggests, have a valuable contribution to make, both in disclosing the negative consequences of the attempted domination of nature and in helping to regenerate those places that have borne the brunt of this failed project. More generally, though, he believes that the arts are crucial in overcoming our amnesia regarding our affective trans-corporeality by providing training in the experience, articulation and production of atmospheres.

In the wider context of Böhme's project of the recovery of the 'nature that we ourselves are' in conjunction with the regeneration of the 'nature that we are not', the translation of inchoate impressions into articulate speech is the necessary precondition for raising the personal experience of atmosphere to the level of a transformative social praxis: for it is only by conversing about atmospheres, and the physical qualities of the things and places that produce them, that we can develop a shared understanding of how we might want to reshape our environs with a view to enhancing our collective well-being as bodily beings amongst others, human and otherwise. From this perspective, literature, in its capacity of verbalizing the 'space of feeling', has a key role to play within the wider field of ecological aesthetics.

Literary instantiations of the ecological aesthetics of atmosphere come in all genres. In fiction and drama, for instance, spatial atmospheres feature whenever the moods or motivations of characters are shown to be inflected by their surroundings. Within non-fiction 'nature writing', the affective force of place is also frequently foregrounded. Yet when Böhme himself discusses literary texts, his examples are most commonly taken from lyrical verse. This is no mere personal preference, for in his analysis, poetic writing, in its vivid imagery and musical qualities, is a particularly effective medium not only for the depiction of atmosphere but also of its production: namely, in the bodily and affective responses of readers. In this way, the space of literature too can constitute an atmospheric place, a *Gefühlsraum*, summoned not by the detailed description of any putative 'real' place but rather by the use of figurative language linking the state of feeling that such words engender with the invocation of an imaginary environment (2001b). For the ideas elicited by words can just as readily affect our physical condition as can the atmosphere generated by the physical environment affect our frame of mind: this is, of course, the principle on which literary pornography, no less than autogenetic training, operates (1995: 75). Recent work in the field of econarratology, informed by contemporary cognitive science (e.g. Weik von Mossner 2016), lends support to Böhme's claim that poetic language, along with other works of art and design, performs the work of ecological aesthetics not so much by representing the experience of atmosphere but by actually producing it: by virtue of the brain's mirror neuron systems (which are believed to underlie our capacity for empathy), the literary reception of *in textu* atmospheres activates the same, or overlapping, neural pathways as would be in play in their experience *in situ*, eliciting an actual affective response to a virtual space of feeling.[7]

The link between poetic language and aesthetic experience was certainly clear to Baumgarten, who first introduced this definition of aesthetics as a science of sensory perception in his *Meditations on Poetry*. For Baumgarten (1954), poetry was to be valued precisely as a 'sensible discourse', affording a different kind of truth from that conveyed by 'logical discourse', by means of its capacity to arouse affects. To a greater or lesser extent, this has perhaps always been a dimension of the work of art. However, it only acquired programmatic status during the eighteenth century in response to the perceived deficits of rationalist reductionism. Romantic landscape painting and music, as well as much Romantic literature, foreground the phenomenon of atmosphere. In German Romanticism, it came to define an entire sub-genre of lyric poetry: the *Stimmungsgedicht* (mood/atmosphere poem), of which Joseph Freiherr von Eichendorff was the supreme master (Rigby 2012). As already noted, it also finds an early theoretical articulation in Goethe's studies into the 'sensual-ethical' effects of colour. Similarly, Alexander von Humboldt's concept of the 'physiognomy' of landscape, in part inspired by the work of his friend and sometime collaborator, Goethe, is hailed by Böhme as a forerunner of his ecological aesthetics. Departing radically from earlier conceptualizations of physiognomy as the art of deducing human character traits from facial features, Humboldtian physiognomics is concerned not with what might be revealed about a human other in their appearance but rather with the impressions made by things and places on a human observer. When Humboldt refers to the 'character' of a landscape, then, he is not alluding to an inner essence but to an external 'atmosphere', measured in terms of the mood it engenders in a perceiving subject. It is this unconventional usage of physiognomy to refer to the impressions formed by the 'speaking face' of the land and sky that Böhme adopts and adapts as one of the key terms of his aesthetic theory (1995, 101–52).

Wordsworth's poetic project of attending to 'the moods/Of time and season, to the moral power,/The affections and the spirit of the place', then, might be seen as part of a wider movement to decolonize the trans-corporeal lived body, or *Leib*, from its rationalist reduction to the status of an objectified *Körper*. As Noel Jackson demonstrates in *Science and Sensation in Romantic Poetry*, Wordsworth, far from being the poet of 'sublime disembodiment' targeted by an earlier New Historicism, 'explicitly conceived his work as an experiment in embodied aesthetic response' (2008, 4, 202). In the next section of this chapter, I consider how Keats' ode 'To Autumn' might be read along similar lines. However, in my own response to the poem, I attend also to the discordant feelings aroused by Keats' invocation of pre-industrial seasonal atmospheres when read in the changing climate of an anthropogenically altered planetary atmosphere.

Seasonal atmospherics and affective ecopoetics in 'To Autumn'

In his landmark recontextualisation of Keats' ode, alongside its apocalyptic counterpart, Byron's poem 'Darkness', in relation to the climatic, and associated socioecological, impacts of the Tambora volcanic eruption in April 1815, Jonathan Bate (1996) announced the inauguration of a post-natural 'global warming criticism', informed not only by climate science but also by the science studies of Michel Serres and Bruno Latour. Countering what Serres termed the 'Modern Constitution' of knowledge, severing the natural from the human sciences, Global Warming Criticism would disclose the inextricability of 'nature' and 'culture' as disclosed, paradigmatically, in the experience of weather. This early formulation of the ecomaterialist promise of environmental literary studies, pre-empting by nearly two decades more recent articulations of a 'material ecocriticism' (e.g. Iovino and Oppermann 2014), was as methodologically innovative as it was geohistorically prescient. My rereading of the affective ecopoetics instantiated in 'To Autumn' is to some degree an extension of this project. In the era of Global Warming Criticism, when the weather itself bears witness to the industrial disruption of natural systems, the literature of weather-borne atmospheres acquires a special interest: in the phenomenon of the weather, the aesthetic and meteorological meanings of atmosphere are bridged. However, whereas Bate focusses on what Keats' ode *says* about 'living with the weather' from within the matrix of the ecological networks gestured to in the text, my concern, in the first instance, is directed towards what the poem *does* on the level of affect.

Although Keats abandoned medicine for poetry, he was exposed to new thinking regarding the interrelationship between mind and body during his studies at Guy's Hospital in London. In a letter to Benjamin Bailey from 22 November 1817, Keats exclaimed, 'O for a Life of Sensations rather than of Thoughts!' (qtd. Jackson 2018: 327). As Jackson observes, modernist critics of Romanticism commonly misread this as 'a call to irrationality, evidence of the primitivism and puerility of Romantic literature'. In light of more recent research into eighteenth-century theories of the entanglement of psyche and *soma*, this can now be recognized as 'an appeal for a more embodied way of knowing – a claim that thinking based in physical sensation could potentially engender a higher form of knowledge than that obtained through what Keats calls in the same letter "consequitive reasoning"' (2018: 327; see also Bari 2012): a claim that he explored in the affective ecopoetics of his verse.

'To Autumn' belongs to the well-populated sub-category of nature poetry that responds to the phenomenality of the seasons, weather or time of day. 'Daybreak', 'dusk', 'the wind', 'the heat': nominal expressions such as these refer to atmospheres that have acquired a thing-like character, or what Böhme terms 'the atmospheric' (1995: 66–84). What such literature discloses is the tincturing of terrestrial environments by the motions of the heavens, the coalescence, as it were, of earth and sky. For readers who are familiar with the relevant cultural codes and literary conventions, seasonal atmospheres are commonly summoned by means of what Böhme terms verbal 'insignia': metonyms that have acquired emblematic status. Keats reckons on such recognition in the opening stanza of 'To Autumn', which swiftly swerves away from the autumnal feelings potentially evoked by the title, and reinforced in the first line ('mists', 'mellow fruitfulness'), to plunge the reader instead into a more summery atmosphere by means of a series of insignia drawn from the pastoral tradition. Thus, for example, in the Harvest Home section of Theocritus' *Idylls*:

> Lark and goldfinch sang and turtle moaned, and about the spring the bees hummed and hovered to and fro. All nature smelt of the opulent summer-time, smelt of the season of fruit. Pears lay at our feet, apples on either side, rolling abundantly, and the young branches lay splayed upon the ground because of the weight of their damsons.
>
> (VII, 135)[8]

For readers with experience of those climes in which late summer brings such opulent flowering and fruiting, buzzing and bird-song, and familiarity with the corresponding verbal insignia, affects associated with this time of year will have already been summoned by the imagery of the opening stanza, long before this season is called by name in the final line. Within Greek pastoral, the presiding deity of summer is of course the randy Pan, who ghosts this stanza in the voluptuousness of Keats' varied tropes of roundness, softness and swelling:

> Season of mists and mellow fruitfulness,
>   Close bosom-friend of the maturing sun;
> Conspiring with him how to load and bless
>   With fruit the vines that round the thatch-eves run;
> To bend with apples the moss'd cottage-trees,
>   And fill all fruit with ripeness to the core;
>   To swell the gourd, and plump the hazel shells
> With a sweet kernel; to set budding more,
>   And still more, later flowers for the bees,
>   Until they think warm days will never cease,
>   For Summer has o'er-brimm'd their clammy cells.
>
> (l. 1–11)[9]

Vines loaded with fruit, moss'd cottage-trees bent with their load of apples filled with 'ripeness to the core' and the swelling gourd and plump hazel shells: all this conspires to lend a startling literalism to 'bosom-friend' of the second line, which now ceases to be a sentimental personification of autumn, suggesting a more physical intimacy than would conventionally be connoted by this (at that time gender-neutral) term, perhaps even triggering an amorous desire to reach out and caress your friend's bosom, or indeed for them to caress your own swelling parts, which are blossoming along with all those flowers, and perchance even 'o'er-brimming', like the honey oozing from the beehives' 'clammy cells'.

What makes this imagery so deeply erotic, in my reading, is that it foregoes the representation of human bodies viewed from the outside, that is, as objectified *Körper*, in favour of evoking the atmosphere of sexual arousal as experienced from within the lived body, *Leib*. Moreover, as in that 'oldest and sweetest' of Hebrew love songs, as J. G. Herder described the biblical *Song of Songs* in his commentary of 1778 (Herder 1987), this is achieved through the medium of natural imagery, thereby embedding human sexual desire into the wider Eros of the living Earth. This is also consistent with Erasmus Darwin's depiction of the 'entire material world as dominated by love' (Reno 2016: 35) in *The Loves of Plants* (1789) (republished as the second part of *The Botanic Garden*, 1791). Informed by empirical research in the emerging field of botanical science, with which Keats had some familiarity, this idea can be traced back to pre-Socratic natural philosophy, and it appears also in Hesiod, whose *Theogony* figures 'Eros as an underlying biotic energy, driving all moments of creation' (Sharkie and Johnson 2017: 72). In its affective ecopoetics, then, Keats' verse affords the reader an embodied sense of participation in the erotic burgeoning of more-than-human life.

If we allow that the overriding atmosphere of the first stanza is one of sensuous desire, then that of the second surely approaches the post-coital, making good the promise of mellowing announced in the opening line:

> Who hath not seen you oft amid thy store?
>   Sometimes whoever seeks abroad may find
> Thee sitting careless on a granary floor,
>   Thy hair soft-lifted by the winnowing wind;
> Or on a half-reap'd furrow sound asleep,
>   Drows'd with the fume of poppies, while thy hook
>   Spares the next swath and all its twined flowers:
> And sometimes like a gleaner thou dost keep
>   Steady thy laden head across a brook;
>   Or by a cyder-press, with patient look,
>   Thou watchest the last oozings hours by hours.
>
>   (l.12–22)

The echo of classical pastoral continues here in the atmosphere of drowsiness summoned in the central line: 'Drows'd with the fume of poppies'. This noontide mood also belongs to the presiding deity of pastoral, Pan. What is somewhat surprising here, though, is that Keats has relocated it from its conventional locus of lolling about in wooded meadows to the hard-working agrarian landscape of georgic. While a certain suturing of pastoral and georgic can also be found in eighteenth-century verse, Keats does this to rather different effect. In James Thomson's *The Seasons* (1730), for example, the georgic valorization of human working on the land is artfully blended with pastoral pleasantry in such a way as to implicitly endorse the historical project of agricultural 'improvement', by means of which food production began to be intensified in the eighteenth century. By contrast, the second stanza of 'To Autumn' modulates into a meditative mood that effectively undercuts the idea of human mastery that might otherwise be connoted by the activity of winnowing, reaping, gleaning and pressing the apple harvest. Instead, the bustle of the harvest is interrupted by a moment of quiet reverie: the thresher is 'sitting careless on the granary floor/Thy hair soft-lifted by the winnowing wind', the reaper is dozing on 'a half-reap'd furrow', the gleaner is steadying herself 'across a brook' and the cider maker is sunk in patient contemplation of the 'last oozings'. This last image recalls the bees' 'o'brimming' honeycombs in the first stanza, but in place of erotic ardour, we are now given a meditative sensation of the self on the verge of merging with its surrounds.

In 'To Autumn', reverie, which, as discussed in the previous chapter, underpins contemplative ecopoetics, is itself disclosed as an 'affective stance', which, as Allison Dushane observes, 'collapses the distinction between the subjective and the objective, the vital and the material, the soul and the body' (2016: 128). In this moment of reverie, the agricultural labourers no longer experience their own bodies, qua *Körper*, as a means to the end of instrumentalizing the environment (whether primarily for their own, or, more likely, another's benefit), but as transcorporeal *Leiber*, enmeshed in what Merleau-Ponty termed the 'flesh of the world' (1968: 130–55). In this way, Keats implicitly counters the instrumental logic of the enlightenment project of agricultural improvement with its agenda of maximal economic exploitation, with a vision of mindful working with, rather than on, the land, linked to a form of ecological selfhood that resists the hyperseparation of human from nonhuman, mind from body.

As has been frequently observed, 'To Autumn' concertinas several months and maps them onto the passing of a single day, beginning with a misty morning in late summer, moving through an afternoon during harvest-tide and concluding in late autumn. By disappointing our initial expectations of an autumnal mood, Keats' verse creates what Schmitz terms an experience of 'ingression' and perhaps even 'discrepancy'. While our bodily state of being is perpetually being played upon by the people and things in whose company we find ourselves in any given place and time, it is above all on first entering a space with an atmosphere that is markedly different from the one that we have left ('ingression'), or at those times when the prevailing atmosphere contrasts strongly with our own pre-existing mood ('discrepancy'), that we become aware of this spatial dimension of feeling (Böhme 2001c: 46–48). Returning the reader to the autumnal atmosphere invoked by the title only in the third stanza, Keats enhances its affective force, inviting reflection on the trans-corporeal phenomenon of atmosphere in and of itself:

> Where are the songs of Spring? Ay, where are they?
>   Think not of them, thou hast thy music too, –
> While barred clouds bloom the soft-dying day,
>   And touch the stubble plains with rosy hue;
> Then in a wailful choir the small gnats mourn
>   Among the river sallows, borne aloft
>   Or sinking as the light wind lives or dies;
> And full-grown lambs loud bleat from hilly bourn;
>   Hedge-crickets sing; and now with treble soft
>   The red-breast whistles from a garden-croft;
>   And gathering swallows twitter in the skies.
>
>   (l.23–34)

When we finally arrive there, the atmosphere of a misty autumnal evening, foreshadowed in the opening line, is summoned predominantly by means of acoustic insignia. In his discussion of the phenomenon of 'acoustic atmospheres', Böhme explains how sounds too modify the space in which they are heard, informing the listener's disposition, sometimes reaching 'directly into his or her corporeal economy'. Particular combinations of sounds contribute to the acoustic character of specific life worlds, 'be they natural ones, like the sea, the forest or other landscapes, or be they the life worlds of cities and villages' (2000: 16). When we find ourselves out-of-doors, or even indoors, but listening to what is leaking in from outside, some of the sounds that assail us are likely to be weather-borne. To go outside is to enter what Tim Ingold terms the 'weather-world', a world not of static objects but of 'comings and goings', of 'formative and transformative *processes*' (2011: 117), in which, as we move through it, we are corporeally caught up – and which, ensconced in our air-conditioned interiors, we forget at our peril. 'As an experience of light, sound and feeling that suffuses our awareness', Ingold writes, 'the weather is not so much an *object* of perception as what we perceive *in*, underwriting our very capacities to see, to hear and to touch' (2011: 127). Drawing on Böhme, Ingold insists that acoustic atmospheres, whether weather-borne or otherwise, should not be thought of as 'soundscapes', as this implies objectification rather than immersion. For, as Böhme observes, those who attend to acoustic atmospheres

> are dangerously open; they release themselves into the world and can therefore be struck by acoustic events. Lovely tunes can lead them astray, thunderclaps can shatter them, scratching noises can threaten them, a cutting tone can damage them. Listening is a being-beside-yourself [*Außer sich sein*]; it can be the joyful experience of discovering oneself to be alive.
>
> (2000: 18)

Deep listening has long been integral to pastoral poetry (Gifford 2016). In 'To Autumn', it is the quietude of the previous stanza that opens the speaker up to an ecstatic immersion in the more-than-human sounds of the weather-world, in which the music of human words joins the choir of other-than-human vocalizations: specifically, of gnat, lambs, hedge-crickets, red-breast and swallows. Here, though, in discovering yourself to be alive, a sensate human speaker/hearer/reader in the presence of a diversity of other communicative living beings, you might also be reminded that living inevitably entails dying. This is where Keats' rendition of the 'music' of autumn turns out to be taking us, piling up imagery of immanent death as the counterpart to the imagery of burgeoning life with which the ode opened: 'soft-dying day'; gnats 'borne aloft/Or sinking as the light wind lives and dies'; and 'full-grown lambs', who will soon be taken off the fields for slaughter. There are hints of the mood of pastoral lament here: yet, even though the gnats' hum is anthropomorphized as 'wailful', the dominant affect is not necessarily melancholy, inclining rather to a peaceful acceptance of death as integral to life, a feeling arrived at as an outcome of the meditative mood invoked in the middle stanza. As Timothy Clark has observed, in Keats' ode, 'autumn's implicit projection of future death is muted by its imprint in a circular trajectory that also entails renewal' (2015: 42). Moreover, by inviting empathy towards the short-lived animals named as singers in the autumnal choir, into whose acoustic atmosphere the reader has been summoned, this ecopoetic text affords a sense that human singularity as knowingly mortal does not set us apart and above other living beings but rather calls us towards compassionate responsiveness towards fellow creatures. Here, then, Eros gently modulates into Agape, not by means of any prudish repudiation of the flesh, however, but rather through a heightened sense of trans-corporeal participation in creaturely existence (of which, more in the following chapter).

Yet the affects elicited by *in textu* atmospheres, not unlike but even more so than those experienced *in situ*, are inevitably inflected by sociocultural dimensions of subjectivity and refracted through the knowledge, assumptions and beliefs we bring to the text. Rereading this poem in the horizon of anthropogenic climate change and accelerating extinctions lends it an aching sadness: its 'consolatory effect', as Clark put it, fails in light of the knowledge that inevitable death, rather than being folded back into life, is becoming displaced by what Deborah Bird Rose calls 'double death' (2004: 175–76), in which, with the erosion of Earth's vital life support systems, renewal is no longer possible. What then are we to make of an affective ecopoetics when 'living with the weather' and its mood-altering atmospheres can no longer be taken for granted but becomes instead an anxiety-ridden alertness to possible anthropogenic impacts? In my view, it is precisely in light of that very disjunction that ecological aesthetics acquires a new significance, namely as a reminder of human psycho-physical susceptibility to environmental conditions.

Unsettling atmospheres and Anthropocene affects in the Antipodes: From Harpur to Hart

The disorientating experience of discordance between seasonal expectations and prevailing weather conditions, which is now going global, was well-known to European settlers in colonial Australia. Together with its odd vegetation and wildlife, fickle waterways and unfamiliar topography, Australia's erratic climate, which even in the temperate regions fails to conform to the regular four seasons that were nonetheless projected onto it, contributed to the sense of alienation that assailed many colonizers. It also hampered their endeavours to induce the land to grow European crops, until assisted by the full arsenal of industrial agriculture: a sorry tale, to which I will return in the final chapter. While 'acclimatization societies' set about importing species that were regarded as 'useful, aesthetic or respectably wild to fill the perceived gaps in primitive Australian nature' (Griffiths 1997, 3), nineteenth-century poets endeavoured to render the colonial earth less alien by accommodating it to the poetic discourse of European pastoral.

One of the most successful of these was Charles Harpur (1813–68), whose 'Midsummer Noon in the Australian Forest' effectively conjures the lazy, hazy, drowsy, dreamy mood of quiet reverie associated with summer noontide in the European pastoral tradition:

> NOT a sound disturbs the air,
> There is quiet everywhere;
> Over plains and over woods
> What a mighty stillness broods!
>
> All the birds and insects keep
> Where the coolest shadows sleep;
> Even the busy ants are found
> Resting in their pebbled mound;
> Even the locust clingeth now
> Silent to the barky bough:
> Over hills and over plains
> Quiet, vast and slumbrous, reigns.
>
> Only there's a drowsy humming
> From yon warm lagoon slow coming:
> 'Tis the dragon-hornet – see!
> All bedaubed resplendently,
> Yellow on a tawny ground –
> Each rich spot nor square nor round,
> Rudely heart-shaped, as it were
> The blurred and hasty impress there
> Of a vermeil-crusted seal,
> Dusted o'er with golden meal.
> Only there's a droning where
> Yon bright beetle shines in air,
> Tracks it in its gleaming flight
> With a slanting beam of light,
> Rising in the sunshine higher,
> Till its shards flame out like fire.
>
> Every other thing is still,
> Save the ever-wakeful rill,

Whose cool murmur only throws
Cooler comfort round repose;
Or some ripple in the sea
Of leafy boughs, where, lazily,
Tired summer, in her bower
Turning with the noontide hour,
Heaves a slumbrous breath ere she
Once more slumbers peacefully.

Oh, 'tis easeful here to lie
Hidden from noon's scorching eye,
In this grassy cool recess
Musing thus of quietness.[10]

As environmental historian Tim Bonyhady (2000) has shown, by no means all settler Australians shared the widespread view of the colonial earth as hostile and deficient. Not unlike the artists discussed by Bonyhady, Harpur had an aesthetic appreciation of the Australian 'bush' (specifically, the dry sclerophyll forests of his natal New South Wales), which he construes in this poem as a *locus amoenus* in the manner of Theocritus, Vergil or indeed Keats. Yet it is clear from this text that the European insignia of summer cannot be translated seamlessly to the Australian environment. Among these, as we have seen, are swelling fruits and – at least in the Romantic hybridization of pastoral and georgic – ripening grain: harbingers of the harvest to come. Harpur, however, has fled the agrarian landscape and escaped into the bush in order to find his *locus amoenus*, the tenuousness of which is suggested by his reference to 'Noon's scorching eye'. Indeed, in Paul Kane's reading, Harpur's would-be idyll ends up morphing into more of an 'anti-pastoral' (2004), hinting that Australian summers are not as benign as might be suggested by the mood of easefulness that the colonial poet invokes in his strained effort to adapt the insignia of European seasonal poetry to the antipodean environment: as he well knew, there would be many years when that 'ever wakeful rill' would fall silent, while the oil-filled 'leafy boughs' above it were bound, sooner or later, to burst explosively into flame.[11] Here too we see the problematic colonial move away from the European Romantic valorization of non-instrumentalizing modes of encounter with earth and sky in more-or-less anthropogenic environments towards a celebration of wild places, set apart from human habitation: places, that is to say, where the long history of Indigenous place-making was in the process of being erased, or at least suppressed.

Among contemporary Australian writers, the preeminent poet of summer is unquestionably Kevin Hart. Hart's preoccupation with the phenomenality of heat, typically experienced in urban environments, has a biographical index in the shock of arriving in Brisbane in the midst of a steamy sub-tropical summer as an eleven-year-old immigrant from London, the son of 'ten pound poms' (beneficiaries of the Assisted Passage Migration Scheme established by the Australian government in 1945 in an effort to populate the country with suitably white British citizens). As a scholar of literature and religion, Hart has influentially brought Derridean deconstruction and, more recently, Michel Henry's phenomenology into conversation with negative theology; and, not unlike Lilburn's, his poetry is profoundly informed by the apophatic variant of the Christian contemplative tradition. Yet while the concerns of his verse often have a religious dimension, his poetic language is intensely physical, and not infrequently erotic. As in the pastoral tradition (and in Hart's own adolescent experience in Brisbane in the late 1960s), summer and sex are intimately connected, and generally languidly and lusciously so. Yet in Hart's urban post-pastoral, this is not always the case. In one of his many poems simply entitled 'Summer', for example, the enervating atmosphere of inner-city Melbourne on a scorcher, when 'A trip to the corner shop can take all day', assumes a menacing character through its association with imagery of casual sexual objectification ('the youngish wife outside with her long legs/And her big husband off in Singapore/For what must be his second month up there/Doing software'), along with all that remains unspoken at the end, 'about the booze/The crying in the backyard late at night,/About the smell of thunder in the dark/And that walk back' (2008, 13).

The year after Hart published the collection *Young Rain*, in which this poem appeared, Melbourne experienced a record-breaking heatwave, during which birds, possums and fruit bats fell dead out of the trees, and koalas, who normally do not need to drink, staggered into suburban gardens looking for water. So many people died that underground carparks had to be repurposed as temporary morgues. Occurring towards the end of a decade-long drought, this heatwave brought three consecutive days with temperatures above 43°C to downtown Melbourne. When it peaked on February 7 at 46.4°C, much of the state of Victoria was engulfed in the so-called Black Saturday firestorm. Until the apocalyptic summer of 2019–20, this was the worst fire disaster in Australian settler history, but it is one of several extreme weather events this century that have been linked to anthropogenic climate change. The sense of foreboding that Australia's ever hotter summers have come to engender among those who live with the knowledge of global warming was anticipated by Hart in a poem from the 1980s, entitled 'That Bad Summer':

> Vast cobwebs in the sky. No wind for months.
> Airports deserted, and the trains on strike;
> Odd bits of cargo litter Lygon Street
>
> Beneath a Fokker hanging by a wing.
> A dull fierce silence everywhere you go:
> Suburbs and parks crisscrossed by shade all day;
>
> Your childhood dreams of camping out in tents
> All summer long has just about come true,
> Though kids are kept inside on sedatives.
>
> The air gone thick and bad. Some days it takes
> An entire afternoon to cross a road,
> Some days an hour to wink at one you love.
>
> What's worse, the hottest year this century!
> Our bedroom windows have begun to sweat,
> Reflections in mirrors cannot stay awake,
>
> While numerals peel off the Town Hall clock.
> Better, perhaps, to sleep the summer through.
> No longer shocked, good citizens lie down
>
> Beneath skylights, observing spiders mate
> – the bluest movie curving round our sky –
> Or watch that regiment attack the webs,
>
> Ballooning past grey clouds with guns and knives.
> Nothing much happening in parliament
> Yet food supplies, I know, are running thin.

> And here he comes again, that little man
> With a bald patch, still puffing door to door,
> Intently peddling jars of human breath.
>
> (2015, 45–46)

Composed in one of Hart's favourite verse forms, the tercet, reminiscent of Dante's *Divine Comedy*, the opening line makes it clear that we are in a place less idyllic than hellish: a place of 'wicked heat', to recall the title of one of Hart's most sultry collections (1999). Many of the insignia of summer in the pastoral tradition are recalled here but qualified in such a way as to evoke a distinctly uncanny atmosphere: the prevailing stillness is disquieting, for there has been 'no wind for months'; the silence is 'fierce'; shade persists 'all day'; drowsiness has deepened into torpor, inclining the speaker 'to sleep the summer through'; and the heat is so enervating that libido is all but quenched – 'Some days it takes/An entire afternoon to cross a road,/Some days an hour to wink at one you love.' There is no 'grassy cool recess' here, for the weather-world out-of-doors has turned hostile: 'The air gone thick and bad'; 'kids are kept inside on sedatives.' And in place of the hum, drone and twitter of bees, beetles and birds, there is only the bizarre spectacle of spiders mating overhead, observed through skylights: 'the bluest movie curving round our sky', the source, as we discover, of those vast cobwebs named in the opening line. The uncanny atmosphere of this 'bad summer' is rendered yet more disturbing by the signs of sociopolitical disarray: 'Airports deserted, and the trains on strike', and 'Nothing much happening in parliament/Yet food supplies, I know, are running thin.'

This is, as we learn in the central line of the poem, 'the hottest year this century!' Evidently construed as a 'natural disaster', the cause of all this trouble has been projected onto 'nature over yonder', tapping into primal fears that have fixed upon those alien others who have allegedly taken possession of the sky, and whose webs are being vainly attacked by a 'regiment ... Ballooning past grey clouds with guns and knives'. This arachnophobe's nightmare recalls the colonial Australian discourse of battling with a hostile environment: one that has begun to be reactivated in response to extreme weather events that should be recognized as warning signs of anthropogenic climate change but are instead attributed to a violent and amoral nature beyond the human realm (Rigby 2015a: 10–13). That the attribution of responsibility to alien arachnid invaders is a similarly delusional denial strategy is hinted at in the opening and closing stanzas of 'That Bad Summer'. By referring to the debris littering Lygon St (a hip street of restaurants, bars and upmarket shops close to the

University of Melbourne and just outside the central business district) as 'cargo', Hart deftly discloses consumerism as the dominant popular religion of this dystopian urban world. Together with fossil-fuelled transportation, recalled metonymically in the 'Fokker hanging by a wing', the consumerist idolatry of objects of similarly fossil-fuelled human manufacture is a significant contributor to climate change, as well as an impediment to effective mitigation. Yet instead of recognizing the alien sky of this Anthropocene anti-pastoral as anthropogenically altered, blame is deflected onto 'nature'. Meanwhile, those with a commercial interest in so doing are ecocidally set on maintaining practices that produce high levels of carbon dioxide emissions: troped here as 'that little man/With a bald patch, still puffing door to door,/ Intently peddling jars of human breath' (i.e. carbon dioxide).

As I read it, 'That Bad Summer' is powerfully evocative of the uncanny atmosphere and sense of threat engendered by the weird weather of an anthropogenically changing climate. Yet in its amusingly satirical diagnosis of maladaptive denialism, this text passes beyond an affective ecopoetics into the terrain of the ecoprophetic: terrain to be explored further in Chapter 4. In concluding this chapter, though, I want to reiterate the value of the kind of ecological aesthetics discussed here in honing our awareness of the affective force of our physical environs. This enhanced appreciation of our trans-corporeal susceptibility to environmental conditions, in terms of our affective embodied experience no less than our physiological health, should inform discussions and policies intended to conserve or create spaces and places conducive to both personal well-being and collective flourishing. As mentioned previously, ecological aesthetics has much to contribute to fields such as architecture, urban planning and landscape gardening. In my view, an affective ecopoethics is also pivotal to the cultivation of 'cultures of nature and wellbeing'. For while there is undoubtedly plenty of evidence of the physiological and psychological benefits of a dip in the sea, for example, or a walk in the woods, the readiness to even participate in such activities and experience the sense of well-being they potentially afford is socially contingent and culturally inflected – just as making them available for all is an ecopolitical matter of environmental justice.

In the UK, for example, a 2019 study commissioned by the Campaign to Protect Rural England found that around half of the country's most socially deprived areas are situated more than fifteen miles by road from England's ten national parks and forty-six areas of outstanding natural beauty (AONBs). With the defunding of rural bus services, and in the absence of other public transport links, this has put England's national parks out of reach for many poorer people.¹² Yet the impetus for their creation came not only from middle-class environmentalists, inspired by Wordsworth's vision for the Lake District, but also from the likes of Benny Rothman of the Young Communist League in Manchester. Rothman was one of the leaders of the mass trespass of 500 men and women, largely from working-class Sheffield and Manchester, onto the privately owned moorland at Kinder Scout in Derbyshire's Peak District in 1932. In the subsequent court hearing, Rothman argued, 'We ramblers, after a hard week's work, in smokey towns and cities, go out rambling for relaxation and fresh air. And we find the finest rambling country is closed to us... Our request, or demand, for access to all peaks and uncultivated moorland is nothing unreasonable.'¹³ The jury were unpersuaded, and he and four others were jailed for between four and six months. But their actions inspired further, and larger, protests, ultimately contributing to the passing of the National Parks and Access to the Countryside Act of 1949, which was intended to secure access to 'nature reserves' and 'open country' for all. The National Parks and AONBs that were subsequently created, like Wordsworth's Lakes and Rothman's Peak, are all peopled places, featuring a range of past and present land-uses, often involving farming and commoning, where biodiversity conservation and human well-being are understood to be intimately entwined.

Today, efforts are underway to enable a wider diversity of people to enjoy the health benefits and affective affordances of rambling in such places. These include collaborations between the National Health Service and the National Trust to increase access for the disabled,¹⁴ as well as citizen initiatives, such as Bristol's Black2Nature, a project created by a remarkable British Bangladeshi teenager, Mya-Rose Craig, to advance race equality with respect to nature and well-being and to encourage other people of black, Asian, ethnic minority (BAME) backgrounds (who currently make up on 1 per cent of visitors to England's National Parks, although they constitute 17 per cent of the population) to experience the benefits of spending time in enlivening outdoor environments.¹⁵ Yet you do not necessarily have to leave the confines of the city to seek these out. Let me conclude this chapter, then, by introducing you to a place where an ecopoetic culture of collective flourishing has taken root in Melbourne, not far from Hart's Carlton.

My father grew up between the two world wars quite close to Lygon St, but a couple of suburbs further out in what was then the working-class suburb of Coburg, in a small weatherboard house with a corrugated iron roof, right across the road from the looming granite walls of Pentridge Prison. About half a mile away, the little Merri Creek makes its way down to the Yarra River, and he and a friend liked to go adventuring on its banks. Among its many attractions, as he recalls in his memoirs, 'were a rather tricky but climbable basalt cliff and the nearby "Coburg Badlands", a severely eroded area replete with little caves and gullies, to several of which we gave our own names, such as "Dead Man's Gulch"' (T. H. Rigby 2019: 30). By the early 1980s, however, when ecophilosopher Freya Mathews moved to Brunswick (situated between Coburg and Carlton), the Merri had been turned into 'an utterly degraded little gutter, winding past the backs of factories and under flyovers, choked with [invasive] fennel and blackberry' (2005: 134), along with the carelessly discarded detritus of the destroyer-consumer society of the Great Acceleration. All that, however, was about to change. Thanks to the efforts of the Friends of Merri Creek, in collaboration with other community groups and the local authorities, the creek was cleaned up and native vegetation replanted along its banks, luring back both native birds, such as the Sacred Kingfisher, which had long since been driven away, and local kids. Today, walkers and riders along the bike path that was subsequently constructed from Dight's Falls, where it joins the Yarra River in trendy Abbotsford, all the way to the socioeconomically deprived outer northern suburbs, are hailed by the gold spires of the Russian Orthodox Church, built by parishioners over many years, the Aboriginal flag of the Wurundjeri Healing Place, and the windmills and African grass hut rooftops of the Centre for Education and Research in Environmental Strategies (CERES) (Mathew 2005: 135).

As its name suggests, the CERES Community Environment Park conjoins environmental science with ecosophical mythopoiesis: Ceres, after all, is the Roman counterpart of the Greek goddess of agrarian fertility, Demeter. Under her auspices, this 4.5-hectare site by the Merri Creek, once part of the well-tended country of the Wurundjeri people, then a settler society quarry, then a tip, has become a vibrant place of socioecological renewal:

> The soil, originally compacted and barren, became fruitful again. The ground sprouted with gardens and groves; animals (particularly pigs, sacred to Demeter) made their home there; and people, especially school children came from far and wide to visit the site and learn about the ways of renewal, exemplified in windmills and solar generators, methane digesters and grey water systems, worm farms and native permaculture. There was music and dancing and art.... There were many festivals, notably the annual Kingfisher Festival.
>
> (Mathews 2005: 202)

As Mathews stresses in her article 'Singing up the City' in the inaugural issue of *Philosophy Activism Nature* (i.e. *PAN*, in honour of the presiding deity of pastoral), this did not arise from a modernist grand plan that was imposed on the site, but rather emerged in an improvisational manner as 'a result of piecemeal creative initiatives and spontaneous adaptation to changing conditions and contexts' (2000: 9). This has contributed to the distinctive ecological aesthetics of the site, in which:

> Different aspects of life intermingle and permeate each other: offices are situated in the midst of food gardens; in the gardens themselves, cross-species mutuality rather than species apartheid is fostered; animals wander around the café; children run freely; sociability informs work; functional areas are inscribed with 'art', which endows the mundane activities that take place in those areas with larger meanings, and lifts the tone of daily life to a ritual or poetic level.
>
> (2000: 10)

Many social enterprises are now housed at CERES, including several devoted to contemplative and creative practices, along with 'fair food', 'fair wood' and bee-keeping, among others. There are courses in sustainability, hospitality, and horticulture, and each year CERES reaches out to some 200,000 school children across metropolitan Melbourne and rural and regional Victoria. And while local kids get to muck around once more by the restored creek, CERES Global offers participatory, cross-cultural, educational and skill sharing programs with far-flung communities on Yolngu country in Arnhem Land in Australia's Northern Territory, as well as in India, Indonesia, China and Cuba. The Kingfisher Festival is no longer an annual event, but there are many others, including a Harvest Festival that honours the place's presiding deity.[16]

None of this, in isolation, is going to stop the seasons from coming unstuck. Yet the heightened awareness of human psycho-somatic susceptibility to our physical environs, including weather conditions and their weirding, afforded by the ecopoetics of atmosphere, is conducive to the cultivation of a wider culture of 'nature and wellbeing', within which ecological considerations are increasingly salient.

3

'piping in their honey dreams': Creaturely ecopoetics

In what was to be the final issue of the *Athenäum* (1800), Friedrich Schlegel published a lightly fictionalized account of the debates about the nature, history and value of literature, which had animated the discussions of the Jena circle over the preceding years. Distributing their differing perspectives among a cast of seven speakers of mixed gender, the 'Conversation on Poetry' (*Gespräch über die Poesie*) bears witness to what Schlegel termed the 'symphilosophical' and 'sympoetic' conviviality of Early German Romanticism. This short-lived experiment might not have ushered in that new epoch of the arts and sciences about which he had speculated in a letter to his brother, August Wilhelm: one that would arise should 'symphilosophy and sympoesy become so generalised and intensified, that it would no longer be unusual for many complementary natures to create works collaboratively'.[1] In retrospect, though, this can be seen as a noteworthy precursor to contemporary calls for an ecologically oriented praxis of sympoiesis: to 'make-with – become-with, compose-with – the earthbound', as Donna Haraway (2016: 102) puts it. For the model of co-creativity that gave rise to, and was embodied in, the *Athenäum*, was also understood to extend beyond the human.

As Schlegel observes in the foreword to the 'Conversation', human creativity grows out of, and remains indebted to, the 'unformed and unconscious poesy of the living earth', of which we are ourselves a 'bloom'. This primal poesy, which 'stirs in the plant and shines in the light, smiles in a child, gleams in the flower of youth, and glows in the loving bosom of women', Schlegel avers, has always been humanity's privileged 'object and source of activity and joy'. The human capacity to 'hear the music of the unceasing action' (*unendlichen Spielwerks*) of natural becoming, and 'to understand the beauty of [this] poem', arises because we are ourselves 'a part of the poet, a part of his creative spirit lives in us and never ceases to glow with secret force under the ashes of our self-induced unreason'. For the young Schlegel, at the height of his romantic avant-gardism, this poetic deity (*Gottheit*), like Schelling's 'world soul', was located within nature *qua natura naturata* ('nature naturing'), which he too had come to understand as a creatively self-organizing and dynamically self-transforming meta-organism (1967: 339).[2]

Here, then, the continuity between human creativity and natural becoming is seen to arise from the agency of the One (*natura naturata*) operating within and across both spheres. This leaves open the question of whether some among the Many (*natura naturans*, 'nature natured') might not actively co-create, sympoietically, across species lines, in the interests of collective creaturely flourishing: might the 'many natures' referred to in Schlegel's letter, in other words, be more than only human? If so, what forms might their collaboration take, and how might that be traced in poetic works of merely human words? These are the questions that I pursue in this chapter with reference to the 'creaturely ecopoetics' of John Clare, and its counterpart in poems by the African American poets, Audre Lorde ('The Bees', 1974) and Natasha Trethewey ('Carpenter Bee', 2009). If contemplative ecopoetics entrains a praxis of non-appropriative attentiveness to things beyond the self, while affective ecopoetics turns that attention back upon the self in its trans-corporeal responsiveness to its environs, creaturely ecopoetics highlights human entanglements, at once material and moral, with other living beings: entanglements that entail shared, if unevenly distributed, vulnerabilities, as well as shared, if variegated, communicative capacities; entanglements that harbour the ever-present risk of conflict and harm, as well as opportunities to co-create emergent multi-species worlds no longer constrained by the colonizing logic of human-nonhuman hyperseparation, and hence freed to explore more felicitous forms of coexistence in risky times.

Creaturely co-becoming and biosemiosis

The term 'creature' belongs originally to the lexicon of those monotheistic, and in a European context, predominantly Christian, religious traditions, according to which all things ultimately owe their existence to the *poiesis* of a divine Creator. In my secular re-deployment of this word, I propose to winkle it away from its theological origins, whilst retaining its connotation of radical indebtedness: the recognition, that is, of how your own existence, and that of every other living being, is contingent upon the lives and deaths of those who have gone before and upon whom you are dependent in the present. In addition, I take creaturely life to entail an inherent vulnerability. For Anat Pick, whose 'creaturely poetics' follows the philosophy of Simone Weil, the 'fragility and finitude' of our creaturely condition implies a 'recognition of life's value as material and temporal', calling us to respond compassionately towards fellow creatures, human and otherwise, in their abandonment to what Weil termed the '"pitiless necessity of matter"' (Pick 2011: 3, 4). For Judith Butler, following Levinas, vulnerability is parsed as 'precarity', and in Deborah Bird Rose's reading of Butler, the face of the other 'awakens us to the precariousness... of all lives', enjoining a responsibility to respond, as best we can to their pain and peril (2013: 11). Creaturely coexistence, then, at least from a human perspective, is an ethical undertaking. Before that, however, and for all concerned, it is a biophysical affair: one that Ralph Acampora terms 'symphysis' (2006: 76). As such, creatureliness also presupposes communication, and it is this that opens the possibility of more-than-human *sympoiesis*.

Unsurprisingly, Haraway's deployment of the term 'sympoiesis' is derived not from the Jena Romantics but rather from contemporary biological science: specifically, the work of a Canadian environmental science graduate student M. Beth Dempster, who proposed it in a 1998 paper to refer to 'collectively-producing systems that do not have self-defined spatial or temporal boundaries'. In such systems, Dempster explained, ' (i)nformation and control are distributed among components. The systems are evolutionary and have the capacity for surprising change' (qtd. in Haraway 2016: 61). Sympoiesis, Haraway insists, is 'a word proper to complex, dynamic, responsive, situated, historical systems' (58). With respect to evolutionary systems, it refers to the ways in which '[c]ritters... make each other through semiotic material involution, out of the beings of previous such entanglements' (60). These communicative interchanges, which enable the co-becoming of living organisms, evolutionary processes and ecological systems, are currently being explored in the burgeoning field of biosemiotics.

Biosemiotics proceeds from the premise that 'living nature', as Jesper Hoffmeyer puts it, is 'essentially driven by, or actually consist(s) of, semiosis' (2008: 4).[3] Among the diverse vehicles of communication that are perpetually composing, recomposing, decomposing and interconnecting the multifarious life forms that co-constitute Earth's biosphere are sound, scent, movement, pressure, texture, taste and shape, as well as more elusive but nonetheless powerfully efficacious phenomena such as electrical fields and chemical effusions. From a biosemiotic perspective, the whole world – or, rather, all worlds, since, as Uexküll discovered, each organism has its own – is, as Peirce put it, 'perfused with signs' (qtd. Wheeler 2011a: 271), from the level of the individual cell, within which genes must be interpreted in order to help build a body within a particular biophysical environment, to that of the literary critic who interprets a poem to help build understanding within a particular sociocultural environment. Biosemiotics is a fast-growing field with diverse disciplinary manifestations, ramifications and cross-fertilizations. Claus Emmeche's succinct definition from 1992 nonetheless still holds good:

> Biosemiotics proper deals with sign processes in nature in all dimensions, including 1) the emergence of semiosis in nature, which may coincide with or anticipate the emergence of living cells; 2) the natural history of signs; 3) the 'horizontal' aspect of semiosis in the ontogeny of organisms, in plant and animal communication, and in inner sign functions in the immune and nervous systems; and 4) the semiotics of cognition and language.
>
> (Qtd. Hoffmeyer 2008:4)

Biosemiotics proper, as Hoffmeyer observes, was invented independently several times over during the latter part of the twentieth century. It is widely accepted, however, that the preeminent figure who 'had the broadminded intellect and indefatigable energy to assemble all the threads that would serve as the foundation for the modern biosemiotic project' (2008: 364) was the Hungarian-born American linguist Thomas Sebeok (1920–2001), to whom Hoffmeyer's authoritative introduction to the field is dedicated. The two main threads out of which Sebeok wove his synthesis were the 'semeiotic' philosophy of American Pragmatist Charles Sanders Peirce and the *Umwelt* theory of German-Estonian biologist Jakob von Uexküll, which he explored in depth with Jakob's grandson, the medical researcher Thure von Uexküll. Sebeok was fascinated by nonhuman animal and human-animal communication, and in Peirce he found a theory of sign relations that was not restricted to human verbal communication (unlike the semiology of Ferdinand Saussure that was taken up so enthusiastically in French structuralism and post-structuralism, contributing to the pronounced anthropocentrism of the kind of theory that was so eagerly assimilated into literary and cultural studies from the 1970s onward).

In order to advance the theory of 'zoosemiotics' that he had postulated in the early 1960s, Sebeok needed to be able to account for the process whereby animals come to translate corporeal sensations into meaningful perceptions. It was in the revised second edition (1928) of Jakob von Uexküll's

Theoretische Biologie, which he read in the original German in 1978, that he found the key: namely, in Uexküll's redeployment of the existing German term *Umwelt* (environment) to designate a species-specific and more-or-less individually nuanced phenomenal world, a world, that is, composed of signs. As Hoffmeyer observes, Uexküll 'was working very much within a nineteenth century Romantic intellectual culture that was still vibrant in Estonia, while the science of Darwin's England was increasingly utilitarian, mechanistic and Malthusian' (32). Among his most important (and under-researched) influences, moreover, were Schelling's *Naturphilosophie* and the developmental or 'epigenetic' biology of Goethe and Karl Ernst von Baer, among others (Kull 2001: 4).

Uexküll's research into the perceptual worlds of other-than-human animals revealed how every organism's *Umwelt* is borne out of the functionality of its particular bodily constitution and conditioned by its developmental stage and life experience. This is correlated with a mental model of reality, or *Innenwelt*, that determines whether and how any entity that enters an animal's physical environment might become a bearer of meaning – one that the animal will be called upon to interpret wisely in order to interact with it appropriately (e.g. as predator, prey, playfellow, mate or the source of some other kind of potential trouble, pleasure or interest). The relationship between an organism and its environment is dynamic, being continuously renegotiated through what Uexküll termed the 'functional cycle' of perception and action that 'effectively "couples" the ever-changing system that is the organism to the ever-changing system that is the world' (Favareau 2009: 32). In his work of natural philosophy, *On the World Soul* (*Von der Weltseele*, 1798), Schelling prefigures von Uexküll's discovery of species-specific semiospheres in his discussion of what he terms the 'sphere of characteristic impressions' (*Sphäre eigenthümlicher Eindrücke*) (2000: 248), by means of which all organisms (including humans) read the world and make their way within it.[4] While Sebeok and others have since extended this zoosemiotic line of inquiry, other biosemioticians have gone on to explore the sign relations that obtain within organisms ('endosemiosis'), among plants ('phytosemiosis') and even in inanimate nature ('physiosemiosis').

Most biosemiotic research hitherto has been conducted by natural scientists. However, it has also begun to attract the attention of a growing number of researchers in the environmental humanities. It is not hard to see why: by repositioning articulate human language on a continuum with the varied semiotic transactions with which all other organisms are also involved, biosemiotics opens a pathway out of the dead end of human exceptionalism, affording new ways of understanding and practicing forms of multispecies *sympoiesis*. In addition to restoring communicative agency to nonhumans, moreover, biosemiotics expands our understanding of human sign relations. As 'whole creatures', in Wendy Wheeler's felicitous phrase (borrowed from Goethe), humans also participate in a host of corporeal communications that generally transpire below the level of consciousness (2006). It is for this reason, as Peirce stressed, that we always know more than we think we know. Caught up, as we tend to be, in the world composed by the words that are forever running through our heads, passing out of our mouths, into our ears or being traced by our eyes or fingertips, much of what we know viscerally, so to speak, does not make it into our field of awareness. Occasionally, though, some of the signs that our mindful bodies are perpetually decoding might be felt in the flesh, such as the approach of a threat whose source we have not yet identified, or intuited as a hunch, which could give rise to one of those creative insights that Peirce termed 'abductions'. In his *System of Transcendental Idealism*, Schelling refers to this phenomenon as an 'aesthetic intuition' (*ästhetische Anschaung*), and he argues that it is by means of the 'poetic capacity' (*Dichtungsvermögen*) that these kinds of intuitions find their initial articulation in figurative language: metaphor, in this sense, constitutes a bridge whereby that which is as yet unknown enters into the sphere of the known (Wheeler 2011b). Aesthetic intuitions, or abductions, are clearly also in play in those affective responses to circumambient 'atmospheres' discussed in the previous chapter.

Biosemioticians consider human articulate language as probably the most complex sign system to have evolved so far on this planet; and with growing complexity, they argue, come increasing levels of what Hoffmeyer calls 'semiotic freedom'. This has enabled the intergenerational creation, perpetuation and transformation of symbol-based communal cultures, which, under certain geohistorical conditions, have in turn facilitated the emergence of greater social complexity and the augmentation and acceleration of communication across time and space through the development of new media (from writing to the Internet), thus enabling the creation of new kinds of knowledge, along with enhanced technological capacities. Increasing levels of semiotic freedom nonetheless also have a downside, as they imply also an ever-expanding margin of potential misunderstanding, along with the risk of entrapment in inherited ideas, images and narratives. Yet it is that same semiotic freedom which also allows us to reflect upon our own assumptions, critique oppressive imaginaries and prefigure alternative possibilities. Undoing those 'mind-forg'd manacles', as Blake put it, including those that have led some cultures down the path of human exceptionalism, is in itself a cultural task, entailing, among other things, new conversations about the material-semiotic world-making practices of other critters.

Haraway provides a startling example of the role of communication in interspecies sympoiesis in the case of bee orchids and their pollinating insects. As seen by their human researchers, Carla Hustak and Natasha Myers, 'the orchid and its bee pollinators are mutually constituted through a reciprocal capture from which neither plant nor insect can be disentangled' (qtd. in Haraway 2016: 68). This reciprocal capture, moreover, is inherently semiotic, dependent upon the male bee's enthusiastic response to what he perceives as the plant's enticing signals: namely, its mimicry of the colour, shape and scent of the female bee's sexual organs. Departing from the neo-Darwinian orthodoxy that construes such inter-relationships as purely exploitative, evidence of the 'selfish gene' in action, Hustak and Myers work 'athwart the reductive, mechanistic, and adaptationist logics that ground the ecological sciences' to 'offer a reading that amplifies accounts of the creative, improvisational, and fleeting practices through which plants and insects *involve* themselves in one another's lives' (qtd. in Haraway 2016: 69). Theirs, then, is an 'affective ecology in which creativity and curiosity characterize the experimental forms of life of all kinds of practitioners, not only humans' (qtd. in Haraway 2016: 68).

Among bees, whose virtual company we will be keeping throughout this chapter, the more sociable species have also acquired some remarkably poetic ways of collaborating with one another for mutual benefit. Bees are thought to have co-evolved with the glorious appearance of flowering plants during the Cretaceous era, possibly as early as 130 million years ago. Sometime over the next 50 million years, some bee species adopted a social lifestyle, acquiring marvellous artisanal proclivities and communicative capacities in the process. There are – still – an estimated 20–25,000 species that are known to science, but only a small number of these are honeybees: the kind in which sweet-toothed humans have understandably been most interested (Goulson 2013: 42–51). Following Karl von Frisch's pioneering work on the role of dance in honeybee communication, Seboek has demonstrated that this entails the use of symbolic (or 'arbitrary') as well as indexical and iconic signs, thereby subverting the great divide between humans as the sole *animal symbolicum*, as Ernst Cassirer put it, and all the rest (Bühler and Rieger 2006: 71–72). The research of ethologist James I. Gould (2002) lends further support to the claim that the 'waggle dances', whereby forager bees inform their coworkers of the direction, distance and quality of the nectar source they have found (the scent of which they are also conveying), are evidence of apian 'cognitive mapping', entailing the capacity to form concepts, develop insights and communicate these insights via signs that are actively interpreted. Apian *poeisis*, then, extends beyond what they *make* (hives and honey) to what they *say*, and the artistry of how they do so. If, for Petrarch, the bees' fabrication of honey was analogous to the writing of poetry, contemporary cognitive ethologists and biosemioticians are disclosing the 'more-than-metaphoric poetry of the bee' (Brown 2006: xv). Moreover, research conducted by Frisch's student, Martin Lindauer, provides evidence of argumentation among different 'scout' bees regarding the best site for a new nest when part of the colony is preparing to swarm. In view of these findings, Catriona Sandilands (2014) posits that honeybees might even be seen to practice a form of democratic politics, with the majority determining which pitch for a new nest site is most persuasive. While Sandilands readily concedes that 'these ideas of "honeybee democracy" are every bit as much located in historically specific political desires as were the post-Elizabethan invocations of Charles Butler in his 1609 "The Feminine Monarchie,"' she concludes that there are 'sound reasons for us to think of bees as having a public realm of their own' (163): one that is enmeshed with ours in ways that are increasingly precarious for all concerned.

Within the literary and visual texts of diverse cultures around the world, there is evidence of an extremely long history human-bee interaction in ancient cave paintings, as well as in the songs and stories of oral cultures, some of which persist into the present, despite the depredations wrought by sundry imperialist regimes, such as those of the Damara people of southern Kunene in Namibia (Sullivan 1999). Elsewhere in Africa, petroglyphs dating from around 10,000 years ago that have been found in present-day Zimbabwe also depict honey harvesting from wild bees. The most ancient surviving rock art in the world, confidently dated at 28,000 years old, adorns a rock shelter in Arnhem Land in Australia's Northern Territory. Although these do not include images of honey hunting, rock paintings found elsewhere in Australia do show bees' nests, honey hunting and/or the sticks used to pierce the hives or 'sugarbags', as they are called in Aboriginal English: it appears that First Nations Australians have been appropriating the fruits of apian labour for a very long time indeed (Fijn 2014). It was not only the honey they were after either: some rock art is painted with soft bees wax, which also came to be used for a variety of other purposes, such as forming the mouthpieces of didgeridoos; to wax and preserve string; for decorative hairpins, necklaces, pendants and headbands; and for toys like spinning tops, model animals and human figurines (Prideaux 2006: 8).

Where conditions conducive to the invention and expansion of agriculture emerged in the wake of the last Glacial Maximum, human-bee entanglements deepened, with the conversion of pre-existing vegetation to irrigated crops doubtless benefiting some bee species and disadvantaging others, while farmers' yields were – and remain – dependent upon bees for pollination. In some of these farming communities, ready access to the bees' sweet produce was significantly enhanced by the invention of beekeeping. Although the oldest surviving written works concerning beekeeping are Hittite texts from around 1,300 BCE, it seems that bees had already begun to be domesticated – to the extent that they ever have been, which is not entirely – in Egypt from around 4,500 years ago. That this practice was subsequently most avidly taken up in Europe has less to do with any special human bee-taming prowess in those parts than with the propensities of a particular bee species found there: namely, the Western honeybee (*apis mellifora*), who is a gentler critter than many other honeybees, although armed with that infamous sting. This constituted one of many unpleasant surprises for First Nations Australians, previously accustomed only to stingless bees, following the invasion of their country by resource-hungry Europeans and their mightily disruptive biotic entourage. For, having proven particularly amenable to cohabiting with humans in artificial hives, *apis mellifera* was thence later transported to all the parts of the world European nations have colonized (Preston 2006: 10).[5]

Bees also figure significantly within European literature, notably in pastoral and georgic poetry. In Theocritus's *Idylls*, as in much subsequent pastoral literature, bees are invoked as part of the retinue of summer in the meadows: 'Sure bedstraw there doth thrive/ And fine oak-trees and pretty bees all humming at the hive' (I, 104). As such, they are recruited to provide a kind of virtual mood music. From an ecophenomenological perspective, however, as we have seen in the last chapter, this is hardly trivial. 'Humming' is of course onomatopoeic, and in this way the written text bears a zoopoetic trace of an other-than-human voice. In conjunction with other metonymies of place and time (the grasses and wildflowers offering 'bedstraw', soft ground on which to lie, under the shady green canopy offered by the 'fine oak-trees'), this apian mood music summons the atmosphere of dreamy, drowsy easefulness arising from a creaturely somatic-affective responsiveness to particular socio-environmental conditions: noon, in a shady spot in the meadows, on a warm summer's day, when you are released, however briefly, from your labours (or, as in the admittedly idealized case of the Theocritus' imagined herdsmen, when the work itself allows periods of leisure) and in the absence of any overwhelming physical or emotional discomfort.

In the *Idylls*, as in much subsequent pastoral, this *locus amoenus* is nonetheless wedded to a potential source of considerable suffering, as well as intense pleasure: namely erotic love. Here, too, bees play a part, and an interestingly ambivalent one at that. In the embedded narrative recounted in Idyll 19, mischievous young Eros gets stung while stealing honey from the hive. When he complains about this to his mother, Aphrodite wryly observes 'What?... art not a match for a bee, and thou so little and yet able to make wounds so great?' (XIX, 1). Here, bees are entertainingly construed as resisting their recruitment to the service of human amorousness, as instigated by the honey-hungry boy-god, by giving him a taste of his own medicine with a painful piercing, the diminutive counterpart of his love-dealing arrows. That Eros is said to have encountered such apian opposition might be related to the widespread assumption that bees did not reproduce sexually, a zoological error that led to their association with the medieval Christian veneration of the Virgin Mary, and the notion that they alone of all creatures had escaped from the Garden of Eden untainted by the Fall (Preston 2006: 76–78).

The classical poet, however, was happily untainted by the Christian dualism of Eros and Agape. This is evident from the first Idyll, in which Theocritus enlists bees, not for their presumed chastity but rather in service of the love-sick goatherd Daphnis, the prototype for all subsequent pastoral poets. Having pledged himself exclusively to his first love, Daphnis is pining away for love of another, possibly Aphrodite herself, but is graciously fed by bees when incarcerated by a malicious king. The humble goatherd shares this distinction with several Greek deities, including the big boss, Zeus himself, who was fed by bees as an infant after his mother hid him in a cave to protect him from his violent father, Kronos, earning him the sobriquet, *melissaios*, bee-man, from the Greek for honey-bee, *Melissa*. Melissa also became the name of a bee nymph, and in some accounts, it was she who hid the baby-god and fed him honey. Pan and Dionysus, key figures in the mythic landscape of pastoral literature, were also fed exclusively by bees as infants, and it was the latter who is said to have taught humans how to keep bees. Dionysus, like the Roman Bacchus, was in fact originally the god not of wine but of mead, which is believed to be the most ancient alcoholic brew in the world. It is perhaps as a consequence of mead's capacity to induce altered states of consciousness that bees also became linked with prophecy: Apollo's Temple at Delphi was built of beeswax and attended by bees. Apian mysteries also crossed gender boundaries: the Delphic oracle was female, and the priestesses of Cybele, Artemis and Demeter were called *Melissae* (Preston 2006: 115–20). In this shared denomination, another boundary-crossing quality of the bee becomes apparent, linking earth mothers with virgin huntresses, the domestic and the wild.

It is precisely in this contact zone that the pastoral is located, and it is through the story of Daphnis, friend to all wild creatures, yet blessed with exceptional gifts of human speech and song, that the poet acknowledges his indebtedness to the *poiesis* of bees. This has both a metaphoric and a material dimension. To begin with, the sweetness to the ear of Daphnis's voice is likened to 'honey to the lip' (VIII, 81) in an apian trope for eloquence and insight that is also at play in the accounts of numerous other bee-fed writers (Sophocles, Pindar and later Vergil and Lucan), philosophers (Xenophon, Plato) as well as Christian saints (Basil of Caesaria, Ambrose and especially Bernard, who became known as *doctor mellifluous*, patron saints of bees, bee-keepers, wax-melters and candle-makers). Additionally, the pipe that Daphnis bequeaths to Pan is referred to as 'pipe of honey breath,/Of wax well knit round lips to fit' (I.,128): an acknowledgement of the human appropriation of a product of bee-manufacturing prowess in the construction of works of human culture; and (perhaps especially for contemporary readers) a reminder that in the absence of the *sympoiesis* of the more-than-human world, in which bees are such key singers in the choir, there would be no *poiesis* of merely human words.

Beekeeping enters European pastoral literature in its more labour-intensive moiety, the Georgic, pioneered by Vergil in his work of that name from around 29 BCE, but pre-figured in Hesiod's *Work and Days* (*c.* 700 BCE), a farmer's almanac in which honeybees are recruited to provide an exemplar of cooperative rural labour (with the exception of the drones, to whom the poet likens good-for-nothing women and sluggards). In his *Georgics*, Vergil composes an agrarian counterpart to the more 'idyllic' – albeit by no means untroubled – world of his earlier *Eclogues* (42–37 BCE), which responded more directly to the Theocratic prototype. Celebrating 'husbandry', the *Georgics* endorse a human (and, like Hesiod, specifically male-gendered) dominion, an attitude that became infused with a biblical mandate in later Christianized variants of this pastoral sub-genre (Gifford 2014: 20). The georgic poet nonetheless also warns against hubris by insisting that successful farming demands close attention to the peculiarities of weather, water and soil, and the ways of vegetal growth and animal conduct. Nowhere is this acknowledgement of the potentially resistant agencies of the nonhuman more pronounced than in Book 4, which is entirely devoted to the art of bee-keeping. In her ecocritical rereading of the *Georgics*, Rachel Nisbet observes that the restocking of Aristaeus' hives is framed as a restorative act of atonement that 'augers well for the cultivation of egalitarian social relations in Vergil's slave-free Mantua after a civil war', in the course of which Aristaeus had raped Eurydice ('wide Justice') (2018: 32). In his restorative labours, force is replaced by seduction: Aristaeus orchestrates a mini pastoral idyll for the free-living bees as a way of luring them to make themselves at home in the artificial hive. This, we learn, should be sited near 'clear springs and moss-green pools' (l. 19), surrounded by the bees' favourite flowering plants growing in a shady nook, with appealing access provided by little bridges of carefully positioned stones and willow-branches strewn across the hurrying brook. In this *sympoietic* vision of multispecies world-making, bee-keeping is conceived as ideally benefiting all concerned, on the premise that if the bees are not happy with their treatment and surroundings, they can and will simply up and leave (a privilege admittedly not shared by the more thoroughly domesticated livestock that Vergil's farmer is entrained to 'husband').

Following the recovery, recasting and repurposing of classical pastoral during the Renaissance, the Virgilian dyad of georgic and bucolic modes gave way during the eighteenth century to a stark divide between the idealizations of Augustan pastoral, on the one hand, and the subversive realism of labouring-class 'anti-pastoral', as exemplified by Stephen Duck's *The Threshers' Labour* (1730), on the other (Gifford 2014). As I have argued previously, Romantic neo- or counter-pastoral verse at its best forged a new synthesis, celebrating the more-than-human life of the countryside – and sometimes also, as in William Wordsworth's London Bridge sonnet, of the city – in the shadow of industrialization, from a standpoint of resistance to the encroaching objectification, instrumentalization and commodification of the natural world (Rigby 2004b: 234–56).

The late Romantic poet John Clare carried forward the vision of present pleasure and immanent holiness of Wordsworth's earlier verse, while introducing a whole new attentiveness to the particularities of the poet's other-than-human fellow creatures, and the varied perils that they faced. For pioneering ecocritic Jonathan Bate (2000: 153–68), Clare's verse exemplified the art of *ecopoiesis*, understood (with Heidegger) as the verbal 'making of the dwelling place', in that it resembled the bird's nests that abound in his work: it opens a space, woven of words, within which life can come forth and be nurtured. But is this to put too parental a spin on it? After all, most of the animals that haunt Clare's extensive zoopoetic oeuvre are not domesticated, and they are commonly framed both as strangers, respecting their other-than-human alterity, and as neighbours, with the full ethical freight that concept carried in a Christian culture (where neighbourliness was of course always meant to be extended to the stranger, but in which that welcome, when practiced at all, had historically been largely confined to other humans). In my reading, then, Clare's ecopoetics is less about nesting, connoting care for your own kith and kin, than about kin-making across the boundaries that separate different kinds: a tricky practice of multispecies *sympoiesis* beset by friction, fraught with risk.[6]

'piping in their honey dreams': Clare's wild bees

The bees that leave their traces in the two poems discussed here are identified from the outset as 'wild', suggesting that we are in the territory of pastoral idyll rather than agrarian georgic. Yet, while this might be partially true of the earlier of this contrasting pair, it is definitely not the case with his untitled sonnet from the 1830s, and both are in differing ways hybrid forms.

Wild Bees
These children of the sun which summer brings
As pastoral minstrels in her merry train
Pipe rustic ballads upon busy wings
And glad the cotters quiet toils again
The white nosed bee that bores its little hole
In mortared walls and pipes its symphonies
And never absent couzin, black as coal
That Indian-like bepaints its little thighs
With white and red bedight for holiday
Right earlily a morn do pipe and play
And with their legs stroke slumber from their eyes
And aye so fond they of their singing seem
That in their holes abed at close of day
They still keep piping in their honey dreams
And larger ones that thrum on ruder pipe
Round the sweet smelling closen and rich woods
Where tawny-white and red flus[h]ed clover buds
Shine bonnily and bean fields blossom ripe
Shed dainty perfumes and give honey food
To these sweet poets of the summer field
Me much delighting as I sawn along
The narrow path that hay laid meadow yields,
Catc[h]ing the windings of their wandering song
The black and yellow bumble first on wing
To buzz among the sallows early flowers

> Hiding its nest in holes from fickle spring
> Who stints his rambles with her frequent showers
> And one that may for wiser piper pass
> In livery dress half sables and half red
> Who laps a moss ball in the meadow grass
> And hurds her stores when april showers have fled
> And russet commoner who knows the face
> Of every blossom that the meadow brings
> Starting the traveller to a quicker pace
> By threatning round his head in many rings
> These sweeten summer in their happy glee
> By giving for her honey melodie[7]

Although only lightly sketched, the apian others of 'Wild Bees' (1820s) differ from the generic critters of earlier pastoral in being clearly differentiated into diverse kinds. In fact, so attentive is Clare to the particularities of his strange apian neighbours that the entomologist Jeff Ollerton has been able to identify most of them with a reasonable degree of zoological confidence: these are, in order of appearance, the male and female Hairy-footed Flower Bee (*Anthophora plumipes*), since, as Ollerton explains on his 'Biodiversity blog', the latter 'is all black except for its orange pollen brush on its rear legs, and... also nests in old walls'; the Buff-tailed Bumblebee (*Bombus terrestris*), 'the queens of which tend to emerge earlier than other, similar species, hence *"first on wing"*. It also usually nests in rodent holes'; the Red-shanked Carder Bee (*Bombus ruderarius*), 'the only red and black bee in the UK that makes a mossy nest above ground'; and the Common Carder Bee (*Bombus pascuorum*), 'which is as common as the name suggests, and is renowned for foraging on a wider range of flowers than most others, and therefore *"knows the face of every blossom"*' (2016).

As Clare avers in his short essay on 'Taste' from the mid-1820s, a contemplative mode of comportment towards ones more-than-human environs was by no means restricted to men of means:

> to stand & muse upon the bank of a meadow pool fringed with reed & bulrushes & silver clear in the middle on which the sun is reflected in spangles & there to listen the soulsoothing music of distant bells this is a luxury of happiness & felt even by the poor shepherd boy.
>
> (1983: 285)

Yet by comparison with Wordsworth's, Clare's poetic musings display the whole new attention to empirical detail that is evident also in his prose writings. In his Natural History letter of 25 March 1825, for example, he observes with respect to the bees 'singing a busy welcome to spring' how he had 'often wonderd how these little travelers found there homes agen from the woods & solitudes were they journey for wax and honey', noting that he had 'seen them to day at least 3 miles from any village in Langley wood working at the palms & some of them with their little thighs so loaded with the yellow dust as to seem almost unable to flye' (1983: 59–60). Here, and elsewhere, Clare's natural history writings exemplify a 'gentle' or 'delicate' empiricism, to use a Goethean coinage (*sanfte Empirie* Goethe 1988: 307), allowing things to disclose themselves on their own terms, in their complex and dynamic interrelations with other entities and phenomena (including their human observer). His perspective is participatory and self-reflexive, embodying a mode of contemplation keyed to compassion as much as to curiosity, open to empathy as well as alert to alterity, mindful both of the potential impact of his presence on the critters he is observing and of his own affective responses to what he perceives. Clare certainly participated in the popular practice of collecting 'specimens', assisting his friend and mentor Joseph Henderson in the collection of birds' nests, snail shells and orchids. Henderson was head gardener at Milton Hall when Clare was working as a gardener at Burghley Hall, and it was from him that Clare learnt how to use a killing jar for insects and how to display them on a cork board (Heyes 2019; see also Heyes 2015). In much of his writing, and especially in his verse, though, far from seeking to pin things down as the object of a reifying gaze, Clare lets us glimpse them in the horizon of a shared creatureliness – one which might proffer pleasure aplenty but is also rife with risk. Disclosing also the entanglement of natural and human histories, as Irvine and Gorji (2013) have remarked, Clare's creaturely ecopoetics construe his rural environs as a multispecies *oikos* rather than as scenery, a mere backdrop for human dramas.

'Wild Bees' opens in a distinctly pastoral mode, with a reminiscence of Daphnis' 'pipe of honey breath'. Here, though, it is the bees themselves that are identified in the opening stanza as 'pastoral minstrels', who 'Pipe rustic ballads upon rustic wings'. That the happy hearer of the bees' balladry is not a herdsman but a toiling cottager nonetheless throws us into georgic terrain; but in place of the solicitous husbandry of Vergil's model beekeeper, Clare foregrounds the independent agency of his free-living apian neighbours, inviting us to consider the distinctly other-than-human semiosphere that they inhabit, as well as how it is enmeshed with ours.[8] In the case of those of the 'white nosed bee' and his 'never absent couzin', this includes taking advantage of the fruits of human labour in their evaluation of the 'mortared walls' constructed to enclose human homes as a suitable location for their own nests. Similarly, the 'larger ones that thrum on ruder pipe' find sustenance not only among the wild flowers of the woods and meadows but also in the bean fields. The 'black and yellow bumble' avails itself of other creatures' nests, taking shelter below ground from spring showers, while the 'one that may for wiser piper pass' is said to make provision for leaner times, as she not only 'laps a moss ball in the meadow grass' but also 'hurds her stores when april showers have fled'. These critters are shown to be actively interpreting the bee-shaped *Umwelt* they inhabit, with the 'russet commoner' said to be one 'who knows the face/Of every blossom that the meadow brings'. Through their interpretations and interactions, they co-create the multispecies *oikos* that the villagers too inhabit in their human way. Deploying what might be considered a strategic anthropomorphism, moreover, the speaker hails his apian neighbours as fellow poets, 'piping in their honey dreams'.

In keeping with the pastoral tradition, Clare construes this multispecies *oikos* as a gift economy, but one in which gifts are neither intended as such nor directly returned, but rather circulate in felicitously haphazard ways. These, then, are on the way to being true gifts, as Derrida (1992) would have it, spiralling outwards, rather than locked in a closed cycle of reciprocity, running on, as does Clare's verse, from line to line, unconstrained by punctuation, and without reaching a definitive conclusion. Plants, pursuing their own purposes as beneficiaries of the ministry of sun, rain and soil, 'shed dainty perfumes and give honey food' to the bees, whose piping, although not intended for human ears, cheers the cottager. And while human walls and fields provide similarly unintentional affordances for some bees, these 'sweet poets of the summer fields' greatly delight the speaker as he strolls 'along/The narrow path that hay laid meadow yields,/Catching the windings of their wandering song'. The human poet, meanwhile, taking up the 'rustic ballad' of the bees, responds in kind with his own gift of words in honour of his apian counterparts. Foregrounding his musical kinship with these strange neighbours, Clare, who once averred that he 'found his poems in the fields' (qtd. Bate 2003: 15), frames his own verse as a work of *sympoiesis*, inspired and enabled by the summery symphonies of wild bees, which are in turn inspired and enabled by floral flourishing and open to whatever unforeseeable reception Clare's variously situated readers might afford his words.

The imagined gift economy of 'Wild Bees' is exemplary of the generosity of what Bresnihan terms the 'manifold commons', affirming 'the many different natures which unfold through ongoing, negotiated and changing relations between people and things' (Bresnihan 2013, 71). This pastoral idyll might be seen as a kind of heterotopia, lodged precariously within a socially stratified and increasingly capitalistic rural economy. Read in that context, Clare's likening of the cousin, 'black as coal', of the white-nosed bee to an Indian who 'bepaints its little thighs/With white and red bedight for holiday', is subtly suggestive of the vulnerability of the commons to colonization.[9] Importantly, Clare's 'biopolitics' (Washington 2014) of co-becoming does not demand a return to a putative paradise, in which, according to the Christian conceit recalled in Wordsworth's 'Vernal Ode' (1820), the bee had not yet acquired its sting. Here, as elsewhere, Clare admits conflict and suffering as an inevitable dimension of creaturely coexistence, remarking the propensity of that 'russet commoner' to startle the 'traveller to a qu[i]cker pace/By threatning round his head in many rings'. The risky dimension of multispecies world-making might also be discerned in the bees' very piping: for while this might recall Daphnis, and by extension, the mythic pastoral *locus amoenus* governed by Pan, it could also connote a cause, if not necessarily for panic, then at least for caution, as 'piping' is the term used by beekeepers to refer to the noise coming from the hive of social bees busily preparing to swarm. It is as much in such recollections of a shared capacity to inflict and receive harm as in the invocation of more felicitous forms of co-becoming, or 'embodied conviviality' (Acampora 2006: 96), that Clare's ecopoetics is distinctively 'creaturely'.

In the sonnet known as 'Wild Bees Nest' (*c.* 1832–7), this aspect of vulnerability predominates:

> The mower tramples on the wild bees nest
> And hears the busy noise and stops the rest
> Who carless proggle out the mossy ball
> And gather up the honey comb and all
> The boy that seeks dewberrys from the sedge
> And lays the poison berrys on the hedge
> Will often find them in the meadow hay
> And take his bough and drive the bees away
> But when the maiden goes to turn the hay
> She whips her apron up and runs away
> The schoolboy eats the honey comb and all
> And often knocks his hat agen the wall
> And progs a stick in every hole he sees
> To steal the honey bag of black nosed bees

As in other animal poems from this period, humans are figured as compounding the precariousness of other critters' lives. The opening line locates us firmly in a georgic world, but one in which the focus is not on the human craft of working with sundry sometimes resistant other-than-human actants to make a living from the land but rather on the price exacted on free-living critters by human activities in rural places. This is foregrounded starkly in the opening line: 'The mower tramples on the wild bees' nest'. The damage in this case (as in Robert Burns' famous 'To a Mouse') is evidently accidental and regretted, for the mower 'hears the busy noise and stops the rest'. The rest of the poem, however, focuses on the actions of those who do not share the mower's attentiveness to the well-being of others, who instead 'carless proggle out the mossy ball/And gather up the honey comb and all'. The greediness of this action, which is evidently not a matter of honey harvesting for subsistence purposes but of an excessive form of consumption, 'careless' of consequences, is emphasized by the repeated reference to taking 'the honey comb and all' (l. 4 and 11). And while the speaker of the earlier poem simply garners aesthetic pleasure from the 'symphonies' piped by those bees that avail themselves of the fruits of human labour by nesting in walls, the schoolboy of the sonnet 'knocks his hat agen the wall/And progs a stick in every hole he sees/To steal the honey bag of black nosed bees'.

There is also an element of carelessness in the description of the schoolboy who, in gathering a wild harvest of dewberries, comes across poisonberries (of the *Solanum dulcamara*, or nightshade plant), which he 'lays on the hedge', thereby risking their consumption by other children or animals, who have not learnt to decode them as dangerous. This reference to natural toxins also recalls human creaturely vulnerability to potentially hazardous aspects of their lively rural *oikos*, and the concomitant requirement to take care on one's own accord, as well as for the sake of others. A further failure of care with respect to the threat posed by the bees' defensive sting is alluded to in the following lines, describing the schoolboy driving the bees out of the hay with his stick, while the maiden who 'goes to turn the hay... whips her apron and runs away'. Here, human violence towards other species is implicitly allied with male sexual aggression towards females, imbuing the imagery of greedy consumption ('eats the honey comb and all'), striking ('knocks his hat agen the wall') and poking ('progs a stick in every hole he sees') with connotations of rape. This echoes Theocrates' analogy of the bees' sting and Eros' arrows, both in turn carrying phallic connotations; but there is a darker strain here that undercuts the pleasurable promise of consensual libidinous dalliance amidst the hay so familiar from earlier pastoral, recalling perhaps the sexually predatory propensities of the hyper-phallic Pan in his pre-pastoral aspect as the god of wild nature. Rather than naturalizing, and hence excusing, human rapacity, however, the empathetic responsiveness towards its victims, human and otherwise, invited by Clare's creaturely ecopoetics seems pitched towards the melioration of aggressive tendencies through ecocultural practices of considerate *sympoiesis*.

As has been well-documented, Clare's concern about the well-being of fellow critters was by no means unique during the Romantic period. In Britain especially, advocacy for the humane treatment of animals, which had been growing since the late seventeenth century, burgeoned around 1800, with generally unloved and widely exploited species, such as insects, vermin and beasts of burden, featuring prominently in literary texts calling for greater respect for the lives of nonhuman others. Among these are several that query the hierarchical dualism of 'man' versus 'beast', such as Coleridge's 'To a Young Ass' (1794), with its pledge of bio-inclusive emancipation in the imagined Paradise regained of Pantisocracy, and Blake's more quizzical 'The Fly' (also 1794), which leaves a space for difference with respect to the life of the mind, while nonetheless affirming creaturely continuities. The promotion of animal rights, whether by way of a Christian ethic of kindly stewardship, Jeremy Bentham's utilitarian argument against the infliction of pain on sentient beings (*Principles of Morals and Legislation*, 1789) or, more radically, the Buddhist-inspired call for liberation of all beings from human domination advanced by John Oswald (*The Cry of Nature*, 1791),[10] could only gain limited traction at this time on account of many people's continuing economic dependence on the exploitation of animals for labour, food, wool, skins and bones. Opposition to live vivisection, recreational hunting and the mistreatment of domestic animals nonetheless became widespread in Britain, leading to the introduction of animal protection legislation in 1822 and the foundation of the Society for Prevention of Cruelty to Animals in 1824 (Perkins 2003). Some, including Percy Shelley, called also for the adoption of a vegetarian diet (commonly referred to as the Brahmin diet, with reference to the very different dietary norms encountered by the British in India). Shelley's arguments against meat consumption in his 'Vindication of Natural Diet' (1812) incorporated considerations of social justice as well as animal liberation, as he believed that a larger number of people could be fed more equitably on a vegetarian diet. Moreover, he maintained that such a diet was more 'natural' and therefore healthier for humans, whose teeth and digestive system more closely resembled those of 'frugivorous' animals like the 'orang-outan' than of carnivorous beasts of prey (Oerlemans 2002: 98–122; see also Morton 1994).

Shelley's appeal to anatomy exemplifies the growing recognition of human kinship with (other) animals on the basis of the early evolutionary theories of Erasmus Darwin in England, and of Schelling and Goethe in the German region. Contrary to the widespread assumption that the Romantics were anti-scientific, most took a nuanced view of the burgeoning research being undertaken by the inheritors of Bacon's 'new organ' of knowledge. Many might have shared Anna Letitia Barbauld's concern about the potential suffering caused by scientific experimentation, as articulated in her poem 'The Mouse's Petition' (1773), addressed to her friend, the physicist, Joseph Priestly. But there was also considerable interest in the emerging biological evidence for the immensely long history and continuing process of human co-becoming with other kinds, such that, as Goethe's confidante Charlotte von Stein put it in a letter to a mutual friend in 1784, it seemed 'probable that we were first plants and animals' and that 'what nature will make of us will remain unknown to us' (qtd. Kuhn 1987: 12). Evolutionism, however, was (and remains) by no means incompatible with human exceptionalism. Wordsworth's enthusiastic reception of Darwin's *The Botanic Garden* (1791) and *Zoonomia, or, the Laws of Organic Life* (1798) inclined him to honour in all things an inward enjoyment of their own existence, regretting only the artificial strictures that interfered with such enjoyment within human society: what 'man has made of man', as he laments in 'Lines Written in Early Spring' (1798). Coleridge's reading of Schelling, by contrast, led him to conclude in his 'Theory of Life' (1816–18) that humans are the most highly evolved species, that is, the most fully individuated in accordance with its predetermined 'ideal' (one from which the coloured races had in Coleridge's view fallen away, due to adverse environmental conditions), leaving a 'wide chasm between man and the noblest animals of the brute creation' (qtd. Oerlemans 2002: 135).

Within the wider spectrum of Romantic-era reconceptualizations of human relations with other critters (of which I have only been able to provide a glimpse here), Clare stands out for his close engagement with horizontal ecological interrelations in space, rather than with vertical evolutionary processes of co-becoming over time. Moreover, while the forms of (inter-and intra-specific) friction and injury alluded to in the bee poems discussed above might be described as run-of-the-mill dimensions of rural life, which Clare also targeted in his counter-pastoral critique of traditional practices such as badger-baiting and hedgehog eradication, his tender attentiveness to the lives of fellow creatures also informed his response to the enclosures that were rapidly transforming the Northamptonshire countryside during his lifetime. In 'The Lamentations of Round-Oak Waters' (1818), for example, the felling of woodland, straightening of waterways and conversion of moors and meadows to commercial crop production are shown to affect not only subaltern humans (gypsies and the rural poor) but the entire multispecies collective that co-constituted the commons:

humans, animals (wild and domesticated), plants and even the free-flowing brook itself, whose watery lament it is that the poet translates into human words. Reactivating the ancient mythic notion of the indwelling *genius loci* for the purposes of ecopolitical protest, Clare positions himself as a mediator of the circumambient sentience that inheres in the inter-specific co-becoming of the commons, the many voices of which were being silenced by the conversion of this 'animated, sensible landscape' (Irvine and Gorji 2013: 124) into a mere storehouse of 'natural resources': land to be rid of 'pests', such as the moles 'hung … as traitors', as Clare puts in 'Remembrances' (1984: 260), and rendered 'productive', no longer of vibrant multispecies collectives but of cash crops and, thereby, taxable income for private land-owners. Among those whose lives were imperilled in this process, as the *genius loci* of Clare's 'Lament of Swordy Well' protests, are bees, who now 'flye round in feeble rings/And find no blossom bye/ Then thrum their almost weary wings/Upon the moss and die' (1.81–84).

Crucially, Clare does not allow his dismay to carry over into hostility towards the waged workers, among whom he himself was numbered on occasion, who had been commanded to fell the trees and straighten the stream (Bate 2003: 106). On the contrary, in 'The Lamentations of Round-Oak Waters', he invites empathy also for their 'aching hands', recognizing them as fellow victims, whose labour is exploited in the accumulation of wealth for the few:

> But sweating slaves I do not blame
> Those slaves by wealth decreed
> …
> No no the foes that hurt my field
> Hurts these poor moilers too
>
> (1.165–174)

Clare's loaded reference to 'slaves' locates his protest against the destruction of the commons in his own little corner of Northamptonshire within a wider national and transnational horizon. The commodification of land and its evermore intensively farmed produce, facilitated by enclosure, constituted a form of internal colonization during the era that Anna Tsing and Donna Haraway have dubbed the 'Plantationocene'. Beginning in the sixteenth century with 'the devastating transformation of diverse kinds of human-tended farms, pastures, and forests into extractive and enclosed plantations, relying on slave labor and other forms of exploited, alienated, and usually spatially transported labor' (Haraway 2015: 162), this is an era, which, in the absence of fossil-fuelled industrialization, may not have left a trace in the future geological record; but it is one that, in conjunction with the latter, continues to cause far-reaching socioecological ruptures. And it is to the creaturely ecopoetics, manifest both in writing and beyond the page, of some of the descendants of the enslaved Africans set to work in the plantations of the Americas that I now turn.

Sympoiesis forestalled: Lorde and Trethewey

For African Americans, rural and wild places bear the trace of some very different personal experiences and historical memories from those found in white American pastoral literature, even in its more complex forms, such as Thoreau's *Walden* (1854).[11] As Camille Dungy explains in the introduction to the first anthology of African American 'nature poetry', for the writers, spanning four centuries, whose verse she has brought together in this volume, 'moss, rivers, trees, dirt, caves, dogs, fields' are 'elements of an environment steeped in a legacy of violence, forced labor, torture and death' (2009: xxi). And yet, the exquisite photo featured on the front cover suggests that this is not the whole story. Gordon Parks' 'Boy with June Bug, Fort Scott, Kansas, 1963' images in profile the head and shoulders of a child resting, eyes closed, in long grasses, some in purple flower. This scene is redolent of the mood of lazy, hazy noontide in the fields on a summer's day invoked within European pastoral poetry; except that on the boy's forehead, making its way determinedly towards his hairline, is a beetle tethered to a string that the boy is either playing out or reeling in through his raised hand. This is, to be sure, an ambiguous, and potentially discomforting, image. Parks' photographic documentation of African American lives, exposing poverty, segregation and racism, played a significant role in the Civil Rights Movement.[12] In the relationship between boy and June bug, though, it's evidently the former who holds the reins. Yet while there is perhaps a hint here of the casual cruelty of children towards insects and birds that troubled Clare (not least because he himself had once been among the nest raiders), this photo is also suggestive of the boy's easygoing intimacy with the earth, plants and critters of his rural environs. In fact, while many of the anthologized poems 'implicate the natural world in a personal or collective history of trauma', others 'reveal the astonishing degree to which [some] African American poets and their subjects have aligned themselves with the natural world' (Dungy 2009: xxxi, xxii) in a range of places, including those cityscapes where most African Americans now reside. The two poems that I focus on here fall into the latter category. They are among a number in Dungy's collection that feature bees, but these are particularly noteworthy for the empathetic gaze that they bring to their potentially pesky subjects in view of the forestalling of multispecies coexistence.

'The Bees' (1974), by lesbian womanist writer, scholar and Civil Rights Activist Audre Lorde, appears in Dungy's third cycle of poems, 'Dirt on Our Hands', highlighting 'the barriers that have been established between humans and the natural world … encouraging destruction and disaffection, discouraging cooperative thinking, and eventually ushering in certain trauma and death' (xxx). Here, it is, in the first place, a colony of bees that dies in the process of swarming to their new hive:

In the street outside a school
what the children learn
possesses them.
Little boys yell as they stone a flock of bees
trying to swarm
between the lunchroom window and an iron grate.
The boys sling furious rocks
smashing the windows.
The bees, buzzing their anger,
are slow to attack.
Then one boy is stung
into quicker destruction
and the school guards come
long wooden sticks held out before them
they advance upon the hive
beating the almost finished rooms of wax apart
mashing the new tunnels in
while fresh honey drips
down their broomsticks
and the little boy feet becoming expert
at destruction
trample the remaining and bewildered bees
into the earth.

Curious and apart
four little girls look on in fascination
learning a secret lesson
and trying to understand their own destruction.
One girl cries out

'Hey, the bees weren't making any trouble!'
and she steps across the feebly buzzing ruins
to peer up at the empty, grated nook
'We could have studied honey-making!'

(in Dungy 2009: 78–79)

Lorde's attention to the apian labour that has been laid waste, as highlighted by the qualifiers 'almost finished' and 'new', gains added poignancy in light of current understandings of the communicative feats of collective decision-making that will have preceded the construction of, and flight to, the new nest site. Lorde's bees are no passive victims, but their defensive stings only invite a more concerted attack.

As in the case of Clare's sonnet, this scene of devastation is strongly gendered and implicitly sexualized, with the image of the 'fresh honey' that 'drips/down their broomsticks' not only metonymic of wastage but also metaphoric of rape. While one might wonder about the source of the fear and anger that underlies the boys' violent hostility towards the swarming bees, Lorde focuses our attention on the perspective of a group of four girls who 'look on in fascination'. As we discover in the second stanza, it is they who are the subject of the opening lines: 'In the street outside a school/what the children learn/possesses them.' And what these girls are 'trying to understand' in view of this display of masculine aggression towards the Other, the denial of the bees' agency and the negation of their efforts to craft a new abode, is 'their own destruction'. They too, however, are not passive victims: what they learn, implicitly, is the need to forge another *modus vivendi* embracing multiple differences, including that of species.

The horizon of multispecies coexistence and potential *sympoiesis* that is so brutally foreclosed in this poem is explored in prose fiction by Sue Monk Kidd in her novel *The Secret Life of Bees* (2002). Set in the segregated South right around the time when Parks photographed 'Boy with June Bug', this novel imagines a gynocentric heterotopia, in which the narrator, sixteen-year-old Lily Melissa Owens, finds refuge and reconnection with her African American maternal inheritance among the bee-honouring honey-harvesting Boatman sisters. Charming though this narrative might be, Natasha Trethewey's poem 'Carpenter Bee' (2000) is more symptomatic of the current state-of-play in human-bee relations beyond the page. Appearing in Dungy's fourth cycle, 'Pests, People too', addressing 'power negotiations between humans, insects and other troublesome creatures' (xxx), Trethewey's bee poem is in some ways even more harrowing than Lorde's precisely because it does not entail violent hostility. Moreover, it departs from the historically contingent reverse sexism of Lorde's womanist poem, which implicitly elides the 'complexity of difference' (Cudworth 2005) – that is, the complex intersections of distinct forms of socioecological domination – by targeting masculinity as the primary driver of oppression and violence. By contrast, Trethewey discloses how the everyday home-making efforts of a woman of colour, who in other contexts might herself experience domination on the basis of race and/or gender, unhouse and imperil her apian neighbours:

> All winter long I have passed
> beneath her nest – a hole no bigger
> than the tip of my thumb.
>
> Last year, before I was here,
> she burrowed into the wood
> framing my porch, drilled a network
>
> of tunnels, her round body sturdy
> for the work of building. Torpid
> the cold months, she now pulls herself
>
> out into the first warm days of spring
> to tread the air outside my screen door,
> floating in pure sunlight, humming
>
> against a backdrop of green. She too
> must smell the wisteria, see
> – with her hundred eyes – purple
>
> blossoms lacing the trees. Flower-
> hopping, she draws invisible lines,
> the geometry of her flight. Drunk
>
> on nectar, she can still find her way
> back; though now, she must be
> confused, disoriented, doubting even
>
> her own homing instinct – this beeline,
> now, to nowhere. Today, the workmen
> have come, plugged the hole – her threshold –
>
> covered it with thick white paint, a scent
> acrid and unfamiliar. She keeps hovering,
> buzzing around the spot. Watching her,

> I think of what I've left behind, returned to,
> only to find everything changed, nothing but
> my memory intact – like her eggs, still inside,
>
> each in its separate cell – snug, ordered, certain.
>
> (in Dungy 2009: 142–43)

Not unlike the bumblebees said to nest in stone walls in Clare's poems, the Carpenter bee is wont to avail itself of human constructions by drilling into the exposed timber of human homes. Unfortunately, as I discovered from the website of the Orkin pest control company, '[w]hile fairly harmless, Carpenter bees increase the number of nests over the course of years, causing noticeable damage to wood'. Moreover – horror of horrors – '[t]hey can also create stains with their feces'.[13] The speaker of Trethewey's poem, then, does have what some (not least those who make a living by eradicating undesirable animals from human domiciles) would consider reasonable grounds for having brought in workmen to plug the Carpenter bee's hole. Yet her verse is devoid of self-justification, foregrounding instead her empathetic response to the impact of this decision, in so far as this can be discerned from within a human semiosphere and conveyed by human words, on the banished bee – one who had in fact been a prior resident of this place, as we learn in the second stanza. The enjambment of the phrase that loops across the stanza break here is suggestive of the branching tunnels of the nest. As this looping pattern continues through the following tercets, it links into the *topos* of entry and egress across a threshold, a necessary passage shared by the speaker, who, as we read in the opening stanza, has passed beneath the bee's nest throughout the winter, and the bee, emerging to forage for nectar after her winter hibernation, yet returning to find her entry barred.

Here, and throughout the poem, Trethewey couples the affirmation of creaturely kinship with the recognition of alterity. While the winter has not stopped the speaker from being out and about, the bee has been '[t]torpid/the winter months', and having now pulled 'herself/out into the first warm days of spring', it is to 'tread', not the ground, but 'the air ... floating in pure sunlight, humming/against a backdrop of green'. As in Wordsworth's 'Lines Written in Early Spring', Trethewey hints at a sense of enjoyment in existence that crosses species boundaries, yet while her speaker affirms that the bee 'too/must smell the wisteria', she sees the 'purple/blossoms lacing the trees' differently, ' – with her hundred eyes – '. Moreover, the flowers that presumably afford aesthetic pleasure to the speaker are a source of vital nourishment for the bee and her brood. Having brought to mind the bee's labour in building her nest, her eager 'yes' to the alluring colours and scents of the spring blooms, and her skill in negotiating her *Umwelt* – 'Drunk/on nectar, she can still find her way/back' – Trethewey's speaker speculates that the bee 'must be/confused, disoriented, doubting even/her own homing instinct' on finding 'the hole – her threshold – / covered ... with thick white paint, a scent/acrid and unfamiliar'. Witnessing the bee 'hovering/buzzing around the spot', she is reminded of her own experience of returning to what she has left behind, 'only to find everything changed, nothing but my memory intact – like her eggs, still inside,/each in its separate cell – snug, ordered, certain' (143). Yet while those memories might yet be reawakened through mental recollection, the bee's young will surely perish without their mother's ministrations and in the absence of a way out of the nest.

The unhousing of this one Carpenter bee as a consequence of the ordinary everyday activities of a human home-maker, herself bearing a history of dislocation, is emblematic of the trajectory of the Plantationocene, 'which continues with ever-greater ferocity in globalized factory meat production, monocrop agribusiness, and immense substitutions of crops like palm oil for multispecies forests and their products that sustain human and nonhuman critters alike' (Haraway 2015: 162). Among its victims are insects, including many species of free-living pollinators (Sánchez-Bayo and Wyckhuys 2019). Domesticated honey bees, meantime, have been subjected to a whole new regime of industrial exploitation, nowhere more thoroughly than in the United States, where they are bred and transported around the country wherever required to pollinate some $40 billion worth of cash crops annually, representing around one-third of all food consumed. These bees have become vulnerable to a lethal mix of parasites and pests, pathogens and pesticides, compounded by harsher climatic conditions, reduced genetic diversity and poor nutrition – including, obscenely, being fed on corn syrup in place of their own honey – apparently giving rise to the appalling phenomenon of Colony Collapse Disorder (Sánchez-Bayo and Wyckhuys 2019: 12–13). If the 'honey dreams' of Clare's buzzing minstrels still carried the ancient cultural connotation of the Delphic oracle, today's apian messengers have become prophets of a different sort. As Preston observes mournfully, 'the substances they gather in water, nectar pollen and even blood gas (are now) analyzed for ecological changes and health hazards. As animal monitors of these various toxins and dangers, bees are likely to perish in the very act of bringing us the dire tidings of our own terrible technologies' (2006: 165–66). There is an appalling irony in all this. For it appears to be precisely because of their communicative intelligence and collaborative way of life that bee colonies are so vulnerable to neonicotinoid poisoning, which disrupts the neurotransmitter acetylcholine in insects, interfering 'with worker bees' ability to navigate, and thus to bring back pollen for the hive and also to bring back information about the world to be shared and debated' (Sandilands 2014: 164). Meanwhile, many of their free-living counterparts have also declined dramatically as a consequence of the loss of their food sources, together with toxins ingested from flowering crops, and the impacts of climate change (Miller-Struttmann 2016; Sánchez-Bayo and Wyckhuys 2019: 12). Among these are the Red-shanked Carder Bee, celebrated by Clare as the 'russet commoner who knows the face,/Of every blossom that the meadow brings', which has seen a huge decline throughout its range (Ollerton).

Sympoiesis beyond the page: 'Migration and me'

Discerning connections between the plight of pollinators and the dislocation of particular human groups in the course of the Plantationocene, however, can also provide impetus for new practices of multispecies hospitality and conviviality. This is the case, for instance, with an initiative of the US multi-faith conservation organization Faith in Place. The 'Migration & Me' programme was developed by Veronica Kyle in response to the resistance that she encountered to Faith in Place's environmental stewardship initiative when she first endeavoured to introduce it among largely African American and Latino American churchgoers in Chicago. Herself African American, with a family history of negative experiences on the land and in the woods, she could readily relate to responses such as these:

> 'I ain't going in the woods where bad things have happened, I ain't going to get my hands dirty.' 'Why should we care about some woods, when folk don't care about our neighborhoods?' 'I promised the good Lord that if I made it North, I would never get my hands dirty again. I ended up still cleaning white folks' toilets and taking care of their children, but when it came to digging in the dirt I drew the line.'
>
> (Kyle and Kearns 2018: 12)

Yet she also realized that her own and others' experiences of dislocation, marginalization and migration as African Americans could open an axis of connection and care with respect to other species: to begin with, this was specifically the Monarch Butterfly. Parts of Illinois, including Chicago, are on the Monarchs' flight way between Mexico and Canada, and as this annual migration is inter-generational, the females need to lay their eggs on route. However, they will only do this on milkweed, which has fallen prey to intensive farming, which, together with cities featuring largely exotic horticulture, has consumed some 99 per cent of native prairies in this state. In order to engage congregations in responding to their plight, Veronica initiated storytelling circles, in which participants share their own experiences of marginalization and migration, and she shares 'the story of this beautiful delicate creature, the Monarch ... where the Monarchs come from, why they migrate, what they need along their journey to survive, and how we as humans could provide such "hospitality"' (49). In this way,

> [p]articipants learn that hospitality for the Monarchs and other creatures means clearing the invasive plants, planting milkweed, perhaps planting a butterfly native garden, and providing hospitality in terms of familiar desired foods, both for caterpillars and people ... Ranging from preschool to senior citizens, representing a diversity of race, class, religious affiliation, and cultures, they understand the need to do for 'the least of those' in our ecological community. The program now averages at least a dozen major stewardship and recreational outings a year to our local forest preserves, beaches, and city parks, which have hosted hundreds of individuals.
>
> (49)[14]

These activities become the stuff of further stories, which, as sociologist of religion, Laurel Kearns observes, 'lay the basis for an ecological identity to grow, or help to revive an earlier one, perhaps left behind in childhood or another place' (Kyle and Kearns 2018: 52). Moreover, such practices of hospitable *sympoiesis* can enable personal and social, as well as ecological forms of healing:

> To understand ... all the brokenness that the Faith in Place program 'mends' is to go beyond the immediate places of the Southside of Chicago. *Migration & Me* creates a space for African Americans and other people of color to reclaim a lost heritage, to reclaim a place in the natural world that is healing and not harmful, and to reclaim the connection to land interrupted by slavery and forced migrations from place after place, then uprooted once again in the migrations to the cities. And it helps to break open the 'white spaces' of the environmental movement and nature preserves – preserves often created ... by moving indigenous people, communities of color, and poor people out of them first.
>
> (54)

As the growth of cities continues to accelerate worldwide, with ever more people, plants and animals displaced from their former abodes by environmental and climate change, there will be a growing need to cultivate the arts of multicultural as well as multispecies *sympoeisis* in urban, no less than in rural spaces. Better understanding the communicative capacities and creative agency of other living beings, as disclosed through biosemiotic research, will be invaluable in such endeavours. And while we can never fully enter into the semiospheres of other critters, ecopoetic works of human words can engage our empathetic interest in them, deepening our appreciation of our entanglement with them and potentially firing up our desire to put *sympoiesis* into practice beyond the page.

4

'the wrong dream': Prophetic ecopoetics

In concluding his 'Defence of Poetry' (1821), Shelley famously proclaims that poets are 'the unacknowledged legislators of the world' (2002: 535). What is less frequently remarked is that he had previously aligned this poetic vocation with another elevated calling: namely that of the prophet. Among the early German Romantics too, some had aligned poetry with prophecy. Friedrich Schlegel, for example, in his *Literary Notebooks*, declared that 'Poetry is theosophy; no one is a poet except the prophet' (Schlegel 1957: 187). Novalis, rather more cautiously, casts this connection in terms of analogy: 'The sense for P[oetry] has a close kinship with the sense of prophecy and for the religious, oracular sense in general' (Novalis 1984, 685). And yet, with the notable exception of William Blake, few Romantic writers frame their works as explicitly prophetic texts.[1] Indeed, Blake himself only identified two of his works as 'prophecies' – *America* (1793) and *Europe* (1794) – even though prophetic language, carrying strong biblical resonances, permeates much of his writing. In fact, as Ian Balfour has observed, in both British and German Romantic literature 'taken as a whole the prophetic is at once marginal and pervasive' (2002: 19).

In this chapter, I identify a specifically ecopoetic variant of the prophetic mode of Romantic literature, as exemplified above all by Blake. Here, the ecopoetic arts of contemplation, affective attunement and creaturely *sympoiesis* open onto a call for radical ecopolitical transformation: one that took inspiration from biblical prophetic and apocalyptic writing. For Blake and other Romantic writers, a creative engagement with biblical texts, no longer bound by doctrinal strictures, was facilitated by new understandings of the scriptures as historically situated, culturally contingent and poetically crafted works of literature. Among the biblical prophets who ghost Blake's work was Jeremiah, who has been hailed by environmental and climate ethicist Michael Northcott as 'the first ecological prophet in literary and religious history' (2007: 12). In the latter part of the chapter, I discern an echo of Jeremiah's ecoprophetic call to heed the cry of the earth, as manifest in the drying out of soil and dying out of plants and animals, in a poem by the Australian author and activist Judith Wright. It is from Wright's poem 'Dust' (1945), composed on the cusp of the Great Acceleration, that this chapter takes its title. While the socioecological ills, and deceptive cultural imaginary, discerned by Wright pre-dated current concerns about climate change, Jordie Albiston's poetic sequence 'Lamentations' (2013) returns to the biblical 'Lamentations of Jeremiah' to find a prophetic mode of response to the Victorian firestorm of January 2009, in which the dire implications of anthropogenic global warming for that part of Australia became horrifically legible.

For the Romantics, as we shall see, prophetic language was held to be performative: its value lay in the change that it effected, both in individuals and in the wider society. Among twentieth-century Australian poets, Wright was undoubtedly the most significant inheritor of this Romantic conception of the poet as prophet. Towards the end of her life, though, she despaired of the political efficacy of the poetic word: the idealist project of engendering a new imaginary, a better dream, by purely literary means had begun to look like another 'wrong dream'. Throughout this book, I too have stressed the insufficiency of poetry in the face of the complex socioecological challenges of the Anthropocene. Following Wright, then, this chapter concludes with a consideration of a contemporary example of ecopolitical activism in Australia, which takes prophetic ecopoetics well beyond the confines of the literary field.

Heeding Earth's cry: Blake's *apokalypsis* of the Ploutocene[2]

In Shelley's account of the literary calling, the poet 'essentially comprises and unites' the 'character' of legislator and prophet:

> For he not only beholds intensely the present as it is, and discovers those laws according to which present things ought to be ordered, but he beholds the future in the present, and his thoughts are as germs of the flower and the fruit of latest time.
>
> (513)

The law and the prophets: for Shelley's contemporaries, the biblical reference would have been obvious, most likely bringing to mind Jesus' assertion in Mk. 12.40 that '[o]n these two commandments', namely love of God and love of neighbour, 'hang all the law and the prophets': a passage that is recited in every communion service of the Church of England to this day. If so, they might have been all the more powerfully struck by the revolutionary way in which Shelley is appropriating the Bible for his literary project: one that is as much political as it is poetic. Biblical ideas, allusions, narratives and imagery had abounded in European literature for virtually a millennia. What changed during the Romantic period was that the Bible had become newly available as a work of literature; or rather, as a compendium of diverse literary texts, a wildly heterogeneous anthology, liberated from doctrinal usages and dogmatic beliefs (Prickett 1996).

This secular reception of the Bible was facilitated in large measure by the work of sundry enlightened clergymen, who were quite comfortable in considering their sacred text as both the work of human hands and a source of spiritual nourishment. Among them was Robert Lowth, whose 1754 doctoral thesis, subsequently published in English as *Lectures on the Sacred Poetry of the Hebrews* (1787; second edition 1815), provided the first detailed analysis of the poetic character and structure of those Hebrew texts that had been incorporated into the Old Testament of the Christian Bible. Further attention was given to the literary and linguistic aspects of the prophetic books by Richard Hurd in his inaugural William Warburton Lectures at Lincoln's Inn Chapel in 1768, published in 1772 as *Twelve Sermons Introductory to the Study of the Prophecies*.

Across the Channel, meanwhile, J. G. Herder was arguing for the necessity of appreciating not only the literary and, as he saw it, mythopoetic character of the Old Testament but also the geographical and historical circumstances that informed what he called the 'spirit of Hebraic poetry' (*Vom Geiste der Ebraischen Poesie: Eine Anleitung für Liebhaber derselben, und der ältesten Geschichte des menschlichen Geistes*, 1782 [1987]). Herder's geohistorical recontextualization of biblical literature, a form of ecocritical historicism *avant la lettre* (Rigby 2017a: 33–35), also informed his effusive discussion of the Song of Songs not as an allegory of Christ's love of the church, as interpreted in the de-sexualizing Christian exegetical tradition, but as a gloriously erotic exemplar of ancient 'Oriental' love poetry (*Lieder der Liebe: Die ältesten und schönsten aus Morgenlande, Nebst vier und viergiz alten Minneliedern*, 1778). This historicizing angle had previously been advanced by Baruch Spinoza in his *Tractatus Theoligica-Politicus*. Published anonymously in 1670, and swiftly banned, Spinoza's *Tractatus* argues that the Jewish Torah, which also constituted the first five books, or Pentateuch, of the Old Testament, was not sole-authored by Moses, as traditionally believed. Rather, Spinoza postulated that this was a compilation of partly fragmentary texts produced at different times by assorted writers, which had subsequently been edited, translated and re-interpreted by others in various ways and for diverse (often political and frequently repressive) purposes. Herder, a Lutheran minister and outspoken enthusiast for Spinoza, believed that the Bible was best appreciated as a multi-authored 'book written by people for people', as he put it in his *Letters Concerning the Study of Theology* (*Briefe, das Studium der Theology betreffend*, 1780–81; in Herder 1994: 145). In other words, he saw the Bible as a work of fallible human witness, rather than as direct divine revelation.

J. P. Eichhorn, the non-clerical professor of oriental languages at the University of Jena, incorporated the Hebrew Bible into the emerging canon of 'world literature' (*Weltliteratur*, a term coined by Goethe). Eichhorn made this case in his *Introduction to the Old Testament* (*Einführung in das alte Testament*, 1804–1814), 'one of the earliest full-scale attempts to study the Bible from a relatively "disinterested" position of scholarship' (Balfour 2002: 114). However, it was another Lutheran minister, Friedrich Schleiermacher, who would further develop the modern historical-critical method of biblical hermeneutics in a theological context, as foreshadowed in his talks on religion 'to its cultured despisers' (*Über die Religion: Reden an die Gebildeten unter ihren Verächtern*, 1799). Here, he explains (in the first instance to his anti-Christian friends among the Jena Romantics) that, like the documents of all positive religions, the Bible is composed of much extraneous material –'worldly wisdom and morals or metaphysics and poetry' (1988: 210) – written by different authors under a variety of historical circumstances, often very different from those of its subsequent readers. Its meaning, then, was emergent, rather than fixed, as it was forever being reinterpreted by diversely situated readers across many times and places. This implies that biblical revelation was ongoing: its truth was being unveiled over time and was certainly not to be found in any kind of literalist fixation on the words on the page. In addition, this old anthology could potentially be extended by the incorporation of new texts: 'The holy writings have become Scripture by their own power, but they prohibit no other book from also becoming Scripture' (1988: 220). Inspired by Schleiermacher, Friedrich Schlegel came to regard the Bible as the model for the Romantic conception of the book, namely as a polylogical, *sympoietic* combination of poetry and prose, philosophy and narrative, history and mythology (Prickett 1996: 203).

In Britain, around 1800, the biblical translations and commentaries produced by Alexander Geddes became one of the primary vehicles for the reception of eighteenth-century German biblical scholarship. Geddes was 'a heterodox

Scottish Catholic who ended up finding favour in the radical Protestant circles around the publisher Joseph Johnson' (Balfour 2002: 121). These circles included, among others, William Blake, William Godwin, Mary Wollstonecraft and Thomas Paine. English poetological and German historical-critical rereadings of the Bible, in the context of the revolutionary sociopolitical changes underway at this time, were key to the recovery of the prophetic mode among writers on both sides of the Channel.

This influence is clear in the way Shelley qualifies the prophetic vocation of the poet in his 'Defence'. Insisting that 'to behold the future in the present' was not to be confused with making predictions, Shelley parts company with the predominant popular understanding of prophecy, as recorded in Samuel Johnson's *Dictionary of the English Language*: namely, 'a declaration of something to come, prediction', and, as a verb, 'to predict; to foretell; to prognosticate' or 'to foreshow' (1755:1588). Such definitions of prophecy, and the prophet, as, to quote Johnson again, 'one who tells of future events; a predictor; a foreteller' (1588), Shelley dismisses as 'the gross sense of the word' and 'the pretence of superstition' (513). Instead, he draws closer to the Judaic understanding of the prophet as disclosed by the new biblical scholarship: that is, as one who is able not to 'foretell the form' but rather to 'foreknow the spirit of events' (513). Similarly, Herder interpreted the prophetic speech of the *nābî*, a Hebrew word of uncertain derivation, inadequately translated into the Greek of the *Septuagint* as *prophétés*, as a form of 'political art' (*politische Kunst*) (Balfour 2002: 111). As mediators of the voice of God, prophets such as Isaiah, Jeremiah and Ezekiel were possessed of what Herder, translating the Hebrew *davar*, meaning both word and act, termed the 'deedful word' (*thatvolles Wort*). And what their speech acts sought to accomplish was 'to persuade a recalcitrant people to change its ways and to reorient that people to its new future' (Balfour 2002: 117).

In this respect, ancient Hebrew prophetic writing differs from both Jewish and Christian apocalyptic writing of the late Hellenic period with respect to the position that it assumes towards what Martin Buber (1957) terms 'the historical hour'. Apocalyptic shares with prophetic the revelation that humans, for all their self-proclaimed apartness, belong to a more-than-human community of fate, in that all creatures are seen to be afflicted by the anticipated destruction of the prevailing order. However, it tends to constitute history as predetermined in its outcome, leaving human agents little option other than to prepare themselves for the millennial end that heralds a glorious new beginning: God's creation of 'a new heaven and a new earth' (Rev. 21.1) By contrast, the prophetic voice insists on the ever-present possibility of a change in direction in the present. In the absence of that change, there is no promise of redemption. The prophetic voice, moreover, while understood as uttering the speech of heaven, does not speak from a place of purity: the prophet is both implicated in and wounded by the wrongdoing that he or she diagnoses as the fault that is driving the world headlong into catastrophe (Rose 2008: 165). Prophetic speech is inspired by the imaginative capacity to see through and beyond those conventional attitudes, assumptions and patterns of behaviour that engender or support oppression and wrongdoing. It is propelled by the hunger for justice, underpinned by compassion, which cannot tolerate complacency in the face of another's suffering. Breaching the fortress of 'royal consciousness' (Brueggemann 2001: 21–37) – the mindset of mastery and privilege that renders us insouciant to the suffering of others and unmindful of our own vulnerability – the prophet speaks with the voice of grief, but also, implicitly or explicitly, of hope.

The sociocritical words of warning uttered by the prophet, then, were underpinned by a recognition of the potentially catastrophic tendencies of the times together with the conviction that things were meant to be otherwise and that they could (perhaps) yet be turned around. In both aspects, the prophet is 'enabled to perceive/Something unseen before', as Wordsworth has it with respect to the prophetic voice of the poet, in the 1805–6 version of *The Prelude* (XII, l.304–5). For Shelley too, the poet *qua* prophet is one who reveals the world anew: 'Poetry lifts the veil from the hidden beauty of the world, and makes familiar objects be as if they were not familiar' (517). This revelatory role also qualifies his take on the poet as 'legislator'. Shelley insists that the poet should not be seen as a moralist in a narrow sense, let alone a legalist. The poet's role is not to propound 'his own conceptions of right and wrong, which are usually those of his place and time' (517). Rather, 'his' task is to extend the reign of love by fostering the imaginative capacity to empathize with another's situation and experience: 'A man, to be greatly good, must imagine intensely and comprehensively; he must put himself in the place of another and many others; the pains and pleasures of his species must become his own' (517). God, to be sure, has been bracketed out here, but the love of 'neighbour' taught by that 'extraordinary person' (524), Jesus of Nazareth, be that neighbour a stranger or even an enemy, remains a guiding thread of Shelley's poetics.

In his own prophetic writing, Shelley nonetheless eschews biblical paradigms in favour of English folklore, in *Queen Mab* (1813/1822), and classical mythology, in *Prometheus Unbound* (1820). In both cases, though, Shelley's utopian vision bears a distinct echo of Isaiah's redemptive promise of the peaceable kingdom, in which 'the wolf also shall dwell with the lamb, and the leopard shall lie down with the kid' (Is.11.6). For Shelley, too, history evidently has a *telos*, albeit one that is no longer dependent upon divine providence. In *Queen Mab*, the realization of the ecotopian vision of an emancipated humanity dwelling on a newly habitable earth is the result of conscious human agency acting in consort with Nature, understood as an unfolding process tending towards a peaceable future. This optimistic view of natural becoming was shared by some of the Jena Romantics, notably Novalis (Rigby 2017b). Shelley himself came to have doubts about this, however, and the vision of *Prometheus Unbound* is more emphatically anthropocentric, looking forward to a time when Earth no longer hides any of her secrets, and 'Man' commands even the lightning. Here, the dismissal of divine overlordship equates with the deification of humanity; human sovereignty, however, remains subject to the transcendent power of Love, which 'folds over the world its healing wings' (IV, l.561).

While Shelley's relationship to biblical traditions was relatively oblique, Blake's was considerably more upfront, albeit no less unorthodox. Blake also came closest of all the Romantic-era writers on both sides of the Channel to creating an entirely new mythology and a new revelation (*apokalypsis*, in biblical Greek): one that was pitched simultaneously against religious dogmatism, mechanistic scientism and political tyranny. The mythopoetic potential of literature to propel cultural revolution was widely championed during the Romantic period. Among the first arguments of this kind was presented in an anonymous tract, entitled 'Oldest System Programme of German Idealismus' ('Ältestes Systemprogramm des deutschen Idealism', 1797). Although the manuscript is in Hegel's handwriting, Hegel probably co-authored it with Schelling and Hölderlin. Here, mythopoetic literature is framed as a form of aesthetic education intended to mediate the new (post-Kantian) philosophy to the masses, liberating them from questionable inherited beliefs, and cultivating all of their mental faculties in tandem, as the necessary foundation for the creation of a liberated society. Such a proposal for a new 'mythology of reason' (Hegel 1984: 13) appears to be poles apart from Blake's mythopoetic writing, in which rationalism, as embodied in the figure of Urizen, is a primary target of critique. Yet for Blake too, 'Mental Fight', as he puts it in the Preface to *Milton* ('Jerusalem', l.13), is the favoured means for overthrowing tyranny in the wake of the violence that had ensued in France as the emancipatory endeavours of the Revolution morphed into the bloodshed of the Terror. Moreover, the authors of the 'Oldest System Programme' did not equate 'reason' (*Vernunft*) with the positivistic and mechanistic scientism targeted by Blake in his critique of Bacon, Newton and Locke. Instead, they looked forward to a new physics that would conjoin philosophical self-reflexivity, empirical experience and 'sensuous religion' (13), reconnecting reason, feeling and imagination. Poetry, as the primal and perennial 'teacher of humanity' (13),[3] would usher in this new science.

Hegel subsequently abandoned this project in favour of the philosophical abstractions of dialectical idealism, but Hölderlin sought to put it into poetic practice, and Schelling continued to make the case for a new enlightened mythology in his lectures on the philosophy of art (1802–3 in Jena and 1804–5 in Würzburg). He presents the task as entailing not only the reconciliation of reason and feeling, and science and religion but also the sublation of the opposition between paganism and Christianity, by restoring the divine to nature (1989: 75–77). This too might appear to be at odds with Blake's project, which famously derides the 'natural religion' of his day in favour of the divinization of the human. Appearances can be deceptive, however. Schelling's 'nature' was not that of the mechanists and atomists but reconceived in terms of his own 'higher physics': nature, that is, as a dynamic process of becoming with an inner psychoactive dimension. Spinoza's 'nature naturing' became, in Schelling's thought, Nature as 'absolute subject'. As such, it could not be disclosed by means of scientific experimentation but only intuited 'ecstatically'. At certain special moments of perception, 'the thinking subject ceases to regard the manifest world as some kind of not-I and thus as in a reflexive relation to itself, and moves beyond itself, thereby allowing the absolute subject to be as itself and not an object of knowledge' (Bowie 1993:134).

As it happens, just such a moment may have galvanized Blake's prophetic project: one in which the materialization of the 'human form divine' embraced the entire living world. The textual trace of this – literally – ecstatic moment is to be found in an occasional poem, addressed to Blake's friend and patron, Thomas Butts. In a letter to Butts dated 2 October 1800 (1988: 711–14), Blake describes a visionary experience. A 'vision of Light', he says, came to him that morning, as he sat gazing out to sea on a sandy beach near the village of Felpham in Sussex, where he and his wife Catherine had come to live a week earlier (and where they remained until 1803). Not unlike Wordsworth's William in 'Expostulation and Reply', sitting on the 'old grey stone' looking out upon Esthwaite Lake, the London poet is practising the contemplative arts of *anachoresis* (withdrawal) and *heschia* (stillness). He is setting aside all 'Care' and 'Desire' (*atoraxia*)and allowing himself to be addressed, and, indeed, 'Astonishd Amazed', by the radiant self-disclosure of the manifold things around him (*prosoche*). What Blake's contemplative poet beholds, though, is something rather more shocking than the 'mighty sum/Of things forever speaking': something that causes him initially to feel 'fear'. Illuminated by individuated, and oddly humanoid, particles of light, all things in creation – 'Each grain of sand/Every Stone on the Land/ Each rock & each hill/Each fountain & rill/Each herb & each tree/Mountain hill Earth & Sea/Cloud Meteor & Star' – are suddenly revealed as 'Men seen afar': that is, no longer as mere objects of the gaze set against a sovereign subject but as persons in their own right. Sensing himself being taken up into what now manifests not as atoms, but as streams of light, 'Heavens bright beams', the poet suddenly beholds himself as an other, looking down from above upon his own 'shadow', together with that of his wife, sister and friend, nestled in the 'fair arms' of their new earthly abode, 'Felpham sweet'.[4] As the vision continues to expand, 'Like a sea without shore', the individuated particles of light resolve into the form of One Man. Blake, the nonconformist Christian, unsurprisingly sees this man as Jesus Christ, in whose 'beams of bright gold' the poet is enfolded. No longer afraid, he is 'soft consumd in delight', sensing himself transfigured, 'Like dross purgd away/All my mire & my clay'.

But that is not all: it is in this transfigured state that the contemplative becomes receptive to the divine call. With soft smile and 'voice Mild', Christ hails the poet as a 'Ram hornd with gold' and declares that 'This' (what exactly is unclear) is His 'Fold'. But the following lines complicate this conventional image of Christ as shepherd by disclosing non-domesticated and even predatory aspects of creation – the 'lion & wolf/The loud sea & deep gulf' – as 'guards of My Fold'. This recalls Isaiah's promise of a time to come when the lamb will dwell with the wolf, whilst implying that such a time is always already coming into being. Casting the beach upon which the poet has been awakened as the 'sides of the Deep', the poem recalls also the primal waters of Genesis 1, the *tehom* (deep), out of which *Elohim* (the divine collective) summons a world of differentiated entities: one that is primordially 'very good'.[5] This suggests, perhaps, that what appears to the unawakened gaze as a merely material reality is in fact the sacred matrix of creation, within which the Word is forever becoming flesh. This, then, would be a vision of 'deep incarnation' (Gregersen 2001; Edwards 2006: 58–60), which takes its cue from St. John's invitation to see the living world itself as the first, and ongoing, incarnation of Christ: 'In the beginning was the Word, and the Word was with God, and the Word was God./The same was in the beginning with God./All things were made by him; and without him was not any thing made that was made./In him was life; and the life was the light of men' (Jn 1.1–4). As Paul realized, this implied that Christ was 'all and in all' (Col. 3.11) and that the divine was at once 'above all and through all and in all' (Eph. 4.6).

What this means for the poet is not spelled out here. The poem simply concludes with a vision of Butts, together with his wife, 'By the fountains of Life': that is, in the presence of Christ, not in some ethereal beyond but here, now; whilst the speaker himself 'remaind as a Child' and 'All I ever had known/Before me bright Shone'. Nor does Blake comment on his vision further in the letter. Yet having been interpolated as a 'Ram hornd with gold', the poet, qua visionary or 'seer', would appear to have an important, dare I say seminal, role to play amongst the flock. This is key to the prophetic calling of the poet, as Blake conceived it. Not unlike Shelley, he was dismissive of the popular 'modern' understanding of the prophet's role. In his annotations to Bishop Watson's *An Apology for the Bible* (1796), he observed that 'Every honest man is a Prophet he utters his opinion both of private & public matters/Thus/If you go so/the result is So/He never says such a thing shall happen do what you will. a Prophet is a Seer not an Arbitrary Dictator' (qtd. Balfour 2002: 129)[6]. The role of the prophet, then, is not to predict the future but (as Terry Eagleton puts it, glossing the Hebraic tradition in his characteristically lapidary style) 'to remind the people that if they carry on as they are doing, the future will be exceedingly bleak' (2004: 175). And if you take seriously the revelation that God is 'through all and in all', there are profound implications for the question of how we should treat our fellow creatures, human and otherwise.

The radical ethico-political conclusion that Blake draws from his contemplative experience of 'deep incarnation' becomes apparent in 'Auguries of Innocence' (1803?). If you can indeed behold 'Heaven in a wildflower', then human mistreatment of other creatures, no less than of one another, is potentially catastrophic:

> A Robin Red breast in a Cage
> Puts all Heaven in a Rage
> A Dove house filld with Doves & Pigeons
> Shudders Hell thr' all its regions
> A dog starvd at his Masters Gate
> Predicts the ruin of the State
> A Horse misusd upon the Road
> Calls to Heaven for Human blood
> Each outcry of the hunted Hare
> A fibre from the Brain does tear
> A Skylark wounded in the wing
> A Cherubim does cease to sing
> The Game Cock clipd & armd for fight
> Does the Rising Sun affright.
>
> (l. 5–18)

Conversely:

> Every Wolfs & Lions howl
> Raises from Hell a Human Soul
> The wild deer, wandring here & there
> Keeps the Human Soul from Care.
>
> (l.19–22)

This litany of evils, and counter-posed instances of good, is, to be sure, presented from a knowingly naïve perspective. These are, after all, auguries of 'innocence'. Read as a work of prophetic critique, though, these seemingly far-fetched attributions of cause and effect ('If you go so/the result is So') confront us with a series of puzzles, asking the reader to try to figure out the underlying connections and insisting that we recognize the entanglement of cruelty to animals with those social injustices that are alluded to later in the poem – the 'Babe that weeps the rod beneath', the 'Beggar's rags', the 'Harlot's cry', the plight of the poor and those pressed into military service. These are disclosed as forming a pattern of wrongdoing that 'Shall weave Old England's winding Sheet'. No matter how powerful imperial Britain might appear to be in the present, from Blake's politically egalitarian and theologically incarnational perspective, any society that tolerates cruelty, violence, injustice and oppression is ultimately doomed. Recalling the imagery of 'To my friend Butts', the poem concludes with the affirmation that:

> God Appears & God is Light
> To those poor Souls who dwell in Night,
> But does a Human Form Display
> To those who Dwell in Realms of day.
>
> (l.129–32)

The 'Human Form' is that of the cosmic Christ, which dwells in all creation, such that, as the Chorus concludes in the 'The Marriage of Heaven and Hell' (1790), 'everything that lives is Holy' (1988: 45).

Blake's egalitarianism informs also his take on the role of the prophet, for, as we have already seen, he held that '[e]very honest man is a Prophet he utters his opinion both of private & public matters'. The calling of the awakened poet, the golden-horned ram, then, is to amplify or potentiate the prophetic voice of a wider collective. Moreover, in *Milton* (1803–08), the capacity to prophesy is extended beyond the human: here 'Trees on Mountains' are said to 'thunder thro' the darksome sky/Uttering prophecies & speaking instructive words to the sons/Of Men' (Plate 26:6, 9–10). As Hutchings remarks, there is a faint echo here of the image of 'Mountains and all hills; fruitful trees, and all cedars' participating in praise for the Creator in Ps. 148.9, along with a more direct allusion to the metaphorical 'two witnesses' of Rev. 11.3-4, the 'two olive trees and the two candlesticks', which 'shall prophesy a thousand two hundred and threescore days, clothed in sackcloth' (Hutchings 2002: 115-16). In general, though, earthly entities in Blake's poetry figure less as prophets in their own right than as a locus of the cry to which the prophet responds: 'Break this heavy chain/That does freeze my bones around!' Earth beseeches the Bard at the beginning of the 'Songs of Experience' ([1794] 'Earth's Answer', l.19).

This is consistent with a particular strand in the Hebrew prophetic tradition, in which the relationship between the people and their God is triangulated by the earth or land (*'ereṣ*), which cries out for deliverance in its own right. Earth's 'cry' nonetheless differs from that of the oppressed people, whose crying out (*za'ak*), as in Ex. 2.23, is a 'cry of misery and wretchedness with some self-pity', potentially denoting also the 'filing of a legal complaint' (Brueggemann 2001: 11). The verbal construction used with respect to *'ereṣ* is not *za'ak* but *'ābal*: a word that is generally translated into English as 'mourning', but which can also denote 'drying up' (Hayes 2002: 14-15). In its mournful drying up, then, the land is said to bear mute witness to human wrongdoing: 'Therefore the land mourns', laments the eighth-century BCE prophet Hosea, 'and all who live in it languish;/together with the wild animals/and the birds of the air,/even the fish of the sea are perishing' (4.3). This lament is taken up again by Isaiah:

> The earth dries up and withers.
> > the world languishes and withers;
> > the heavens languish together with the earth.
> The earth lies polluted
> under its inhabitants
> for they have transgressed laws,
> > violated the statutes,
> > broken the everlasting covenant.
>
> (24.4-5)
>
> The land mourns and languishes.
>
> (33.9)

Similarly, Jeremiah, writing in the shadow of the Babylonian conquest of Jerusalem in 587/586 BCE, cries out in desperation: 'How long will the land mourn,/and the grass of every field wither?/For the wickedness of those who live in it/the animals and the birds are swept away' (12:4). To this, the prophet discerns the Lord responding: 'They made it a desolation,/desolate it mourns to me./The whole land is made desolate,/but no one lays it to heart' (12:11).

Conventionally, this trope might be read in accordance with the logic of the Flood: that is, as a form of redemptive violence wrought by an angry deity, who brings calamity to the whole land community as a means of punishing His wayward people. Yet recent scholarship suggests that this would be to misconstrue the complex causal relations that Jeremiah, in particular, is bringing to light. For the biblical scholar Walter Brueggemann, Jeremiah is the 'clearest model for prophetic imagination and ministry', especially in the mode of critique in the form of poetically 'articulated grief' (2001: 46, 47). His prophetic critique, moreover, had a profoundly socioecological orientation: one that has acquired a new salience in the horizon of anthropogenic climate change.[7] In Michael Northcott's ecotheological reading, Jeremiah discerns that 'the Israelites had been vanquished because they had neglected to worship Yahweh. Instead they had idolised wealth and power and enslaved one another and the land in the process' (2007: 10). Neglecting the Sabbath rest and failing to 'protect the cause of the orphan' and 'defend the rights of the needy' (Jer. 5.27–8), the ruling elite had grown 'great and rich… fat and sleek' (Jer. 5.23–4) at others' expense through treacherous trading practices. As well as engendering social injustice, these forms of wrongdoing are linked by Jeremiah with various indicators of ecological collapse, including crop failures, the pollution of wild places, the inability of domestic animals to bear young and growing desertification. Northcott postulates that Jeremiah is responding to an agricultural collapse that occurred around 600 BCE, which may have been partly a consequence of the intensification of land-use under the late Israelite monarchy. In this region of relatively fragile soils and unreliable rainfall, he explains:

> As perennial grasses are cleared and the land cropped with cereal plants the soil is at risk of salinisation from mineral salts in the subsoil and bedrock which rise through the soil when land is ploughed and cropped with non-native plants… Once the primeval forests on the high lands were cleared the land also became prone to drought and flash floods, and the precious topsoil which grew the surpluses that sustained empires was gradually washed into the ocean. When the soil was washed away and the land became less green, it absorbed more sunlight, there were fewer clouds, the rains failed, and parts of the land turned to desert.
>
> (10)

In connecting these environmental problems with a culture geared towards the accumulation of wealth and concentration of power rather than towards social justice and care for creation, Jeremiah could be seen as 'the first ecological prophet in literary and religious history' (Northcott 2007: 12) (or at least, the first that we know about in Western literary and religious history).

Among Jeremiah's successors is William Blake. This inheritance is nowhere more evident than in his account of the 'desolated earth' that results from the fall of 'Albion' (personifying Britain) in *Jerusalem* (1804–20):

> His Children exil'd from his breast pass to and fro before him
> His birds are silent on his hills, flocks die beneath his branches
> His tents are fall'n! his trumpets, and the sweet sound of his harp
> Are silent on his clouded hills, that belch forth storms & fire.
> His milk of Cows, & honey of Bees, & fruit of golden harvest,
> Is gather'd in the scorching heat, & in the driving rain:
> Where once he sat he weary walks in misery and pain:
> His Giant beauty and perfection fallen into dust:
> Till from within his witherd breast grown narrow with his woes:
> The corn is turn'd to thistles & the apples into poison:
> The birds of song to murderous crows, his joys to bitter groans!
> The voices of children in his tents, to cries of helpless infants!
> And self-exiled from the face of light & shine of morning,
> In the dark world a narrow house! he wanders up and down,
> Seeking for rest and finding none! and hidden far within,
> His Eon weeping in the cold and desolated Earth.
>
> (Plate 19, l.1–17)

Blake's *Jerusalem* articulates a prescient ecoprophetic *apokalypsis* of the Ploutocene. Although he was not in a position to know about the role of carbon dioxide and other greenhouse gases in planetary heating, Blake rightly discerned a perilously climate-altering potential in the worsening air pollution belching forth from London's multiplying coal-fired flour mills, breweries and tanneries, together with the felling of the oak forests south of London to produce charcoal for the iron foundries that were, at that time, churning out weapons for use in the Napoleonic Wars (McKusick 2000: 21). Bearing witness to the appalling working and living conditions of a growing army of industrial workers, Blake's ecoprophetic critique targets also 'the monetisation of value and wealth and its concentration in the hands of merchants' and the 'imperial export of these same processes to the nations' (Northcott 2013: 291).

The counterpart of prophetic criticizing, in Brueggemann's analysis, is the 'energizing' afforded by the prophet's discernment of an alternative path and prefiguration of a potentially redemptive future (2001: 59–80). While Blake's language of critique echoes that of the 'Lamentations of Jeremiah' (Kamusikiri 1990), as energizer, he draws on other Hebrew prophets, especially Ezekiel, as well as on the last book of the Christian New Testament, Revelation. Blake's revelation, however, rewrites John's significantly: just as the conclusion of the 'The Marriage of Heaven and Hell' rejects the theocentric exclusivity of Rev. 15 – 'For thou [God] only art holy' – so too the redemption of Albion is not envisaged in terms of a final judgement that separates the saved from the damned. Rather, in Northcott's reading, it will take place through an overcoming of 'the opposition of heaven and earth, good and evil', which will lead 'to the ultimate restoration of all things' (Northcott 2013: 293). This restorative vision does not entail a return to a pre-industrial, let alone pre-pastoral socioecological, order but rather something more akin to a 'good Anthropocene'. Blake's erstwhile targets of critique, Bacon, Newton and Locke, are also included in this redemptive vision, appearing together with Chaucer, Shakespeare and Milton above the ecotopian city of Goglonooza (Plate 98, l. 9). We are not let in on their conversation, but the suggestion is that the materialization of Blake's New Jerusalem would entail the wedding of reason and imagination, *logos* and *poiesis*, and science and religion, in ushering in not the '*kingdom* of God' but a *commonwealth* of love. Blake's new revelation, then, can be seen as answering indirectly to the early German Romantic call for an 'enlightened mythology': one that effectively reclaimed the Bible 'from all interpretations that would make it the instrument of tyranny and prescription' (Roberts 2010: xi). Notwithstanding the pronounced anthropomorphism of his religious imagery, the emancipatory agenda proposed by Blake as a 'prophet against Empire' (Erdman 1977) encompasses also the liberation of 'the Living Creatures of the Earth' (Plate 98, l.54) from human tyranny.

'the wrong dream': Judith Wright's double disillusionment

My own first ecocritical engagement with the concept of the Anthropocene centred on a reading of a poem by Judith Wright (Rigby 2009). This article was commissioned for a special issue of the Ecological Humanities Corner of the *Australian Humanities Review*, 'dedicated', as editor Deborah Bird Rose explained,

> to a topic inspired by Val Plumwood: 'Thinking about writing for the Anthropocene'. In the last article she wrote before her death, Plumwood spoke passionately about the role of writers in our current time of crisis. She called for

poets and other writers to join in a rethinking that 'has the courage to question our most basic cultural narratives'. In particular, she called for writing that is 'open to experiences of nature as powerful, agentic and creative, making space in our culture for an animating sensibility and vocabulary'. This, she says, is a major task facing the humanities today ('Nature in the Active Voice', *Australian Humanities Review* 46).

(Rose 2009).

In my view, this called for an ecopoetic revival of the prophetic imagination, for which I found a model in Wright's 'Dust'. In the meantime, my concerns about the terminology of the 'Anthropocene' have deepened, whilst the potentially catastrophic impacts of those anthropogenic alterations to Earth's life-support systems, to which it refers, have become increasingly manifest. Here, then, I revisit and extend my earlier reading of this text in the light of those concerns but also with a view to probing Wright's disillusionment with her own Romantic inheritance.

'Dust' dates from what is commonly seen as a crucial turning point in Wright's development as a writer: the time of her rediscovery of the country that 'built [her] heart', as she puts it in her later poem of homecoming, 'Train Journey' (1994: 75). She was already a published author, and her early work was inspired by the nationalist interest in the creation of a modern and distinctively Australian literature, in conjunction with the left-humanist call for new cultural values and more just social relations, as articulated in the literary journal edited by Clem Christessen, *Meanjin*, in which 'Dust' was first published in 1945. Following a formative period of study and work in Sydney and overseas travel, it was only on returning to her natal home near Armidale to help run the family property, Talgarrah station, while her brothers fought in the War, that she found her true poetic vocation, becoming in the process Australia's first significant regional poet. For in the work that she now began to write, Wright responds not to some generalized notion of Australianness but to the embodied experience of a particular place, in which she is beginning to discern traces of the complex entanglement of environment and identity, past and present, memory and desire, and repression and recognition. Recalling her homeward journey in April 1942 through a 'drought-stricken landscape' in a 'haze of dust', she writes that she became 'suddenly and sharply aware' of the New England Tableland as 'my country': 'These hills and valleys were not mine, but me, and the threat of Japanese invasion hung over them as me; I felt it under my own ribs. Whatever other blood I held, this was the country I loved and knew' (qtd. Brady 1998: 84). What lends her lyric its force and importance, however, is not so much this patriotic and quasi-deep-ecological epiphany as her anguished perception that this country, and the society that had shaped it, was profoundly troubled, as a consequence of an invasion, which long predated that now feared from the Japanese. Stolen from the Indigenous people who had learnt over millennia to live sustainably with its peculiar ways by European 'settlers', including Wright's own forbears, the land was sickening under the impact of the very agricultural regime that had afforded her the rural childhood that she so relished.

Lengthy periods of low rainfall have long been characteristic of the climate of New South Wales, with its non-annual weather cycles and frequent extremes, now known to be influenced by the El Niño Southern Oscillation, which affects all of eastern Australia, together with the Indian Ocean Dipole, which affects the southern half of the continent.[8] What Wright was beginning to recognize, however, was that the impact of these dry periods in the mid-twentieth century was connected also with the way that settler Australians had been using the land in what was commonly cast as a 'battle' with the unruly elements of the colonial earth (Robin 2010). At its most stark, this escalated into what Deborah Bird Rose has described as 'a dual war: a war against nature and a war against the natives' (2004: 34). Wright would later write about the depredations of that second war. Here, though, her focus is on the impact on farmers of the continent's unpredictable rainfall and frequent extremes, in conjunction with the propensity of its ancient, worn-down and nutrient-poor soils to get up and fly away when stripped of native vegetation. What 'Dust' discloses, then, is that the agricultural crisis, to which the poem bears witness, is no 'natural disaster'. Instead, the wind-blown, dried-out topsoil becomes legible as *ābal*, 'earth's cry', pointing to human wrongdoing:

> This sick dust, spiraling with the wind,
> is harsh as grief's taste in our mouths
> and has eclipsed the small sun.
> The remnant earth turns evil,
> the steel-shocked earth has turned against the plough
> and runs with wind all day, and all night
> sighs in our sleep against the windowpane.
>
> Wind was kinder once, carrying cloud
> like a waterbag on his shoulder; sun was kinder,
> hardening the good wheat brown as a strong man.
> Earth was kinder, suffering fire and plough,
> breeding the unaccustomed harvest.
> Leaning in our doorway together
> watching the birdcloud shadows,

the fleetwing windshadows travel our clean wheat
we thought ourselves rich already.
We counted the beautiful money
and gave it in our hearts to the child asleep,
who must never break his body
against the plough and the stubborn rock and tree.

But the wind rises; but the earth rises,
running like an evil river; but the sun grows small,
and when we turn to each other, our eyes are dust
and our words dust.
Dust has overtaken our dreams that were
wider and richer than wheat under the sun,
and war's eroding gale scatters our sons
with a million other grains of dust.

O sighing at the blistered door, darkening the evening star,
the dust accuses. Our dream was the wrong dream,
our strength was the wrong strength.
Weary as we are, we must make a new choice,
a choice more difficult than resignation,
more urgent than our desire of rest at the end of the day.
We must prepare the land for a difficult sowing,
a long and hazardous growth of a strange bread,
that our son's sons may harvest and be fed.

(Wright 1994: 23–24)

The speaker of Wright's poem, who hears the earth sighing all night 'against the windowpane', if only in sleep, and so perhaps unconsciously, initially locates the source of the wrong in the land itself: 'The remnant earth turns evil', laments the dismayed farmer, whose address we hear in this poem. In the very next line, however, we are given a hint that the land might actually be the victim rather than the agent of this wrong, for the earth that 'has turned against the plough' is said to have been 'steel-shocked'. Later in the poem, as the speaker moves towards a revised assessment of what is amiss, a metaphoric association is drawn between the loss of topsoil from the ploughed land in the drought and the deaths of men on the battlefields of the war. These men are identified emotively from the maternal perspective of the speaker as 'sons': 'and war's eroding gale scatters our sons/with a million other grains of dust'. In light of this linkage, we might hear in 'steel-shocked' an echo of the First World War expression 'shell-shocked', and in this echo, a suggestion that the agricultural landscape is itself a battlefield of sorts.

This is not how the speaker initially speaks of the land. She recalls happier times: 'Wind was kinder once, carrying cloud/like a waterbag on his shoulder; sun was kinder,/hardening the good wheat brown as a strong man.' Yet again in the following lines there are hints that this 'kindness', that is to say, the amenability of the land to the production of wheat, was not so much gifted as extorted: 'Earth was kinder, *suffering* fire and plough,/breeding the *unaccustomed* harvest.' Here, the connotations of 'steel-shocked' are reinforced, and we are reminded that the earth that was now 'running with the wind' had once been accustomed to a very different kind of treatment: a *kinder* treatment, as Wright had come to recognize, from those Indigenous landholders from whom the speaker's people (who were also, of course, the poet's) had stolen it.

If, at first, the speaker mistakenly perceives the wrong as arising from the land, it is because she is still blinkered by dominant ways of thinking, which legitimate human domination of the Earth, along with settler domination of colonized peoples. In 'Dust', this form of 'royal consciousness' is implicit in the speaker's recollection of her former aspirations with respect to the land: 'Leaning in our doorway together/watching the birdcloud shadows,/the fleetwing windshadows travel our clean wheat/we thought ourselves rich already'. Claimed as private property, land is valued primarily as a source of economic wealth and a vehicle of upward social mobility. By profiting from the land in this way, the speaker and her husband had hoped to free their son from the rural labour that involved so much struggle with this recalcitrant environment: 'We counted the beautiful money/and gave it in our hearts to the child asleep,/who must never break his body/against the plough and the stubborn rock and tree.' Here, the speaker claims our sympathy for the hardship that she and her family have suffered in pursuit of a dream now being dashed by the war that is claiming their sons' lives and by the drought that is ruining their harvest. At the same time, Wright hints that their calculation of future happiness is founded on the standpoint of mastery. It rests on the assumption that they will ultimately claim victory in their battle with the land (the unspoken battle *for* the land evidently being assumed to have been won already).

In reducing Earth to the status of a mere resource under human sway, we become insouciant to other-than-human suffering. Just as royal consciousness silences the cry of oppressed peoples, the standpoint of human mastery silences Earth's cry. This poem traces the moment when such silencing mechanisms begin to break down: 'But the wind rises; but the earth rises,/running like an evil river; but the sun grows small;/and when we turn to each other, our eyes are dust/and our words dust.' In the opening stanza, the dust was described as 'harsh as grief's taste in our mouth', a simile that creates an association between the harshness of the desiccated land and the harshness of the grief felt by the speaker for her own loss. The implication is that this association is one of cause and effect: the speaker grieves because the remnant earth, as she puts it, has 'turned evil'. Once again, evil is seen to be manifest in the land, as the dust runs 'like an evil river' in place of the waterways that have run dry. Now, though, the earlier simile has been displaced by a more intimate metaphoric association between the human subject and the desiccated soil – one that intimates a dawning realization that it is not only the land that is eroding but the perspective from which her people had hitherto viewed and spoken of it: 'our eyes are dust/and our words dust'. As the standpoint of mastery begins to crumble, it becomes apparent that in its drying out, the land is also, in effect, indicting its owners, and the speaker is forced to recognize her own culpability in the wrong to which the dust bears witness: 'O sighing at the blistered door, darkening the evening star,/the dust accuses.'

Ultimately, the grieving speaker is forced to admit, 'Our dream was the wrong dream,/our strength was the wrong strength.' This recognition has come too late to avert disaster. Yet, in keeping with the biblical tradition upon which Wright draws at the same time as departing from it, there remains the possibility of going forward otherwise, incorporating a new covenant, if not with God, then with Earth itself. In the final lines of the poem, addressed to a community yet to come, 'land' bears a double burden of meaning. That which must be prepared 'for a difficult sowing' is not only the land that demands to be farmed otherwise, farmed that is, with a view to making a living *with* rather than *from* it; it is also the self that requires to be thought otherwise, such that (recalling the Parable of the Sower from Mat. 13. 24–30), 'sowing' might be read as the imparting of a truth that not all, perhaps, will be ready, willing or able to receive. Similarly, the recollection of the Eucharistic feast carried by 'bread' suggests that what is at issue here is the soul no less than the soil: the anticipated 'bread' might then be understood not only as a source of nourishment but as a kind of sacrament, seeded by the poetic word in its radical critique of royal consciousness. The possibility of reconciliation that is proffered at the end of this ecoprophetic verse is nonetheless not conventionally Christian. The qualifier 'strange' prefigures the necessary emergence of 'new relationships and forms of thought not yet realised', as Wright put it in her later essay 'The Writer and the Crisis'. Poetic language, as she claims there, 'is at once the bread [man] lives by, and the seed wheat from which will come the bread of future generations' ([1952] 1975: 175). In this way, 'Dust' calls upon its readers to have the courage to surrender familiar patterns of thinking and being, in favour of a different sense of self, consistent with a more life-sustaining way of being-in-relationship not with a God beyond but with one another and with the land. Only thus might the flourishing of future generations be assured.

'Dust' is the record of a painful awakening and a work of ecoprophetic enlightenment. Yet the insight that it offers is presented not so much as the fruit of rational reflection but as having been prompted by the material agency of earth and sky in their resistance to human-all-too-human aspirations. In place of this 'wrong dream', Wright's verse offers no pragmatic solutions or political stratagems, for that is not the task of poetry, which was in her view 'an expression of *being*, of where one is at the time not a political or otherwise active entity' (qtd. Brady 1998: 466). This, at any rate, was how she put it in the late 1980s in the context of explaining why she had decided to quit writing verse. Back in the early 1940s, though, when her writing career was just beginning to take off, she retained a firm faith in the power of poetry to engender a cultural revival, not least by reconnecting human consciousness with the natural world. By the 1960s, she understood this as having an explicitly ecopolitical dimension.

In her talks and essays from the late 1960s and 1970s, Wright argued that the socioeconomic changes which were required in order to stem the tide of environmental destruction could only be achieved democratically through the enlistment of 'human concern, distress and love', in order to facilitate the abandonment of the flawed quest for 'domination of the world' in favour of a renewed 'reverence for life', as she put it in a lecture from 1969 (1975: 207, 202). Sound scientific knowledge and rational argument were indispensable, she believed, but also '[o]ur feelings must be engaged, and engaged on a large scale' (1975: 206). As she had argued the previous year in an essay called 'Conservation as a Concept', modern Western society was faced with the need not only 'to revise most radically our exploitative techniques, but to revise a whole attitude of mind and feeling that are very deeply rooted in our whole history of dealings with the natural world' (1975: 189). In effecting this change of heart, Wright discerned a new role for poetry and other art forms, as well as for scholarship. Prefiguring the project that would become known in Australia in the 1990s as the 'ecological humanities', Wright called for new forms of research and writing that would bridge the divide between the arts and sciences (Rigby 2019b). In the Romantic period, as Wright recalls, Goethe had made a similar call, setting out his ideal of 'a science of living experience, of the whole creature including sensation and idea' (1975: 194). Similarly, in a lecture at the University of Newcastle in 1972, Wright proposed that conservation should be integrated into all areas of study.

She argued that 'the sort of education we really need ought to be embodied in the structure of the educational pyramid itself, at all levels, and in all subjects' and that there should be greater 'cooperation and coordination' between as well as within universities' (1975: 233, 277). In this, our 'first task', as Wright saw it, was 'to discover how value can be restored to a world from which we have so long withheld it'. Her aim was to draw nature out of the 'background' into which it had been cast, by recognizing in its 'incessant creativity' new possibilities of human *poiesis* in partnership with other-than-human entities and processes (1975: 194, 191, 198–99).

By this time, Wright had also become a leading environmental campaigner. In 1962, she co-founded the Wildlife Preservation Society of Queensland (WPSQ), and four years later, she co-founded the national Australian Conservation Foundation. Between 1967 and 1970, she successfully joined forces with artist John Busst and forest ecologist Len Webb (vice-president of WPSQ) to protect the Great Barrier Reef from mining. Their efforts were supported by several powerful national and local trade unions, which threatened to place a black ban on the survey ship *Navigator*, owned by the consortium of Japex and Ampol Petroleum Companies, when it reached the aptly named Repulse Bay (McCalman 2013: 298). In the early 1970s, the New South Wales (NSW) branch of the Communist-led Builders and Labourers Federation termed such bans against environmentally damaging developments (including those that threatened historic buildings, as well as urban parks and peri-urban bushland) 'green bans'. This initiative, which inspired Petra Kelly to name West Germany's fledgling ecopolitical party '*Die Grünen*' (The Greens), is a reminder that, at least in Australia, environmentalism has by no means been an exclusively middle-class affair (Burgmann and Burgmann 1998). Their combined efforts were successful: on 16 April 1970, Prime Minister John Gorton introduced a bill placing the entire Reef and its waters under Commonwealth sovereignty. This was confirmed by a High Court ruling in 1972, and in 1979, an Act originally passed by the Whitlam Labor government in 1975 redesignated the Reef province as a marine park. In 1981, the Great Barrier Reef was accorded UNESCO World Heritage status (McCalman 2013: 299; see also Wright 1996).

For Wright, conservation was also, necessarily, a decolonial project, to be undertaken in solidarity with Indigenous Australians and in support of their struggle for land rights. In the late 1960s, she collaborated with the Aboriginal poet Kath Walker (later Oodgeroo Nunuccal) to create an Aboriginal Cultural Centre. In her poem 'Two Dreamtimes' (1973), addressed to Walker, she admits:

> over the drinks at night
> we can exchange our separate griefs,
> but yours and mine are different.
>
> A knife's between us. My righteous kin
> still have cruel faces.
> Neither you nor I can win them,
> though we meet in secret kindness.
> …
> The knife's between us. I turn it around,
> the handle to your side,
> the weapon made from your country's bones
> I have no right to take it.
>
> (1994: 317–18)

Wright here acknowledges that she and her friend are differently situated with respect to the land, which was stolen from Australia's First Nations and is now subject to corporate capitalist neo-colonization at the hands of 'traders and stock-exchanges' (317). Nevertheless, she has been criticized for 'conflating two remarkably different historical traditions in a genetically similar nomenclature', since the mournful final stanza collapses the titular 'Two Dreamtimes' into a singular 'our dreamtime' (Cooke 2013: 63). In Stuart Cooke's assessment, Wright's poetry overall 'is problematical both because it overlooks the continuation of Aboriginal Australia into the present moment and because, in reaching for the universal, it ignores the specifics and complexities of Australian ecologies' (2013: 67).[9] While this may be true, it would be disrespectful to Oodgeroo to overlook the importance of 'Two Dreamtimes' to its biographical addressee, who responded by affirming:

> Sister poet, this I know,
> Your dreams are my dreams,
> Your thoughts are my thoughts
> And the shadow that made us sisters
> That binds us close together
> Together with us cries.
>
> (qtd. Minter 2015: 71)

In Frank Heimans' documentary *Shadow Sister: A Film Biography of Australian Aboriginal Poet Kath Walker* (1977), Oodgeroo recites these lines on the occasion of Wright's visit with her on Oodgeroo's ancestral country of Minjerriba (North

Stradbroke Island). The friendship of these two very differently situated women poets, Peter Minter argues in his discussion of this film, was generative of a 'unique, feminist mode of decolonised transcultural environmentalism' in Australia (2015: 63). Forged at the intersection of Western environmentalism, critical ecofeminism and the Aboriginal land rights movement, their partnership contributed to the emergence of a distinctively Australian ecopoetics that is at once 'radically ecocentric and variously anti-hegemonic' (Minter 2015: 74).

Wright herself became a tireless campaigner for Aboriginal land rights. In 1979, when she was researching the impact of her own family's pioneering farming activity on Aboriginal people and their land, as recounted in *Cry for the Dead* (1981), she co-founded the Aboriginal Treaty Committee with Herbert Cole ('Nugget') Coombs. Formerly a senior civil servant, and first chair of the Council of Aboriginal Affairs (established 1967), Coombs was then a visiting scholar at the Australian National University's Centre for Resource and Environmental Studies (the later birthplace of the National Working Group for the Ecological Humanities) and had been president of the Australian Conservation Foundation since 1977. Through her friendship and collaboration with Oodgeroo, Wright also became highly critical of the American concept of 'wilderness', which had been adopted by some in the Australian conservation movement. Against this, she argued for the recognition of the ethical as well as the ecological significance of Indigenous land-use practices and called for Aboriginal management of national parks (Brady 1998: 448).

By the late 1980s, Wright was beginning to doubt the efficacy of poetry in the face of an ever-worsening and increasingly global environmental crisis, recognizing that 'the whole situation we've got ourselves into is too immense, too insane as it were, for verse to encompass', as she remarked to Richard Glover in an interview from 1993 (qtd. Mead 2008: 339). Ironically, this was the year after she had become the first Australian to win the Queen's Medal for Poetry (an award first proposed by Ted Hughes), and the year before she won the Human Rights Award for poetry. More recently, Wright has been rediscovered as Australia's first major ecopoet, as well as a significant ecocritical theorist *avant la lettre* (Coralie 2011).[10] The importance of her dual legacy – in literature and the arts, as well as in environmental and Indigenous activism – is now recognized well beyond the narrow confines of the literary field, notably in the biennial 'Two Fires Festival', which is held in the small rural township of Braidwood in New South Wales, where Wright spent the latter part of her life in a property named 'Edge' (not far from the home of her friend, Val Plumwood). It was, in fact, at the inaugural Two Fires Festival in 2005 that I first presented a paper on Wright.

Wright's disillusionment with the ecopolitical potential of the 'deedful word', to recall Herder's take on prophetic language, is nonetheless instructive. For the previous forty years, she had banked on poetry as a primary medium for the sharing of the 'strange bread' referred to at the end of 'Dust'. Her faith was inherited, as she well knew, from that 'Romantic theory' which affirmed 'the power of men to alter their world by altering their ways of seeing and knowing it, and to create great art in cooperation with the creativity of natural forces', as she wrote in her 1958 lecture 'Romanticism and the last frontier' (Wright 1975: 65). Ten years later, she gave a lecture expressing the hope she invested in the capacity of literature and the arts in general to engage people's 'feelings and emotions', enlisting 'concern, distress and love' (Wright 1975: 206). In addition to this hope, she also appears to have been taken for a while by something akin to the Heideggerian notion that the poetic word could 'save the earth' in a more intangible sense: namely, by drawing the manifold phenomena of earth and sky into the horizon of human consciousness in a way that was non-objectifying and non-instrumentalizing. Poetry might thereby counter the tendency of modern technology to construe everything as a totally knowable and infinitely manipulable 'standing reserve'. In doing this, Heidegger argued in his later essays, poetry served the crucial role of inducting us into dwelling. For to truly dwell, for Heidegger, was to enter into a set of relationships with what he called the Fourfold of Earth, Sky, Divinities and Mortals in a particular place and time, within which the other-than-human was to a greater or lesser extent inevitably altered but not in such a way as to prevent its own self-unfolding. To 'save the earth', in this sense, is to 'release it into its own being': and this, he believed, was what poets were for (Heidegger 1971, 89–142).

This view has also been advanced by ecocritics, beginning with Jonathan Bate in *The Song of the Earth* (2000).[11] Many contemporary ecocritics and environmental writers, whether or not they have read Heidegger, also set great store on the salvific power of literature. In this respect, Wright's career might be considered a cautionary tale: for as she painfully came to recognize, the seeds that she scattered over many decades in poems such as 'Dust' fell largely by the wayside, on stony ground or among thorns. There are several ways in which this failure to effect the kind of change that she sought through her vocation as a poet might be understood. The first and most obvious concerns the sociocultural location of the kind of writing that she favoured: put simply, if you are hoping to have an impact on the feelings and imagination of a wider public, you would do better to make a big-grossing feature film or a gripping documentary for a national TV channel than to write intellectually challenging modernist verse.

The very marginality of poetry, which Wright saw as giving it its potentially critical and hence progressive edge, is of course also the reason why it is bound to have a limited resonance in society at large. More generally, though, and this is my second point, Wright's poetic project, like that of many ecocritics, is flawed by what Marxists (perhaps a little too readily and dismissively) term 'bourgeois idealism': that is, the belief that social change comes, as it were, from the top-down, from how people think and feel, rather than from how they make a living, and the wider relations of production and consumption within which they do so. As I have observed previously, if 'the Shoah confronted humanists with the devastating realisation that "a man can read Goethe or Rilke in the evening … and go to his day's work at Auschwitz in the morning" (Steiner 1970: ix) so too, ecocritics must acknowledge that a woman might well read Wordsworth or Thoreau in the evening … and go to her day's work for Exxon-Mobil in the morning' (Rigby 2009: np). Here, I find myself in agreement with Timothy Clark, who observes that the exaggeration of the 'importance of the imaginary' risks 'consolidating a kind of diversionary side-show, blind to its relative insignificance' (2015: 18). Wright herself, as I have already stressed, clearly recognized that poetry was no substitute for politics. What she had also come to realize, however, was that her earlier overvaluation of the 'constellating word', as she terms it in 'Lament for Passenger Pigeons' (1973), was also flawed. The ambition to pit poetry against extinction, 'To sing of Being, its escaping wing,/to utter absence in a human chord/and recreate the meaning as we sing' (1994: 320), might be an effective way of voicing our own sense of loss; but it was powerless not only to restore an extinct species to the web of life but also to render any still living being present to experience in its embodied otherness: that is to say (as discussed in the previous chapters), things might be brought to mind by literary language, and significantly and powerfully so; but that is not the same thing as encountering them in the flesh.[12] The poetic word, far from releasing the manifold things of earth and sky into their own being, captures them in a human-all-too-human 'web of language', as Wright puts it in one of her very last poems, 'Summer' (1994: 421), within which their more-than-human materiality is notable by its absence.

As a thing in and of the world, however, albeit one that is also often at odds with dominant forms of world-making, the poem can certainly do plenty of other things, depending on the ways in which it is received and networked with other forms of praxis. Ecoprophetic writing can, at the very least, perform the crucial work of bearing witness to prevailing socioecological ills and stoking the desire for their remediation. In the case of Wright's 'Dust', composed on the brink of the Great Acceleration, what is witnessed are those socioecological vulnerabilities that have been produced by the Plantationocene. Specifically, this poem bears witness to the conversion of the common lands of the Kamilaroi and Anaiwan people of central New South Wales into pastoral properties, entailing land-use practices that were destructive of Indigenous ecologies and lifeways and ill-suited to the prevailing climatic conditions.

Today, however, as the impacts of anthropogenic global hearing begin to bite ever more deeply, those conditions are themselves changing. Now 'the dust accuses' on a planetary scale: for instance, when it blows from the parched plains of sub-Saharan Africa, where the monsoon has failed yet again on account of the polluted atmosphere of the northern hemisphere. Across the Atlantic, it enters the lungs of children in the Caribbean, who sicken with asthma, for which only the wealthy can afford medicine (Schmidt 2009). Now, it is also the wind that accuses, and never more so than when the cyclonic storms and sea surges cooked up by those who feed on fossil fuels bear down upon the poor of far lower carbon-emitting climes. And now too, wildfire accuses, as destructive blazes proliferate around the planet.

Witnessing 'Black Saturday': Jordie Albiston's 'Lamentations'

The likelihood that climate change was set to exacerbate Australia's historical weather variability, making extremes both more frequent and intense, was already beginning to become apparent in the early years of the new millennium. Wright, once again, was one of the first public intellectuals in Australia to voice concern about this, wondering whether the failure of the resident swallows on her property, 'Edge', to nest and breed in the summer of 1991 was evidence of a changing climate (Brady 1998: 471). But it was the massive firestorm that swept down upon the nation's capital from the forested mountains on 18 January 2003, burning to within a few kilometres of Parliament House, which really began to ring alarm bells, including for me personally. I was in Canberra at the time, and it was this terrifying experience that propelled me into the research project that culminated in my last monograph, *Dancing with Disaster* (2015a: 1–2). Worse was to come. On 7 February 2009, at the height of a decade-long drought and in the midst of an unprecedented heatwave, several of the 400 fires then burning across Victoria converged. The mega-blaze obliterated six small towns and badly damaged many more, taking 173 human lives and displacing over 7,500 survivors. It also burnt out over 450,000 hectares of land, killing 2,150 sheep;

1,207 cattle; an unknown number of horses, goats, alpacas, poultry and pigs; and countless free-living animals.[13]

Not unlike the bushfire disaster that was unfolding as this book went to press, Black Saturday was also noteworthy for the fiery debates that followed regarding its causes and significance. For environmental philosopher Freya Mathews, writing in Melbourne's *Age* newspaper, these 'were not "once in a thousand years" or even "once in a hundred years" events, as our political leaders keep repeating. They were the face of climate change in our part of the world.'[14] Her assessment was consistent with the view of those climatologists who considered it likely that the intensity of the heatwave that precipitated the blaze had been exacerbated by anthropogenic global warming. In response to her opinion piece, Mathews was subject to a torrent of abuse by climate change deniers. Meanwhile, Australia's only national newspaper, the Murdoch-owned *Australian*, led a concerted campaign to undermine any link with climate change, targeting instead those environmentalists who had allegedly prevented the widespread prescribed burning, which, it was claimed, would have stopped the fires from becoming so ferocious. Miranda Devine took this fight against 'eco-terrorism' to *The Sydney Morning Herald*, where she insisted that 'it is not arsonists who should be hanging from lamp-posts but greenies'.[15]

Equally troubling, if somewhat less murderous, are responses such as that of the survivors of the firestorm that virtually obliterated the township of Marysville. At a meeting to plan their first trip back to their burnt-out township, where police were still sifting through the ash for human remains, the displaced residents declared their intention to 'stand together and "loudly reclaim" Marysville from nature'.[16] This defiant stance not only exemplifies the ecophobic conclusion that has been drawn from the experience of a disaster tagged as 'natural'; it also indicates that such defiance could lead survivors to put themselves in harm's way by seeking to restore what they have lost, rather than find new ways, and potentially new places, to live more safely and sustainably as we move ineluctably into a climatically changed future. This maladaptive stance betrays a woeful level of settler Australian ignorance and amnesia regarding the pyrophitic ways of the bush that they value, if at all, either as 'timber' or as 'scenery': that is, a passive background for human endeavours, rather than a dynamic network of volatile forces and other-than-human interests.

Environmental historian Christine Hansen has pointed out that although the severity of the conditions in which this firestorm took hold had an anthropogenic aspect, bushfires of this kind have long been 'a fertility dance that had its origins in the remnant Gondwanic forests of Old Australia' (2018: 229).[17] In making this point, Hansen echoes an observation made at the time by Tom Griffiths (2009), author of the landmark environmental history of Victoria's mountain ash forests (Griffiths 2001) and co-author with Hansen of a book on Black Saturday (2012). The 'dance' is one that has taken place at least every 300–400 years in the mountain ash forests of southeastern Victoria for millennia. For Mountain Ash trees, which, unlike other eucalypts, are killed by these mega-blazes, also require them to reproduce. These trees have evolved to take advantage of the long hot, dry periods, combined with the 'deadly one-two punch' of high winds blowing first from the red Centre, then from the icy South. Inevitably, these winds bring bushfires of varying intensity, followed by a cold change with heavy rainfall (Pyne 1991: 37–38).

An understanding of this fiery fertility dance, such as has been afforded by environmental historians, and encoded in Aboriginal oral narratives, nonetheless remains patchy in the wider settler society, the historical memory of which goes back less than 200 years in this region. Moreover, the associated environmental changes wrought by colonization – the replacement of Aboriginal fire-stick farming, or igniculture, by forestry, grazing and agriculture – have increased the frequency of the firestorms that now threaten a growing population on and beyond the sprawling edges of Australia's second-largest metropolis (Pyne 2006). In 2013, following Victoria's Black Saturday firestorm, Aboriginal elders and community members from the Cape York Peninsula published a book to explain how they use igniculture to both mitigate wildfire and sustain biodiversity (McConchie *et al.* 2013). In Victoria, however, traditional knowledge of place-based ignicultures has been severely eroded as a consequence of the earlier and more intense colonial takeover of Aboriginal lands in this part of the country (principally those of the Woiwurrung, Wathaurrung, Daungwurrung and Dja Dja Wurrung). Current endeavours to recover Aboriginal burning practices as a 'tool' for bushfire mitigation, which fail to confront the violent history of colonization, risk perpetuating settler Australian 'hubris' and 'lack of intimacy with country' (Hansen 2018: 238–39), especially where insufficient regard is paid to both the local specifics and the ecological ethics of Indigenous land management.

As Stephen Muecke has observed, '[t]he stories told about natural disasters are crucial in the organisation of people's responses in the medium to long term. While the stories of individual events are told in the detail, they are nonetheless already broadly scripted by narrative forms of mythical strength' (2007: 260). There is more work to be done to recover and attend to those Aboriginal stories that might have survived the carnage of colonization. Meanwhile, some non-Indigenous

Australians are tapping into their own cultural archives in search of narrative and poetic potentials for reimagining disasters misleadingly framed as 'natural' and for discerning the socioecological messages, at once material and moral, that such disasters bring. One of these researchers is the Melbourne poet Jordie Albiston.

In Australia, as in other regions that fell under the sway of European imperialism, the Christian Bible has been deployed as a culturally, and thereby also ecologically, destructive tool of colonization (Brett 2009). Yet, as we have seen in the case of Blake's 'new revelation', it also has the potential to contribute a decolonizing alternative to those anthropocentric, mechanistic and dualistic constructions of 'nature' and 'natural disaster' that came to prevail in modernity. Seeking a language of response to the horrendous damage and loss of life sustained on Black Saturday in Victoria's Kinglake area, where 119 of the 173 human fatalities occurred, and where the poet herself had formerly resided for much of her life, Albiston sought poetic inspiration from the biblical 'Book of Lamentations', attributed to the prophet Jeremiah. Biblical scholars now think this attribution incorrect, but the position of the Lamentations directly after the Book of Jeremiah frames the former in such a way as to lend a prophetic dimension to this series of songs that were composed, probably by more than one author, in response to the Babylonian sacking of Jerusalem in 586 BCE. Read in conjunction with Jeremiah's searing socioecological critique in the preceding book, these songs of sorrow for the destruction of Jerusalem become linked with a grief-stricken awareness of the sociopolitical ills that had beset the city prior to the Babylonian invasion, which thereby acquires the force of a sentinel event.[18]

Albiston's verses bewailing the destruction of Kinglake and the devastation of the surrounding bushland are composed in the form of alphabetical acrostics. In this, she follows the Hebrew original of the first four poems of the 'Lamentations'. Her acrostics stop each time at the letter V, which stands for 'Victoria' at the conclusion of the first three poems in the sequence (I–III) and for 'vanquished' in the last (IV). The incompletion of this alphabetic series recalls the alphabet of the Hebrew original, which has only twenty-two letters; but it can also be read as an acknowledgement of the inability of words to convey the full horror of this event. Crucially, Albiston also replicates the reversal of the letters P and Q in poems II, III and IV, to indicate that *all is not right*. Other formal features of the 1611 Authorised Version of the English translation are also echoed here, including the seemingly arbitrary use of italics (actually marking words supplied by the translators for grammatical purposes); the sense of local detail; and general desolation as expressed through specific imagery, the music of rhythm and repetition and the use of a formal register of communal grief.[19]

Albiston nonetheless departs from the biblical Lamentations in key ways: firstly, by carefully excluding any suggestion of divine vengeance; and secondly, by emphatically including diverse nonhuman others among the innocent victims of the firestorm. This is how the poem-sequence begins:

I.
Ah, look how the township sits solitary *that* was so full of people: look how she sits
    like a weeping widow, the town that just yesterday! sat queen of
        Murrindindi,
    and of the Great Dividing Range, that sat jewel in the crown of all
        Melbourne.
Black is the only one here: black is the only one left: whichever way we turn it
    is black
    who meets our eye, black who shakes our hand, black who murmurs
        nothing
    in our ear.
Can you believe it?
Do you believe what you see?
Everything is missing now, there is no movement in the bush: everything is
    gone and
        there is no bush.
Flora, fauna, family.
Gone.
How has it all come *to* this?

                                                                (2013: 35)

There is no definitive answer to this question, but in the third poem, the speaker alludes to a number of actors and factors, both human and otherwise, that contributed to the catastrophe:

III
…

Understand the story of firestorm and flame, of north wind and southerly
    change.
Understand the story of drought and of fuel.
Understand, and understand: and understand again.

                                                                     (40)

In an anthropogenically warming world, to 'understand the story of drought and fuel' is not only to recognize the necessity for preventive burning to reduce the 'fuel' that fans the flames on such days. It is also to acknowledge other sources of 'fuel', such as the day-trippers introduced in the retrospective second poem, set just prior to the firestorm. These tourists are among those whose carbon dioxide emissions, the 'fuel' that powers their cars and so much else in their lives, have contributed to the unprecedented heatwave:

> II.
> Ah, today you are bringing your baskets to Kinglake.
> Bread and meat are in your baskets: you are bringing them to Jehoshaphat
> Valley, *and* to
> Masons Falls, and to Kinglake National Park.
> Children are in your cars: you are bringing them with your biscuits to picnic in
> Kinglake.
> Driving up the mountain, you stop to snap shots of flowers, and of the forest,
> and of
> Strathewen far below: and of Melbourne, farther below, *that* is covered with
> cloud in its heat.
>
> (36)

Such privileged day-trippers may value 'nature' aesthetically, happily snapping photos, but they fail to register either the disruptive impact of their fossil-fuelled lifestyle or the warning signs of imminent fire-danger. Ironically, they are hastening the devastation of the very places they like to visit recreationally on sunny Sundays. That devastation, Albiston stresses, calls us into a 'moral community' (Rose 2006) with more-than-human others:

> III
> ...
> Pray: pray for Kinglake.
> Pray for the bush and the paddock and the town: pray for the sky and the
> ground.
> Pray for the possum, the ringtail and brushtail: for the koala and the grey
> kangaroo.
>
> Remember to pray for the spider and the skink: the goanna, the gecko, the pink
> galah.
> Remember the rosella: remember the snake: the heifer, the horse and the
> brown-speckled hen.
> Remember to pray for Kinglake.
>
> (40)

Echoing the prophetic witness of Jeremiah, Albiston's 'Lamentations' not only perform the work of mourning but also carry an ominous note of warning:

>   :   Victoria is altered.
>   :   Victoria is burned.
>   :   Victoria is not, can not be the same.
>
>   ...
>
>   undone is she undone is she
>   > *quiet*
>   vanquished is she on this day of the day of fire.
>
>   (42, 40)

At very least, the rebuilt Victoria should not continue to pursue the values that prevailed before the disaster. Yet, as Hansen notes, by 2016, 'Real estate prices for properties caught in the worst of the fire-storm had not only fully recovered but surpassed the pre-fire prices of 2009 as the bush re-greened and the ash sank into the soil' (2018: 235–36). As the climate has continued to warm and the pieces fell into place for another conflagration, it was evident that Australian settler society had still not faced up to its growing vulnerability, with many blithely ignoring (or actively suppressing) the warning calls of scientists, historians, Aboriginal elders, poets and, indeed, of the land itself.

How this might change in the wake of the catastrophic summer of 2019–20 remains to be seen. In the meantime, though, it is clear that a growing number of Australians, including participants in the Fridays for the Future school strikes and Extinction Rebellion protests, are seeking urgent action on climate change. In this connection, it is worth noting that Albiston's poem was first published under the title 'Kinglake Undone' (2011) in the left-leaning Catholic cultural journal, *Eureka Street*, where it appears alongside an article on 'facing up to climate change' as 'the great challenge of our times' (Rue 2011). Long before Pope Francis issued his landmark encyclical *Laudato 'si* (2015), calling all people of good faith to respond to 'the cry of the earth and the cry of the poor', and sparking the global Catholic Climate Action movement,[20] many religious organizations had already begun to take action on climate change. They include, in Australia, the Pacific Calling Partnership (PCP), founded in 2006 as an initiative of the Catholic Edmund Rice Centre for Justice and Community Education, established a decade earlier. This centre aims 'to challenge popular beliefs and dominant cultural values, to ask the difficult questions, to look at life from the standpoint of the minority, the victim, the outcast and the stranger'.[21] The PCP was initiated in response to concerns about the impact on the people of Tuvalu, Kiribati and Torres Strait islands of those climatic changes, to which Australia, which has the highest per capita greenhouse gas emissions in the world, is a significant contributor, primarily through coal exports to China and India. As their website explains:

> The PCP supports the efforts of Pacific Island communities to make their voices heard through training programs for young activists from Kiribati, Tuvalu and elsewhere in the Pacific, such as the annual Kiribati-Tuvalu-Australia Exchange Program (KATEP). The PCP also supports Pacific Island communities' participation in international conferences such as the 2015 Paris conference (COP21). To educate Australians about the impacts of climate change in the Pacific, the PCP runs workshops and presents talks for schools and community organisations.[22]

Although PCP is a Catholic organization, it works with people of all faiths and none.

Increasingly, concern about climate change and other grave socioecological problems is creating common ground for multi-faith ecoprophetic praxis. Informed by science, the multi-faith ecology movement is also inspired by creative re-interpretations and re-workings of religious texts and traditions, such as Albiston's 'Lamentations'. In 2008, for example, Australia's first national organization based on multi-faith environmental activism, Australian Religious Response to Climate Change, was formed, and in 2013, it merged with GreenFaith Australia, a Melbourne-based multi-faith initiative, created in 2009.[23] The membership of ARRCC-GreenFaith includes Christians of various denominations, Baha'is, Buddhists, Hindus, Jews, Moslems, Mormons, Sikhs, those who describe themselves as 'spiritual seekers' and First Nations Australians who adhere to Indigenous spiritual traditions. In addition to practical conservation initiatives, environmental education and advocacy and participation in ecopolitical protest actions, ARRCC-GreenFaith provides literary and liturgical resources for personal reflection and shared worship, both on their website and through their workshops. Having focused in this chapter on the recovery and reworking of the Hebrew prophetic tradition by Christian and secular authors, past and present, it is fitting to conclude with one of the Jewish texts that appear on this website. The poem below, written by Rabbi Jonathan Keren Black, exemplifies the rabbinic tradition of 'midrash' ('expounding'). Black is the founding president of GreenFaith Australia, and the poem was originally written for the new prayer book of the liberal Jewish community,

Mishkan T'filah World Union Edition (2010). It questions and probes a text from the Torah: specifically, God's repeated assertion in Gen. 8 that He would 'never again' bring a flood to destroy all living things:

> The Rainbow
> SHAFTS of bright sun,
> haze of mist
> and there again
> a perfect bow –
> God's palette;
> the spectrum of promise:
> never again will God bring a flood
> to end humanity,
> to start anew.
> But roll back the scroll,
> read the black fire again
> carefully; read the white,
> the unwritten.
> Our task: to take care
> of God's world.
> Between the letters,
> the warning of our failure.
> God will not flood the earth.
> But we, who thought our tiny choices
> would have no effect on this world…
> We have left it late to awaken.
> The sun still shines,
> the haze of mist
> and there again –
> no need for human hand –
> the perfect bow
> God gave.
>
> (Yonatan ben Chayim)[24]

Read and spoken in the context of collective ecopolitical endeavour, and within the horizon of a shared faith, such words might indeed become a piece of that 'new bread' anticipated by Wright, broken in the midst of calamity and nourishing a commitment to transformative ecopolitical praxis.[25]

5

'Deeper tracks wind back': Decolonial ecopoetics

It has been the argument of this book that to critically and creatively re-inherit European Romanticism in the Anthropocene is to recover and repurpose a series of interconnected ecopoetic arts of resistance to the dualistic logic of colonization, in order to discern regenerative, perhaps even transformative, potentials in the face of ever-worsening socioecological ills. This is not to imply, however, that the ecopolitical legacies of the Romantic period are wholly benign. In this chapter, then, I turn to the question of the historical complicity of aspects of Romanticism in the damage wrought on colonized peoples, places and ecologies by European imperial powers and consider the prospects for a decolonizing ecopoetics in the present.

The geohistorical focus for this consideration is the continent that the British dubbed Australia and claimed as their own right around the time that European Romanticism kicked off with the publication of Blake's *Songs of Innocence and Experience* (1789), the Revolution in France gripped the imaginations of progressive intellectuals and the expansion of coal-fired manufacturing initiated the process that is now cooking the planet. As I outlined in the Introduction, the problematic aspect of the Romantic heritage in an Australian context pertains less to the celebration of 'wilderness' than to the translocation of European pastoral imaginaries and agricultural practices. Here, I explore this 'pastoral imposition' (Kinsella 2007a: xii) in relation to the work of a lesser-known contemporary of Judith Wright's, David Campbell. Like Wright, Campbell was a descendant of pioneering pastoralists; but unlike her, he also worked on the land himself for over a decade following the Second World War. In my reading, Campbell's incomplete journey towards a decolonizing ecopoetics during the 1970s underscores the impossibility of succeeding in such an undertaking in the absence of Indigenous interlocutors. To the extent that Wright arguably advanced further along this path, her friendship with Oodgeroo Noonuccal was a crucial enabling factor. The further development of the transcultural decolonial ecopoetics that began to emerge in the personal friendship, literary interchanges and political alliance of Wright and Noonuccal demands the participation of multiple voices, including, in a contemporary Australian context, those of non-Indigenous people belonging to diverse and mixed minority ethnic groups. Those who inherit the dominant Anglo-Celtic colonial culture, however, are faced with particular challenges and responsibilities with respect to past wrongs and ongoing injustices. Within the limits of this final chapter, I therefore bring the work of one such contemporary Anglo-Australian poet, Anne Elvey, into conversation with that of Wiradjuri writer, Jeanine Leane, from whose collection *Walk Back Over* (2018), this chapter takes its title.

Pastoral impositions and Aboriginal dispossession in colonial Australia

European Romantic re-workings of earlier pastoral and georgic poetry were frequently informed by the eager reception of Native American songs and dances, or *Volkspoesie*, in Herder's influential coinage, together with Rousseauian descriptions of Native American lifeways. This can be seen, for example, in Wordsworth's construction of the biocultural landscape of the Alpine vales in Book 6 of 1805–6 version of *The Prelude*:

> A green recess, an aboriginal vale
> Quiet, and lorded over and possess'd
> By naked huts, wood-built, and sown like tents
> Or Indian cabins over the fresh lawn,
> And by the river side.
>
> (l. 448–54)

Cultural as well as biotic exchanges across the Atlantic in the eighteenth and early nineteenth centuries went in both directions, effectively 'Indianizing' aspects of British culture, whilst partially 'anglicizing' Native American culture (Fulford 2006: 6). Yet this Indianized ideal of rural community bore little resemblance to the geocultural landscapes that the British encountered in Australia, with their peculiar flora and fauna, and peopled by 'savages', whose lifeways they were largely incapable of understanding and commonly viewed with disdain.

One of the telling features of settler Australian culture is the paucity of native plants and animals (apart from fish) that became part of the mainstream non-Indigenous diet. Some Australian animals were certainly consumed in the early years, especially when other food supplies ran short. Among the transportees to 'Van Diemen's Land', it appears that many escaped the authorities by going bush and engaging with Aboriginal ways of living (Boyce 2010). Yet the invaders had arrived with their ark of familiar biota, and these remained the mainstay of the settler Australian diet until the latter part of the twentieth century, when it was diversified by non-Anglo-Celtic migrant communities, in conjunction with an increasingly globalized food trade (Symons 2007). Australia exports huge quantities of kangaroo meat, but it is only in recent decades that it has appeared in supermarkets in Australian cities, and Aboriginal 'bush tucker' remains very much a niche market. If, as Freya Mathews has argued, 'appetite opens the eyes' (1994: 43), then the inability of the Australian colonists to recognize the continent as edible contributed to their flattened, two-dimensional view of the landscape as either 'scenery' or 'resource'. This view is epitomized in Kate Grenville's fictionalized biography of one of her forebears, the emancipist William Thornhill, who was among those who first endeavoured to farm, European-style, along the Hawkesbury River in the early 1800s. For Thornhill, 'the forest had never revealed dinner' (Grenville 2005: 321). His refusal to eat with, and learn from, local Aboriginal landholders, whose invitation to partake in their starchy staple of daisy-roots he disdainfully dismisses, referring to it as 'Monkey food' (197), contributed to the violent conflicts that ensued, leading up to the massacre in which he participated in 1814 (Rigby 2008).[1]

Country that had been lovingly and skilfully sustained for millennia as a highly biodiverse 'nourishing terrain' (Rose 1996), then, was commonly viewed as 'wilderness' in a negative sense: as untended and, as it turned out, frequently resistant land, which needed to be wrestled into submission. Aboriginal prior occupation was tacitly acknowledged during the early decades of settlement in the use of terms such as 'runs', 'stations' and 'hunting grounds', demarcating tribal territories, to which were added 'country' in the 1840s and, in the 1870s, the Kamilaroi word *towri*, which was taken to mean hunting ground or 'kingdom' (Ramson 1991: 13). There was also some recognition of the importance of fire in Aboriginal land-use practices. Surveyor-General T. L. Mitchell, for example, during his expedition to the northern tropical regions in the 1840s, observed how cool fires were used seasonally to keep the woodlands open, flush out small mammals, expose birds' nests and renew the grasslands, on which larger game, notably kangaroos, grazed. This led him to conclude, 'Fire, grass, and kangaroos, and human inhabitants, seem all dependent on each other for existence in Australia; for any of these being wanting the others could no longer continue' ([1848] qtd. Pyne 87). Other explorers and colonists also recorded Aboriginal engagement in farming practices, such as the building of dams and wells; planting, irrigating and harvesting seeds; and storing surplus food in sheds or secure vessels (Pascoe 2018; see also Gammage 2012). In the absence of the plough, though, none of this was seen as equating with 'cultivation'. According to British law, this meant that the entire continent could be classified as 'waste', implying also that it was 'going to waste' and thus freely available to be appropriated by those set on 'improving' it.

The expansion of colonial 'settlement' into 'new country' was referred to as 'taking' or 'opening up', or as the pace quickened, 'throwing open' the land (Ramson 1991: 7). Those who pastured their swelling flocks of sheep and cattle, the 'shock troops of empire' (Martin and Griffiths 1999: 45), beyond the legal 'limits of location', which the colonial authorities vainly endeavoured to maintain between 1826 and 1836, were called 'squatters'. Many became very wealthy, thanks to the wool they shipped back to the textile mills of the industrial homeland, and these 'pastoralists' became known as the 'squattocracy'. There is a terrible irony in the description of this process as 'opening up', in that keeping 'country' (about which, more anon) 'open', namely by means of controlled burning, is a key term in the Aboriginal English vocabulary of land care. As Mitchell rightly discerned, Aboriginal 'fire-stick farming' (Jones 1969) played a crucial role in the creation and maintenance of those rolling grasslands, with their mosaic of grassy woodlands and open forested hillsides, onto which the invaders poured their stock. In combination with the multitudinous hard hooves of introduced grazing animals, the cessation of Aboriginal burning quickly led to the degradation of these grasslands, with succulent kangaroo grass being replaced by less nutritious grasses (and in due course, invasive species), while the thickening of the undergrowth in the fire-hungry dry sclerophyll forests made them more susceptible to violent blazes.

It is a historical cliché that the British initially found the country around the penal colony in Sydney unprepossessing. Yet there is clearly some truth in it. According to Kane, the

> sentiments of Major Robert Ross in 1788 were echoed time and again by the early colonists: 'In the whole world there is not worse country than what we have yet seen of this; all that is contiguous to us is so very barren and forbidding that it may with truth be said – here nature is reversed, and, if not so, she is nearly worn out.'
> (1996: 11)

Australia is a big continent, though. From the northern Tropics, through the desert centre, to the snowy peaks of the lower ranges of the Great Dividing Range and the towering temperate forests of the south, and much else besides, Australia's landscapes are highly varied. And so too, it turns out, are the ways in which they have been perceived by European travellers, sojourners, convicts and settlers. As James Boyce (2010) has shown, the well-watered, temperate and wildlife-rich grasslands and open wooded hills of Van Diemen's Land offered a very different prospect to transportees on the run than did the harsher country around the penal colony in New South Wales. While their appreciation of the land (and to some degree also of those Indigenous peoples who had shaped it over the millennia) was, in the first place, a matter of survival, the French explorer Bruni D'Entrecasteaux was able to take aesthetic pleasure in the 'wilderness of the rugged landscape' that he encountered in 'Recherche Bay' in Tasmania in 1793: 'With each step, one encounters the beauties of nature', albeit 'with signs of decrepitude', where the 'trees seem as ancient as the world, are so tightly interlaced that they are impenetrable' (qtd. Lansdown: 120). Another Frenchman, François Péron, also expressed dismay at the 'mercantile greed' driving the decimation of the elephant seal colony on King Island, where the English 'have organised massacres everywhere, which cannot fail shortly to cause a noticeable and irreparable reduction to the population of these animals' (qtd. Landsdown: 121). A similar concern was shared by some of the British. Robert Ross, for example, might not have fancied the landscape aesthetically; but as commander of Norfolk Island during the 1790s, he introduced 'what was probably the world's first prohibition of cruelty to animals' in order to protect native birds, which he nonetheless recognized as a valuable food source in the absence of supplies from home (Bonyhady 2000: 6). More generally, Bonyhady's legal and art history of colonial Australia demonstrates the existence of much early environmental legislation, together with growing aesthetic appreciation of, and personal attachment to, Australian flora, fauna and landscapes from 1788 onwards.

I have already considered a literary instance of this more appreciative view in Charles Harpur's poem 'A Midsummer Noon in the Australian Forest', discussed in Chapter 2. Returning to this poem in the context of the question of wilderness, what is particularly striking is that, far from being a celebration of the sublime, it effectively 'Arcadianises' the bush (specifically, that of his natal New South Wales): this is an instance not only of a delayed Romanticism but also of a displaced pastoral. Harpur's densely forested *locus amoenus*, moreover, does not form an integral part of the world of herding, as in the pleasant copses of European pastoral, but is set apart from it; and it affords refuge, not so much from the corruptions of city life as from the violence of the elements, above all, the 'scorching sun'. Moreover, in much of Harpur's verse, the bush appears in a far more ambivalent light: as a place not of temporary ease but of final rest; a place of graves, haunted by the frontier violence that would continue to fan out across the country for a century or more (and that, in the absence of proper recognition of its toll on Aboriginal people, who continue to suffer from racialized discrimination and disadvantage, has still not really ceased).

In his best-known narrative poem, clearly modelled on Wordsworth's lyrical ballads, 'The Creek of the Four Graves' (1845), Harpur recounts the story of the murder of four shepherds, as recalled by their master. They are said to have been killed while attempting to cross the Blue Mountains, in search of 'New streams and wider pastures for his fast/Increasing flocks and herds' (4–5).[2] The startling vitality of the rugged forested country they traverse is reminiscent of the way in which the plants, insects and birds of Wordsworth's 'Lines Written in Early Spring' seemingly take pleasure in their own existence. Here too, 'wildly beautiful' and 'sentient' trees seem to be 'thrilling – tingling all/Even to the roots for very happiness' (55–56). Yet this is a 'perilous wilderness' (57), peopled by 'painted savages' (59), who slay all four shepherds: 'Men whose wild speech no word for mercy hath' (60), one of whom the invading settler despatches with his firearm before fleeing for the 'shelter of his longed-for home' (62). Harpur's sympathies were by no means restricted to the settler dead, though. In 'The Spectre of the Cattle Flat', the narrator describes how in 'the elbow of a creek', a tribe 'was pent, and held at bay/Till there, like sheep, in one close heap,/Their slaughtered bodies lay' (qtd. Indyk 1993: 84).

Harpur's attempt, here and elsewhere, to view white settlement from the Aboriginal side as a barbaric invasion finds a counterpart in the journal of his contemporary, the explorer Edward John Eyre. In his reflections on the murder of a white boy by a group of Aboriginal men, Eyre evinces a sophisticated appreciation both of cultural hermeneutics and of human psychology, in affirming that 'Aborigines' too have their dearly held 'laws, customs, or prejudices', and that, finding themselves dispossessed of 'the best and most valuable portion' of their land, such that their entire way of life was unravelling, it was understandable that 'when goaded beyond endurance', the 'rankling passions are but fanned into wilder fury, from having been repressed' (qtd. Lansdown: 126). Eyre's perspective is clearly indebted to European Romanticism's explorations of both cultural-historical difference and human emotions and affectivity. Moreover, in both of these instances of colonial Australian Romanticism, it is evident that the landscape described as 'wild' by the invaders is nonetheless recognized, at least to some degree, as not only inhabited but also culturally inscribed by Aboriginal people. Furthermore, whether in the 'funereal landscapes' (Indyk 1993: 841) of Harpur and his gloomier successor Henry Kendall or in landscapes suffused with what Markus Clarke famously termed 'Weird Melancholy' in his Preface for Adam Lindsay Gordon's verse collection, *Sea Spray and Smoke Drift* (1867), there is little to compare here with the celebration of 'pristine wilderness' that came to prominence in North America during the nineteenth century.

As Jay Arthur has shown in her 'lexical cartography', terms used in Australian English to refer to the land and its biotic community typically bear the trace of a 'default' country, namely Britain, the landscape memory of which, kept alive not least by Augustan and Romantic poetry, constituted the norm against which the colonial environment was judged – and frequently found wanting. Australia might boast the world's second national park, but this 'National Park', as it was designated, was no wilderness area. Located just south of Sydney on the Georges River, it was intended to provide health benefits for the growing urban population, and its creation entailed damming waterways, laying grass, planting many thousands of exotic trees and the construction of facilities for its visitors. In other words, it was more akin to the pleasant landscaped gardens of an English stately home than a wild space in which to enjoy the thrill of the sublime. In a further irony, country that from an Aboriginal perspective was a living entity, a matrix of kinship relations, and flush with food, was seen as vacant and unfulfilled in the absence of familiar flocks: a view that has still not entirely disappeared. For writer and pastoralist Kerry McGinnis, for instance, recalling her first impressions of the property in northern Queensland that her family were considering purchasing in 1963, 'Country without cattle...looked empty somehow, like an untenanted house'. With the introduction of livestock, though, the family could 'turn wilderness into property', transforming this vacant land into 'a home' (2001: 34–35).[3] In reality, this was not so much an 'untenanted house', as a home from which its people had been evicted, if not slaughtered outright. These massacres are now known to have continued up until at least 1928 and were referred to with a host of euphemisms, such as 'doing the needful', 'dispersal', 'chastisement', 'dressing down', 'thumping', 'shaking up' and (appallingly and revealingly) 'snipe shooting' and getting 'a brace of black game' (Reynolds 1996; 49–50). In this context, the deceptively benign term 'settlement' has also functioned euphemistically, masking the violent realities of 'invasion and dispossession' (Mead 2008: 411).

This undeclared and lawless war on the 'natives', entangled as it was with the struggle to subdue the colonial earth, was legitimated by eighteenth-century notions of 'improvement', in conjunction with a linear progressivist view of history. In Australia, as in North America, a key ingredient in this ideological concoction was the stadial theory of historical development, stemming from the Scottish Enlightenment, according to which cultures 'advanced' through a fixed sequence of modes of subsistence, from 'hunting and gathering, generally followed by herding, then agriculture, and finally commerce' (Hutchings 2009: 25). Among those who assumed that all peoples were capable of such advancement, the introduction of pastoralism, agriculture and commerce to Australian shores was upheld as affording native populations the enviable opportunity of joining the high road of civilization (a view that finds a contemporary counterpart in versions of 'sustainable development' that take Western technologies, economies and ontologies to be a universally desirable norm). Under the brutalizing influence of Social Darwinism, however, it became more common to assume that it was in the natural order of things that Aboriginal people, as an inferior 'race', would 'die out': here, progress is essentialized as evolution effected by the 'survival of the fittest'. In either case, the ideology of advancement engenders an insensitivity or indifference towards the suffering of the colonized, thereby intensifying their pain. For Rose, following Emanual Levinas, this lies at the heart of the 'immorality' of colonial societies, since "'the justification of the neighbor's pain is certainly the source of all immorality'" (Levinas qtd. Rose 2004: 7).

Although the trope of the 'promised land' plays a considerably more muted role in Australia than it did in North America, the colonial version of 'improvement' was often also afforded religious sanction. Mary Durack, for example, in her 1959 family history, *Kings in Grass Castles*, describes her grandfather, a prominent pioneer in Western Australia, 'as a patriarch blessed by the Almighty' (Rose 2004: 58). He had, she wrote, ridden 'into the lonely land with his hand in the hand of God', bringing 'people and life to the wilderness' (Durack 1986: 280). In a similar vein, Samuel Shumack, the son of the first 'selector' on the 'Limestone plains', now the site of Australia's federal capital, echoes the biblical narrative of Exodus in the epitaph of his *Autobiography*: 'The Lord your God hath given you the land to possess it' (1967: 170). 'Selectors' (such as my own forebears from Wiltshire) were the beneficiaries of a government scheme introduced in the 1860s to create a class of yeoman farmers by breaking up some of the large pastoral estates, as well as 'opening up' more of the country for agricultural purposes. These small-scale farmers became known as 'wheat cockies' on account of the rowdy cockatoos who were attracted by the bounty of their fields. Enthusiastically observing this process in action in the central western district of New South Wales (NSW) in 1904, one 'Bush Brother' wrote that where there was only recently just 'virgin bush', now 'there are new fences, new tracks, and new houses; trees are being ringbarked, paddocks gradually cleared, tanks sunk, creeks damned [*sic*]; and, in a word, the wild bush is being tamed and reduced to bondage by the power of man' (qtd. Ramson 1991: 15). Not only is this implicitly cast as a fulfilment of the biblical injunction in Gen. 1.28 to 'subdue' the earth; the 'sweat and toil' entailed is also extolled as a form of post-lapsarian redemptive labour that will provide 'cheap bread' for the urban poor 'in the slums of the great cities at home': home, that is, in Britain, which was still thought of as such by Anglo-Celtic Australians for many decades after Federation in 1901.

Pastoral under pressure: David Campbell

In her art history of 'Australian pastoral', Jeanette Hoorn shows how, in the 'grand vistas of land, mountains and sky' that were characteristic of Australian landscape painting in the early twentieth century – such as that of Hans Heysen, Arthur Streeton and Alioth Gruner – there is no sign of Aboriginal people; but nor is there any evidence of rural labour (2007: 232). These are sublime landscapes, to be sure; but far from celebrating 'wilderness', such paintings naturalize a pastoral landscape that had been created by means of colonial conquest. It was into this 'white landscape' (Hoorn 2007) that the pre-eminent twentieth-century neo-pastoral poet of the Monaro Plains David Campbell was born in 1915, 'in a brass bed on a sheep station in NSW not far from Gundagai, the town most often celebrated in the early songs and ballads of shearers, bullockies and bushrangers' (Campbell 1981: 5). Like Judith Wright, Campbell was descended from the pioneering families who had helped to craft the pastoral landscape in which he was raised. His father, Alfred, had trained as a doctor but went into grazing in partnership with his brothers; his maternal grandfather, David Innes Watt, was a prosperous squatter in the Coonabarabran district; and his mother's Blackman forebears, who arrived as free settlers in 1801, had established themselves in the Bathurst and Mudgee districts of New South Wales. Campbell shared Wright's preoccupation with this colonial inheritance, yet his poetry 'has its own distinctive story to tell about language, inheritance, and place' (Mead 2006: 7).

His early years were spent on the family's large 'Ellerslie' estate, which at the time of his birth carried 34,000 sheep and 377 head of cattle (De Groot 1987: 21). Having completed his secondary school education at the Kings School in Sydney, Campbell went to Cambridge in 1934 to read history but soon transferred into English. An outstanding sportsman, he played both rugby and cricket, participating in two test matches for England against Wales and Ireland in 1936. It was not all sport though: his studies with E. M. W. Tilyard proved formative, contributing to the publication of his first poems in Jesus College's literary journal *Chanticlere*. Having learnt to fly with the Cambridge University Air Squadron in 1936–7, he piloted reconnaissance and fighter planes in New Guinea during the Second World War. After the war, following a brief stint as a journalist in Melbourne, Campbell returned with his wife, Bonnie, neé Lawrence, and two children to the Monaro to farm his father's grazing property, Wells Station, just to the north of Australia's expanding federal capital. There he built a house looking across Canberra to the blue-black Brindabella Ranges. In the early 1960s, the Campbell family moved to another station, 'Palarang', near Bungendore to the east of Canberra. In 1968, following his divorce from Bonnie, Campbell moved back closer to the city with his new wife, the noted Australian historian Judith Campbell.[4] The couple settled at 'The Run' outside Queanbeyan, while also retaining Judy's house in town.

In the view of fellow Canberra poet R. F. Brissenden, Campbell was 'uniquely qualified to carry into the latter half of the twentieth century the pastoral mode in Australian verse' (1987: 3). In her chapter on Wright and Campbell in *A Question of Commitment*, Susan McKernan highlights their shared concern with 'the human place in a physical universe at a time when both are under threat' (1989: 165). Yet in the decade following his untimely death from cancer in 1979, Campbell's award-winning verse, which at that point ran to eleven volumes, had still received relatively little critical attention. Nor has that changed much in the meantime, despite the publication of his *Collected Poems*, edited by Leonie Kramer, in 1989, and, more recently, a volume of selected poems, *Hardening of the Light* (2006), edited by Philip Mead. In his introduction, Mead acclaims Campbell as 'one of Australia's most important poets' (7). Brissenden had observed that Campbell's work, 'leaning on ballad, pastoral, love song, meditative lyric', was seen as 'passé' among those favouring more experimental forms in the 1980s, but Mead argues that his best poems are 'some of the purest examples of the language art in the Australian tradition', adding that this is 'particularly true of his sparkling lyric depictions of a region, the high Monaro country of southern New South Wales' (2006: 7). As I have argued previously (Rigby 2007),

Campbell's verse would certainly repay more extensive ecocritical attention. Here, I will confine my discussion to indicating some of the ways in which his writing discloses the difficulty of getting to grips with Australia's colonial heritage from within a poetic tradition with its roots in European pastoral and georgic literature.

The contemporary poet, critic and activist, who has engaged most intensely with this question, not least in and through his own poetry, is John Kinsella.[5] Pondering the question of whether there is 'an Australian pastoral', Kinsella argues that the 'negation of the primacy of indigenous culture is part of whatever version of the European pastoral nonindigenous Australian writers have hybridized', and he targets Campbell, along with Les Murray 'and many others', for implying that European pastoral traditions might legitimately 'claim an indigenous relationship to the Australian landscape' (2007b: 364). Here, I want to complicate Kinsella's summary dismissal by tracing a shift in Campbell's writing from an ecopolitically problematic settler Australian neo-pastoral towards what I read as a form of uneasy ecopoetic post-pastoral. This was prompted, I believe, by his growing recognition both of those Aboriginal lifeways that his own forebears had ruptured and of the ecological damage entailed in the industrialized farming methods in which he himself was engaged during the 1960s.

Although Campbell would later become an influential figure in the burgeoning literary scene of the capital city in the 1970s, one of his poems from the late 1950s, 'Looking Down on Canberra', is suggestive of his disdain for the human-all-too-human life of the polis. In the manner of any number of pastoral poets from Virgil to Wordsworth and beyond, Campbell proclaims that his place is among the hills, there to 'think and sing in solitude':

> The thousand voices of the town,
> The worn phrase, the ruined word,
> In this clear mountain silence drown,
> Leaving the sweet song of a bird
> And coupled stone.
>
> (1989: 62)[6]

Much of the poetry that Campbell wrote from this vantage point of contemplative rural retreat shaped a new style of settler Australian neo-pastoral by melding elements of the nationalist bush balladry of Banjo Patterson, himself a Monaro man, with the heritage of European lyric poetry, from the sixteenth to the twentieth centuries. Campbell claimed that his generation were much taken by Donne and the seventeenth-century metaphysical writers and 'found Shelley and the romantics a bit old hat' (1981: 29). Yet Campbell's antipodean lyrical ballads could be seen as reprising, in a new geohistorical context and poetic idiom, the avant-garde project previously undertaken by Wordsworth and Coleridge and other Romantic experimenters. In the philosophical vitalism that pulses through Campbell's poetry, there is also more than a hint of a very different mode of Australian neo-pastoral from that of the bush balladists: namely, the Neo-Romantic (and Nietzschean-inspired) 'metaphysical pastoral', as Peter Kirkpatrick (1992) has it, of Hugh McCrae and the artist Norman Lindsay (an acquaintance of Campbell's, on whom his close friend Douglas Stewart wrote a monograph). There are no 'satyrs in the top paddock' (Kirkpatrick 1992) of Campbell's verse, but his world is animated by erotic energies that extend well beyond the human.

Campbell's first collection of poetry was *Speak with the Sun* (1949). This title, punning on the homophone 'sun' and 'son', alludes to Henry Vaughan's 'The Night' (1650), which in turn recalls the Gospel story of Nicodemus seeking out Jesus in the night (Jn. 3.2). Vaughan's Christian allegory has been transmuted into a wholly secular meditation on the human mind's intercourse with the phenomenal realm, which is for all that not devoid of mystery. In Mead's reading, 'These are poems of mirages, of self-absorbed stockmen, drovers and trappers whose presence in the landscape is simultaneous with their ambivalent presence in the poet's waking consciousness. Even the river Murray's source "is in the mind"; it rises, not according to the topography of the Snowy catchment, but "at a word it flows" ("Soldier's Song")' (2006: 9). Many of Campbell's early poems also betray a version of white Australian nationalism, centred on an ideal of intimacy with, and belonging to, the land. In his next volume, *The Miracle of Mullion Hill* (1956), for example, this is evident in Campbell's lyrical ballad, 'The Monaro':

> Willy Gray will sit and stare
> On One Tree Hill the whole day long
> And green grass-parrots fly in at his ear
> And lay their eggs of rounded song
> Leaving them there for the words to hatch
> Like floating seed from the thistle patch.
>
> Willy Gray has a ten-mile stare
> And his eyes are droving with a dream of sheep
> Down raddled stock-routes to tread white air

Where Willy Gray has a thought as deep
And rounded as a river-stone –
And over the paddocks goes the daylight moon.

Willy Gray has a lover's eye
And it goes over the twin bare hills
And the blond paddocks to the bleached sky
Until it has come to a thought that fills
His mind with tenderness for this wild
Upland country and her suckling child.

(1989, 33–34)

Here, the denuded hillsides, sheep-wrecked grasslands, spiked with invasive Scotch thistles and 'raddled stock-routes' of the Monaro are naturalized, while the white drover is indigenized: his words bestowed by the songs of parrots, his thought 'as deep/And rounded as a river-stone', he has grown to love 'this wild/Upland country and her suckling child'. Whether we interpret the latter as his own child, construed as a native of this land, or as the still-young nation (one in which Aboriginal people were still not regarded as full citizens), there is no doubt that this variant of Australian neo-pastoral air-brushes aside all traces of the colonial violence, at once social and ecological, by means of which this pastoral landscape had been crafted.

While the figure of the drover Willy Gray together with that of the country he is affectionately contemplating belong to the plebeian world of the bush ballad, the verse form of 'The Monaro', with its shapely sestinas, comes from one of the most high-literary and 'least folkloric' (Mead 2006, 10) antecedents of the English pastoral: Edmund Spenser's *Shepheardes Calendar* (1579). Campbell's most significant pastoral work, 'Cocky's Calendar' (1961), from the following decade, also cuts its figure against Spenser's.[7] Unlike Spenser's, though, Campbell's engagement with the rhythms of the agricultural year was far from purely literary: this is very much a product of his working life on Wells Station. Here, however, the scion of the squattocracy refigures himself as a cockatoo farmer, albeit one whose diction betrays a highly literary, indeed classical, education. In that respect, Campbell's 'squatter pastoral' (Wallace-Crabbe 1987), although composed by a farming man, carries a self-ironic reminiscence of the songs of imaginary shepherds that had been written for English country squires (among others) by the likes of Spenser and his seventeenth-century successors. Following the model of Spenser's 'eclogues', 'Cocky's Calendar' comprises a twelve-part cycle of poems, corresponding to the wheel of the seasons. In place of Spenser's trademark nine-line stanzas, though, each of Campbell's eclogues consists of three four-line stanzas, such that each individual poem echoes the structure of the whole. The voice, moreover, is closer to that of Yeatsian symbolism than that of Spenser's faux shepherd. Thus, for example, the hawk hovering over its prey in the opening and closing stanzas, holding 'all of time in his still stare' (1989: 79), could be seen to symbolize the poet, whose privileged vision penetrates beneath the surface of things, disclosing within the perishable entities apprehended by the senses a trace of the eternal. Appearances, however, can be deceptive.

The lyrical subject of this work turns out to be as much a metaphysician as a farmer, and a decidedly 'cocky' one at that, for whom (after the fashion of Fichtean Idealism), the perceived world is initially cast as a thing of his own mind's making:

> The hawk, the hill, the loping hare,
> The blue tree and the blue air,
> O all the coloured world I see
> And walk upon, are made by me.
>
> (74)

This potentially solipsistic assertion of the world-creating power of the human mind, however, is swiftly complicated in the second eclogue, suggestively entitled 'The Red Cock'. Here, the speaker's cocky proprietorial claim on the world as he perceives it (the cock's crow apprehended 'within *my* brain', the sun rising 'in *my* east', the hills shining 'Like tawny lions in *my* breast', the 'lion and the hogget' lying 'In *my* ringed shade', while '*my* plovers cry') is undercut by an acknowledgement of the way in which his intellections might be disrupted by the material agency of his unbiddable environs:

> About my heart the land is dumb
> And quietly the habit grows
> Of peace, but fires like lions come
> And fill my blackened heart with crows.
>
> (75)

The land that is 'dumb' is one that perdures beyond the world of human words. But it is by no means stupid. In fact, the metaphysics informing this work are thoroughly Romantic in their monistic emphasis on the continuity of human thought with a more-than-human consciousness immanent in the material world. In a conversation with Roderick Shaw at Palerang in the early 1960s (published in *Poetry Australia* in 1981), Campbell observes, 'I think there's a lot of thinking in art – the kind of thinking that formed cells in Nature that built themselves into different animals, trees, shells' (Shaw 1981: 29).[8] In the third stanza of the opening eclogue of 'Cocky's Calendar', moreover, the immanent intelligence of 'nature naturing' is hailed as a locus of love:

> First I would praise the world of sense;
> Then praise that sweet Intelligence
> That hovering far-sighted love
> That sees me and in whom I live.
>
> (74)

This loving geocosmic intelligence is nonetheless not conceived of monotheistically as a transcendent deity, for this metaphysician-farmer's 'marble acres lie/Open to an empty sky', as we read in the third poem, a pantheistic 'Prayer for Rain', in which the hare, who 'Folds his ears like hands in prayer', and the farmer alike are said to participate (75). For Campbell, this intelligence inheres within an entirely immanent evolutionary process, which, like that of artistic creativity, does not follow a preconceived plan: 'this is the thing which does away with God and makes evolution terribly exciting' (Shaw 1981: 29).

Also in keeping with the proto-biosemiotic strand of European Romanticism is Campbell's understanding of human *poiesis* as continuous with the communicative processes in which other living beings also participate. In this, his thinking might have been informed by the aesthetic theory of fellow Canberra poet A. D. Hope, who became professor of English at Canberra University College in 1951. In an essay on 'Poetry and Platitude', first published in *The Cave and the Spring* (1965), Hope writes that the poetic celebration of the natural world entails something other than simply 'paean and praise of the natural order'. Rather, it involves

> also an intellectual assent to the causes that make the natural world an order and a system, and an imaginative grasp of the necessity of its processes. More than this, it involves a sense of communion with these natures and participation in their processes. It is for the poet to feel himself to be not merely the mirror of nature or its commentator but the voice of creation, speaking for it and as part of it.
>
> (2002, n.p.)

In Campbell's variant of this thoroughly Romantic conception of the poetic vocation, however, the poet does not so much speak 'for' nature but rather lends his voice to the multi-tongued choir, by 'aligning himself with the energies of nature and of the world... you're with the world and one of the voices that is expressing it – just the same as a tree with its leaves...' (1981: 31). In 'Cocky's Calendar', then, the exclusively human singing competitions of the herding communities recalled by Theocritus in the *Idylls* are displaced by the diverse voices of a multispecies collective. Among those who are shown to participate in co-creating the living world of the Monaro are plants as well as animals: not only the 'freckled bird with sticks for feet', of the fifth eclogue, 'To a Ground-lark', who 'whittles songs of faded light' as the farmer sows the wheat, but also the 'oaten grain' of the third, which awaits the rain, 'as words wait in the brain', so that 'It may make the world anew'. Included also are 'magpie song', in the seventh, and in the tenth, the call of the pallid cuckoo, along with the lambs, who, 'To cuckoo pipes their dances start/And fill and overflow the heart'. The eleventh features Yellowtails, 'small singers made of light/That stream like stars between the trees', but also the 'thin-voiced weeds that cheat the sun... little blushing flowers that part/the grasses where the sheep-tracks meet'. And as well as the thrush who 'drew out his song' while the speaker and his lover, disporting themselves on the hillside, begot their children, there are wattle trees that 'smoulder into gold' in late winter: trees beneath which the speaker imagines they will later lie once again in death, folded back into the ongoing life of the speaking land.

The countryside of 'Cocky's Calendar' is recognizably Australian. This is a place where rain is often scarce; where, in the autumn, 'tongued like snow, if snow could cry,/The cockatoos flake from the sky', seeking easy pickings on the plains while snow blankets the higher mountains; grassy hillsides are green only when washed by winter storms; and in summer, 'fires like lions come'. In general, though, Campbell seems less interested in rendering the particularity of place here than in recasting the landscape as a terrain of symbolic significance. His Spenserian reminiscences and classical allusions, moreover, effectively Europeanize the Monaro Plains of the poem in a way that is analogous to the European colonization of the land itself.

By the late 1960s, however, Campbell was striking out in new directions. His greatest pastoral work of this period is 'Works and Days' (1970), which answers to 'Cocky's Calendar' by replicating its structure, as well as continuing its engagement with earlier pastoral literature, but in a new key. Here, the lines are longer and looser, the rhyme less regular, the tone more reminiscent of A. B. Paterson than W. B. Yeats and the register considerably more colloquial. In place of the classicizing pathos of such lines as 'But O the flakes that fell last year/No rain will wash from Tempe's hair' (1989: 76), Campbell now offers us a more mundane reality, in which the glory of the harvest is celebrated in a decidedly downbeat and vernacular register: 'Towards dusk by the dump, some sheila's singing a song' (1989: 103).

Recalling in its title the origins of European pastoral in Hesiod, 'Works and Days' constitutes a neo-georgic counterpart to the antipodean eclogues of 'Cocky's Calendar'. Recasting the cycle of the rural year into a thoroughly southeastern Australian mould, Campbell also strives to be true to the historicity of the socioecological world that he discloses in this work. This is no timeless rural idyll, but a landscape in the grip of modern industrialized farming, as we are forcibly reminded in the opening line: 'The tractors are out turning the red soil' (1989: 102). As 'Brodricks, Masters and Harrisons', machines marked by commercial names, continue to plough up the earth, 'Valley and town are red with a mist of dust', and when it comes to sowing in the winter, there is 'Dust and super [superphosphate fertilizer] pitting your eyes like blindness' (102). Yet despite this deployment of heavy machinery and chemical weaponry to subdue the land and render it ever more productive of commodities for sale on the international market, rural life is still shown to be vulnerable to forces beyond human control, above all meteorological events, and dependent upon skilful collaborations with other-than-human beings, notably dogs and horses. Livestock, too, though bred for profit and destined for the knackery, are accorded a measure of independent agency, and a resistant one at that. In the final lines of the last poem, the cattle are said to 'stand four-square and bawl/In yards with threatening horns as the floats back in' (107), while the fabled merinos are referred to, not without affection, as a constant source of exasperation:

> Sheep! They're not dumb, they know every trick in the book:
> Bale up, go down, dig in, at the cry of 'Sheep!'
> Ask the penner-up. Ask Paterson: merinos,
> He wrote, made our men sardonic or they would weep!
>
> (104)

Here, as in 'Cocky's Calendar', and elsewhere in Campbell's verse, crows are called upon as a reminder of the inherence of death in life, the entanglement of gestation and predation. Whereas in the former, though, the solitary crow that appears amongst the flock of white cockatoos 'as a reminder of the night' (76) is the bearer of a vague symbolic significance, the speaker of 'Works and Days' makes clear what they actually do to his sheep during lambing, in consort with the foxes, first introduced by nineteenth-century landowners bent on reproducing the aristocratic pleasures of the hunt: 'When a ewe's/Cast, crows take the eye first (foxes the tongue)/And their beaks are poison' (104).

'Works and Days' is without doubt Campbell's greatest, and most ambivalent, tribute to the pastoral world of the Monaro; indeed, in my reading, it is precisely the ambivalence that marks its significance. It was also something of 'a farewell to the pastoral phase of his life' (Brissenden 1987: 3). In the opening section of *The Branch of Dodona* (1970), where it first appeared, 'Works and Days' is paired with a poem entitled 'My Lai', which opens the collection. Here, a Vietnamese farmer discloses how his 'works and days' have been blown apart by war, recalling that while Australian farmers were assaulting their land with agricultural weapons of mass production, Australian conscripts were helping the US military to lay waste to the countryside of Vietnam:

> I was milking the cow when a row of tall bamboo
> > Was mowed by rifle fire
> With my wife and child in the one harvest,
> And the thin blue milk spilt and ruined.
>
> (1989: 126)

In the face of this evil, of another order entirely than that which bedevilled lambing season in the shape of the ever-present crows and foxes, Campbell felt that it was no longer possible to continue to 'sit and sing in solitude' of life on the land (Hart 1975: 4). Meanwhile, the land itself, far from offering a place of withdrawal from the political, had begun to appear as a site of political struggle. Also included in *The Branch of Dodona* is 'Ku-ring-gai Rock Carvings', a cycle of poems that reframes 'Works and Days' by recalling an Indigenous mode of multispecies co-becoming that had been all but obliterated in the creation of the pastoral landscape that Campbell so loved.

The twenty-four four-line poems arranged in three untitled sub-sections of 'Ku-ring-gai Rock Carvings' constitute a collection of fragments, echoing the fragmentariness of the material traces of pre-conquest Aboriginal life in this area. Most are meditations on some of the hundreds of individual pieces of rock art in Ku-ring-gai Chase National Park. Designated as such in 1894, this is one of Australia's first National Parks. Situated only twenty kilometres north of Sydney's city centre, where the Hawkesbury River reaches the Pacific Ocean, this area of 14,882 hectares was protected from destructive forms of development in order to provide restorative opportunities for townsfolk, in recognition of its 'beauty and solitude', as noted by members of the Drafting Committee of the first Constitutional Convention, who met there in 1891.[9] It is now recognized as an area of exceptionally high biodiversity, containing a 'complex pattern of 24 plant communities, including heathland, woodland, open forest, swamps and warm temperate rainforest, with a high native plant species richness of over 1000 species and an outstanding diversity of bird and other animal species'.[10] This, moreover, is a place of immense cultural significance, containing Australia's largest concentration of sites (1,500 on 15,000 hectares) that bear witness to millennia of Aboriginal lifeways and place-making in this area, including stone arrangements, tool-making sites, middens, rock shelters, birthing areas, initiation sites and burial sites, in addition to rock art.[11]

In Campbell's verse, the Aboriginal rock carvings are rendered animate, such that, for example, 'stone echidnas/Dawdle across the rockface' (115), caught up in the ongoing burgeoning of organic lifeforms in this place:

Ladyslippers tiptoe to the carved birds
    Where the great fire blazed
  Last summer. After the corroboree of flame,
  Black crows complained of two lyrebirds dancing.

(116–17)

Included here are also a pair of poems that recycle words and images from British observers of inter-cultural encounter in the penal colony in Sydney. From Lieutenant General Watkin Tench's diary from 1791, we get a glimpse of both the barbarism of the colonial authorities, as seen through Aboriginal eyes, and the condescending view of the 'natives' on the part of the hardened diarist:

Flesh carvings: for theft, before the assembled tribes,
    A convict was flogged. Daringa,
  Her nets forgotten, wept: while Barangaroo
  Threatened the lasher. A feckless if tender people.

(116)

This is followed by a description of an etching by Augustus Earle of 'the tribe's last king', Boongarie, from the 1820s:

A convict driving nails in a deal coffin:
    They're burying the tribe's last king
  Beside Queen Gooseberry with naval honours,
  His Commodore's uniform (Brisbane's) is in tatters.

(116)

This colonial ritual, with its cruel combination of honouring and mockery (as disclosed above all in the derogatory naming of the 'king's' consort), a performance of regret for the passing of an elevated individual that papers over the violence visited upon the rest of his people, is counterposed to the reminiscence of Aboriginal rites of passage in 'Bora Ring'.

A bora ring 'is a circle of foot-hardened earth surrounded by embankments', where male initiation takes place; but Bora is also the name of the ceremony itself, which entails 'sacred songs, stories and dances'; such rings are also the 'doorways for Biamee, the great creator-spirt, to enter into the world of humans' (Cooke 2013: 42).[12] Stuart Cooke provides this explanation with reference to a poem of the same name by Judith Wright, published in 1946, in which such ceremonies are mournfully consigned to the past: 'the tribal story/lost in an alien tale' (Wright 1994: 8). Although he is writing over twenty years later, Campbell's 'Bora Ring' appears to perpetuate this troubling colonial motif of the 'disappearing native':

> The kangaroo has a spear in his side. It was here
> >   Young men were initiated,
> > Tied to a burning tree. Today
> > Where are such cooling pools of water?
>
> (115)

Campbell returned again and again to the topos of Aboriginal rock art: notably, in the sequences 'Sandstone Country', 'Rock Engravings' and 'Devil's Rock and Other Carvings' from *Devil's Rock and Other Poems, 1970–1972* (1974) and 'Sydney Sandstone (Rock Carvings)' from *Deaths and Pretty Cousins* (1975).[13] His encounter with these traces of pre-conquest Aboriginal culture was integral to Campbell's growing recognition of the devastating impact of colonization, along with its continuing legacies, and new formations. In Mead's view, it also revitalized his poetry:

> Studying Aboriginal carved and painted forms allowed Campbell
> to renew his version of the lyric as a neo-modernist sequence of single
> moments and discrete images. He recognised he could keep the lyric
> intensity but shed stanzaic conventions, and rhyme except where it was
> off-centre or serendipitous (sustain/season ['Spring']; Stewart/sweater
> ['Woolgathering']). Thus he could reconnect with the landscape and
> history of Australia in more immediate and energised ways than his
> previous version of the lyric had permitted.
>
> (2006: 14)[14]

From a contemporary perspective, though, the outcome of this encounter was far from unproblematic. Campbell (rightly or wrongly) sees his own vitalist philosophy mirrored in Aboriginal art. In 'Baiame', this is explicitly counterposed to the imbrication of prudishness and crudeness that he attributes to the dominant urban white middle-class society of post-war Australia, whose denizens like to drive out to the National Park on sunny Sundays:

> Baiame, the All-father, is a big fellow with a big dong
> > And the rayed crown of a god.
> He looks at his Sunday children who snigger and drive
> Home to their home-units. The god is not surprised.
>
> > > > > > > > > > > (118)

As we have seen with 'Bora Ring', however, contemporary Aboriginal people do not get a look-in here. For, as we read in 'Baiami and Lilies' from 'Devil's Rock and other Carvings', 'crowned with fine fire, the god looks up from rock/His tribesmen have withdrawn' (157). This, then, is a haunted landscape, explicitly so in 'Emu Hunt' from this same series:

> Magic haunts the bush. The man-tongued
> > Lyrebird taunts you
> Like the tribes that hunted here,
> Leaving carved emus and a spear.
>
> > > > > > > > > > > (155)

Yet, while the Indigenous tribal way of life in this area might have been destroyed, it seems that the white poet, being himself far from prudish, is able to participate to some degree in the lingering magic and potency of its ancient sacred places, as in the opening poem of 'Ku-ring-gai Rock Carvings':

> 'The Lovers'
>
> Making love for ten thousand years on a rockledge;
> > The boronia springs up purple
> From the stone, and we lay together briefly
> For as long as those two lovers.
>
> > > > > > > > > > > (114)

In the final poem in this sequence, moreover, the Aboriginal sacred site is reinscribed with words belonging to a very different religious tradition from another continent:

'Sri Ramakrishna on Mount Topham'

> By the care of the hands a page blew on the wind
> To catch in thorn-flowers. Its message:
> Only those who see Divinity in all things
> May worship the Deity with advantage or safety.

(118)

Here, the specificity of Aboriginal place-based philosophies and practices of the sacred is dissolved into a transcultural and transhistorical spirituality of divine immanence: one that bears a striking resemblance to Schleiermacher's definition of the shared 'essence' of religion (informed, not least, by early ethnographic reports of Aboriginal culture). What is troubling here is the mobilization of this notion in relation to the trope of the allegedly absent tribes. The white poet is implicitly positioned as the inheritor of the ancient tribal legacy, conceived as a local variant of a universal religious sensibility, effacing the perspectives and practices of contemporary Aboriginal people.

Some of Campbell's verse from the 1970s did nonetheless bear witness to the violent history of Aboriginal dispossession, in which, as he makes explicit in 'South Country' (1974), his own forebears had participated. At the same time, he was turning his attention to the ongoing environmental depredations of settler Australian society. As we have seen, there are hints of this in 'Works and Days' with respect to industrialized farming; now, though, his primary target was deforestation. Of particular interest in this context is 'The Anguish of Ants' ([1975] 1989:176–77), which responds specifically to the replacement of indigenous forest ecologies with commercial pine plantations. Conifers began to be planted outside Canberra during the First World War, but initially only on land that had already been cleared for grazing. During the 1970s, however, the plantations were expanding at the cost of native forests. Campbell's views on this could well have been informed by those of Val and Richard Routley (later Val Plumwood and Richard Sylvan), resident in Canberra at this time, where they published their important early work, *The Fight for the Forests: The Takeover of Australian Forests for Pines, Wood Chips, and Intensive Forestry* (1975).

Not unlike the Routleys, Campbell frames his narrative of resistance to the commercial 'takeover of Australian forests' in martial terms. His fighters, though, are other-than-human: ants, and, as we learn in the opening line, specifically 'meat ants'. *Iridomyrmex purpureus* is a native species, building large underground nests in sandy or gravel soils in urban areas, as well as in forests, woodlands and heath. Nests can house up to 64,000 ants, and these are sometimes linked together by ant paths to form colonies that can stretch up to 650 metres. While they are aggressive towards intruders of other species, 'driving off much larger animals by sheer weight of numbers', border disputes between rival colonies 'are resolved by ritual fighting'. These ants, and other *Iridomyrmex* species, are also 'often involved in mutually beneficial (symbiotic) relationships with caterpillars of different butterflies. The caterpillars supply sugary fluids to the ants, which in turn protect the caterpillars from predators'.[15] Meat ants also provided benefits for Aboriginal peoples. Referred to by D'harawal elder and environmental scientist Frances Bodkin as 'environmentalists of the woodlands',[16] meat ants feature in many traditional stories and songs from around Australia (Rose 1996: 12, 57–58). Bodkin explains how observing the behaviour of meat ants provides vital meteorological information:

> The meat ants put stones on their nests. Now, the colour of the stones will indicate to you how hot, or how cold, the weather is going to be. In the spring equinox, they will start to put light-coloured stones on their nest. And the paleness of the stone will indicate how hot the summer is going to be. In the autumn equinox, they will start to put dark stones on their nest, and the darkness of the stones will indicate how cold the winter is going to be.[17]

Campbell cannot be expected to have known this history of Indigenous human-meat ant interaction. His emphatically post-pastoral 'Anguish of Ants' is nonetheless a multilayered work of creaturely ecopoetics, which shares with Clare's poetry a close attention to the biosemiotic world of another species, whose terrain is being colonized in the interests of human commerce. Campbell's meat ants, however, unlike Burns' 'wee mousie', are not cast principally as victims inviting an affective movement of sympathetic identification. On the contrary, they are disclosed in the opening stanza as the locus of a powerful collective agency. These inhabitants of 'gravel cities' are shown to have their own diplomatic protocols: they 'greet each other/On the hard roads... Cross antennae, bow and turn about/On serious unintelligible business/Of state'. They also have the capacity to join forces to bear off carrion 'three times their weight': 'they lift it like bulldozers, bear it off in a bucket'. In the second stanza, the gently ironic anthropomorphism of this representation of ant etiquette and prowess leads into a more subtle subversion of human-animal hyper-separation, as we are left uncertain as to whose 'sets of feet/Beat this highway, carrying merchandise, news,/Between metropolis and lichened farms?' Reading on, it becomes apparent that we are being invited to recognize a mode of multispecies co-habitation of the same space, albeit one that is composed and read in diverse ways by its more-than-human denizens. While the ant nests are cast as 'cities', the reference to 'lichened farms' implies that these are located on rural land. This multispecies pastoral world is no Arcadia, however. As in the case of Clare's bees, the meat ants' interactions with humans, along with animals domesticated by humans, are shown to be potentially conflictual: the disruption caused accidentally by a 'stray' 'grazing horse…/Planting a hoof in the market place', or intentionally by 'boys in short pants' who 'stir up New York with a stick', elicits a counterattack, signalled by the release of a pine-scented chemical alarm signal, leading to the manoeuvring of 'Archaic/Armies', and the evacuation of 'nurseries', while a diminutive 'Horatio fronts a tractor blade alone'.

For readers steeped in the British literary canon, 'Horatio' is bound to recall the figure of Hamlet's confidante. But a more fitting referent in this context is classical: namely, the historical figure of Publius Horatius Cocles, an officer in the army of the Roman Republic, who, in 509 BCE, is said to have heroically stood his ground to prevent the invading army of the Etruscan king of Clusium from crossing a strategically vital bridge, the Pons Sublicius. Horatius was gravely wounded, but his legendary feats are hailed by Roman historians, such as Plutarch and Livy, for halting the Etruscan advance and saving Rome from being sacked. The story was retold in Thomas Babington Macaulay's poem 'Horatius', published in 1842. Macaulay was an administrator in India, and this poem became an icon of high Imperial culture and its heroic ideal. It was frequently taught in British schools right up to the mid-twentieth century.[18] This classical allusion brings in its train further intertextual referents, recalling in particular the critique of warfare in Vergil's pastoral, in both its bucolic and georgic modes. This in turn opens the possibility of reading 'The Anguish of Ants' as a protest against the impacts of intensive timber production on the wider multispecies collective of this erstwhile rural locale.

This suggestion is confirmed in the final stanza, where the rough-and-ready coexistence of ants and others is shown to be located within a wider matrix of socioecological relations that is being ripped apart by the advance of a commercial monoculture. Whereas, in the opening stanza, ants were likened to bulldozers – ironically, as it turns out – now 'dozers much like ants' are stacking up the timber of fallen blackbutt and candlebark, and the 'scent of resin' that fills the air emanates from the conifers that 'march in green ranks over/The meat ants' thin red lines, each tree/Destined for the paper mill, the morning news'. This scent nonetheless retains its association with danger: 'While tense in the scent of resin/Whole cities perish of anxiety.' Again, there is an ambiguity around the question of whose cities are at stake: an ambiguity that implies a continuing entanglement of human and nonhuman lives and habitations, and their shared, if variously distributed, vulnerability to ever more intensive and extensive industrial regimes during the era of the Great Acceleration. As I read it, however, this is no mere lament: 'green-tongued moaning', as Campbell put it self-deprecatingly in a letter to Douglas Stewart from 10 April 1974, with reference to his anti-logging lyric 'Bellbirds' (Persse 2006: 193). For, since it is clear that this Horatio, unlike the Roman Horatius, is not going to be able to hold off the invaders, the poem implicitly issues an ecoprophetic call to arms to its human readers. Reconsidered in light of the vital role of meat ants in Aboriginal fire-stick farming, the ominous note of the last lines resonates especially strongly in the wake of the Canberra firestorm of 2002, when it was the suburbs adjoining the pine plantations that were ravaged by the fires that also completely destroyed the plantations themselves. Whereas the native forests soon began their miracle of regeneration, the land where the conifers had once stood in neat straight rows was left barren and blasted.

Following the publication of *Deaths and Pretty Cousins*, in which these poems appeared, Stewart wrote to Campbell that this volume 'has something of the feeling of Judith Wright's *Alive* [1973], in that you seem relaxed & at ease in your own country' (Persse 2006: 204). There is a sense, though, in which, far from being 'at ease', Campbell had become profoundly unsettled. Even before he and Judy had to move to Canberra in 1979, as his cancer became terminal, he was no longer living in his 'own country', in the sense that he had long since ceased to farm the land his forebears had transformed into the pastoral world in which he was raised; and, as well as confronting the dire impact of this colonial takeover on Indigenous peoples and ecologies, he was witnessing another kind of takeover, as forests and farms were converted into urban and industrial sites. In 'Wells Station', from his sequence 'Letters to a Friend', addressed to Douglas Stewart, he observes how 'villas shine like eyes on Sammy's Hill', where once he had 'climbed at dawn/To search the rocks with foxes for cast ewes' (153–54). Wells Station has since been entirely converted into Canberran suburbs. It seems unlikely to me that their residents 'share a part of (his) reality' (154), as Campbell had fondly imagined, despite the naming of a park in Gunghalin after Campbell's 1956 volume, *The Miracle of Mullion Hill*.

But then, which reality? Interestingly, much of Campbell's work from the mid-1970s took him away from Australia altogether: in addition to the poems that arose from a trip to Europe in 1975, he collaborated with Rosemary Dobson and Natalie Staples in producing two volumes of Russian poetry in translation (*Moscow Trefoil*, 1975, and *Seven Russian Poets*, 1979). Among his later poems, there are some exquisite works of encounter with free-living birds and animals, both in the bush and around his home. Unsettled from his prior mode of pastoral existence, however, Campbell was unable to come anywhere close to the kind of belonging to 'country' that Aboriginal people were beginning to reassert in the land rights movement of the 1970s: something that Campbell would have encountered, not least, in the guise of the Aboriginal ('Tent') Embassy that was erected on the manicured lawns outside Parliament House in Canberra in 1972 (and remains there still). Stewart's comparison of *Death and Pretty Cousins* with Wright's *Alive* is telling, for it is in that volume that Wright published 'Two Dreamtimes', addressed to Kath Walker, whose 1964 volume *We Are Going* was, in fact, a proud assertion of the persistence of Aboriginal peoples and cultures in Australia, despite continuing marginalization, misrecognition and dispossession. 'Two Dreamtimes', as noted in the previous chapter, has itself come under fire from a postcolonial perspective in recent years (Cooke 2013: 62–65). Yet Wright's personal friendship with Noonuccal and political engagement in support of Aboriginal land rights entailed a commitment to Indigenous-non-Indigenous dialogue, of which there is no trace in Campbell's work. That could well have changed had he survived into the 1980s. As it is, though, the challenge of advancing the transcultural decolonizing ecopoetic dialogue broached by Wright and Noonuccal was left to more recent Australian writers.

'Deeper tracks lead back': Anne Elvey and Jeanine Leane

In addition to the eminent figure of John Kinsella, there is a host of new Australian writers whose work can be described as ecopoetic, including many who are contributing to an emerging 'decolonial geopoethics' to recall the title of the special issue of *Plumwood Mountain*, edited by Peter Minter. Among those who identify as non-Indigenous is the founding editor of the journal, Melbourne poet Anne Elvey, whose verse manifests to varying degrees and in different combinations all of those ecopoetic arts of contemplation, affective self-awareness, creaturely empathy and prophetic critique that I have traced in the Romantic inheritance. The author, thus far, of two poetry collections (Elvey 2014, shortlisted for the Kenneth Slessor Poetry Award, and *White on White*, 2018) and several chapbooks, including *this flesh that you know* (2015; international winner of the Overleaf chapbook competition) and *Claimed by*

Country (2010; shortlisted for the PressPress chapbook award), Elvey is also a distinguished biblical scholar, whose work is informed by ecotheology, critical ecofeminism, material phenomenology and the conversations of the Australian ecohumanities community. In addition, her creative and critical contributions towards a decolonizing 'ecopoethics' have been facilitated by a twenty-five-year-long association with Binnap Partners, an initiative of the Aboriginal Catholic Ministry (ACM).

This organization was founded by Aboriginal Catholics in Melbourne in 1984 with a view to enhancing the visibility and contribution of Aboriginal people and perspectives within the church and beyond. Addressing Aboriginal spiritual, educational and material needs in a context of ongoing disadvantage and dispossession, the ACM is also dedicated to working towards truth and reconciliation.[19] In 1992, ACM created Binnap partners in order to invite non-Indigenous people to share their vision. Binnap, as Elvey explains, is a Wurundjeri word, referring to 'seed from the manna gum, that nourished both Indigenous and, in early colonial times, non-Indigenous people. It was chosen by the group "to symbolise the possibility of sharing and being nurtured by the same source".[20]

Elvey joined Binnap partners in 1995, participating in shared meals, conversations and occasional Eucharists; forming friendships; and attending workshops in Melbourne, a vigil recalling massacres in Victoria, and retreats on Yorta Yorta Country in the Barmah forest in northern Victoria. This experience led her to reflect more deeply on 'the way non-Indigenous people are confronted by the violence underpinning our being here and how it challenges our desire to see ourselves as good people'. Of the Barmah forest retreats, she recalls

> learning from Yorta Yorta the history of their struggle, being invited to quietly listen to the land, seeing the damage to the soil from cattle, and sitting round camp fires in the evening being told ghost and other tall stories. That quality of attentiveness to Country combined with political action, and personal interaction, helped inform my writing in *Claimed by Country*, *Kin*, and *White on White*.[21]

To be attentive to 'Country', Elvey learnt, means more than simply observing more-than-human goings on in the bush, as does Harpur, for example, in his 'Midsummer Noon in the Australian Forest'. To begin with, it entails a form of deep contemplative listening, which, as Elvey notes in *Kin* with respect to her 'Claimed by Country' sequence, is referred to by Ngangiwumirr elder Miriam Rose Ungenmerr-Baumann, of Daly River in the Northern Territory, as *dadirri* (2014: 81). For those of us whose ways of being and thinking have been shaped by a modern Western ontology, it also means stepping into, or at least towards, unfamiliar metaphysical territory, in which the nature/culture dualism (along with many others) does not obtain. I have no authority to speak of this from my personal experience or original research. But any move towards a decolonizing ecopoetics in Australia demands that non-Indigenous writers and scholars attempt to gain some glimpse of the rich meanings carried by 'Country' in contemporary Aboriginal English.

As feminist scholar Aileen Moreton-Robinson of the Quandamooka nation argues, 'Our ontological relationship to land, the ways that country is constitutive of us, and therefore the inalienable nature of our relation to land, marks a radical, indeed incommensurable difference between us and the non-indigenous' (2015: 11). What I understand Moreton-Robinson to be saying here is that 'land' qua Country is not property to be worked; it is a matrix of dynamic (and not always harmonious) interrelationships to which you belong through ancestral kinship ties. This multidimensional matrix, consisting of 'people, animals, plants, Dreamings, underground, earth, soils, minerals and waters, surface water, and air', generally refers to a place that is 'small enough to accommodate face-to-face groups of people, and large enough to sustain their lives' (Rose 2004: 153). But Country also has its own personhood. Here, I have to lean on the cross-cultural bridge-building work of anthropologist Deborah Bird Rose, whose studies with Aboriginal people in northern Australia taught her to think of Country in the following terms:

> Country in Aboriginal English is not only a common noun but also a proper noun. People talk about country in the same way that they would talk about a person: they speak to country, sing to country, visit country, worry about country, feel sorry for country, and long for country. People say that country knows, hears, smells, takes notice, takes care, is sorry or happy... country is a living entity with a yesterday, today and tomorrow, with a consciousness, and a will toward life.
>
> (1996: 7)

When Europeans first set foot in Australia, then, the entire continent, including its surrounding islands and coastal waters, was claimed as their Country by one of the many hundreds of nations and thousands of clans who had shaped its varied multispecies communities over the millennia. Far from being 'wilderness', it was, as Bill Gammage puts it, the 'biggest estate on earth' (2012).[22] Country, like each of the diverse entities that co-constitute its ongoing life, has its own agency and communicative capacity, but its flourishing calls for active human collaboration. Among other things, this entails amplifying the Dreaming songs that tell of its fashioning by ancestral creator figures, who remain active agents within Country (sometimes referred to as 'singing up' country); walking the Songlines that traverse land and sea and interlink each Country with others; and upholding those lively multispecies interrelationships that are enjoined by Law, which is understood as coming up out of Country. In this sense, Country is the vital source of the principles and practices that constitute what Rose has termed 'Dreaming Ecology' (1996: 47–51). The research of Indigenous scholar Victoria Grieves, of Warraimay and Tasmanian descent, indicates that caring for Country is intrinsic to Aboriginal social and emotional well-being (2009). Similarly, John Bradley learnt from the Yanyuwa families, with whom he studied for some thirty years in the Gulf of Carpentaria, that people 'worry greatly about country and speak longingly of places they are unable to visit because it is now a part of a pastoral property, a mining lease, or just too hard to get to without transport' (2010: 228). Country that is ecologically damaged or not actively cared for is referred to as 'wild', a word that generally carries negative connotations in Aboriginal English (Rose 2004: 171–73). People need Country, but Country also needs people. According to traditional understandings of death, the departed remain in Country and continue to sustain it, but their descendants, those who 'follow along behind the Dreamings', are responsible for keeping it open to their presence, which is to say, 'quiet' (Rose 2004: 152, 173). Removing people from Country, or causing it to become degraded, effects another kind of 'double death', 'wiping out the life-giving systems that were the signs of the ancestors, and ultimately ... wiping out the living presence of the dead' (Rose 2004: 176).

What, then, might it mean to be 'claimed by country' for a non-Indigenous Australian? In the triptych of that name that Elvey includes in *Kin*, adapted from a longer sequence previously published as a chapbook under that title (2010), she indicates that this begins with the recognition of the prior and persisting claim *to* country of Aboriginal Australians and of the violence and suffering attendant upon the appropriation *of* country by British colonizers, including some of Elvey's own forebears in Western Australia. All of the places to which these poems refer hold personal significance for Elvey. Yet the opening line of the sequence comprises a disclaimer:

No country claims me
where the picnic chalice lies tossed
among the reeds of Lake Pertobe.

(64)

Lake Pertobe is situated in the coastal city of Warrnambool, an industrial town with a strong Aboriginal presence, in part on account of the former Aboriginal mission that was located nearby in Framlingham.[23] Although located beyond the most popular stretch of Victoria's spectacular Great Ocean Road, which runs for 243 kilometres along the edge of the continent from the Bellarine Peninsula, southwest of Melbourne, to Portland, near the South Australian border, the Lake (which now boasts a large adventure playground) is presented here as a tourist stop for travellers along the way. For Elvey's speaker, it also summons personal memories, which are hinted at, sparely, in the second stanza ('*Let's talk soon,* I write,/as twenty year old wine spills and/dissipates'), along with seemingly awkward questions of faith: it's Easter Monday, and that discarded 'chalice', with its Eucharistic connotations, sits incongruously alongside its qualifier, 'picnic'. The speaker's attention, though, is soon drawn to the insistent materiality of her immediate environs: walking 'by clifftop paths', she has to 'dodge/the dry low brush/insistent/and the nodding puffs of puss tails'; here, it is 'sea/not faith' that 'moves mountains'. As we discover in the final stanza, moreover, the lookout that she is heading for bears the trace of a collective memory that recalls how faith, specifically Christianity, could well have been operationalized to legitimate the violent dispossession of those for whom this place was Country:

> ... at the lookout edge a sign recalls
> a people in two memories and one name:
> *Massacre Bay.*

Here, the incongruity of 'picnic chalice' deepens into a grotesque disjunction: in the previous tercet, the multidimensional matrix constitutive of Country for those who were murdered at this site is framed as a two-dimensional scenic spot, where,

> against a background of ocean, rock and scrub
> children pose for shots for Nanna's wall.

(64)

The second poem has the speaker hesitantly edging closer to a sense of what it might mean to be 'claimed by country' (62). This begins with contemplative attention to 'each dry/pricked leaf, each twig defined/where Lesmurdie water churns/towards its fall'. As the speaker senses how the 'greying otherness of scrub/becomes the genius of place', the canopy wind that descends to her 'lips and cheeks and lifts/my hair' reminds her of how 'a boy' had done so too, 'some/ thirty years ago'. The Lesmurdie Falls are located in the Darling Scarp on the southeastern urban-rural fringes of Perth in Western Australia, where Elvey has family connections. Any sense of familial homecoming that the speaker might have, though, is disrupted by the knowledge that her '*ancestors multiplied/on Nyoongah land*':

> when the Kalamundu bus lurches
> toward Perth, coming into, out of
>
> country with one hundred and fifty years
> of settler shame

The name 'Kalamundu', or 'Kalamunda', here referring to an outer suburb of Perth abutting state forest rising into the Darling Scarp, recalls the Nyoongah word for 'home', *kalil*. The closest words to 'munda' in the 1997 edition of the Noongar-English dictionary are *moonditj*, 'prickly bush', and *moondjak*, 'Christmas tree', but the WA Tourism Information website claims that *munda* means 'forest'.[24] In Elvey's verse, this formerly more extensive forest holds its ground on 'on the city's edge' in the guise of

> three trees as if
> three gnarled concierges
> of country

For the speaker, these seem to 'greet me/as if they know me'. According to Aboriginal diplomatic protocols, it is considered appropriate to call out to your other-than-human kin when travelling into and through Country. As Paddy Fordham Wainburranga, a Rembarrnga man of Arnhem Land, explains, 'The law about singing out was made like that to make you notice that all the trees here are your countrymen, your relations. All the trees and the birds are your relations' (qtd. Rose 1996: 14). Elvey's speaker has not presumed to initiate a greeting, though, and her sense of being addressed is interrupted by post(?) colonial anxiety:

> Three trees as if
> three gnarled concierges
> of country *is this*
>
> *the colonising moment*
> *once again?* greet me
> as if they know me.

In the final line, she writes: 'I wonder *should I call out in return?*' This question, like the line, standing separate from the final tercet, is left hanging.

In 'Claimed by Country 3', she does nonetheless tentatively respond to a sense of communion with the more-than-human life of the land, albeit on country where she is not herself at home, and from a position marked as marginal to the event being recalled: a National Aboriginal and Torres Strait Islander Catholic Commission bush mass in the MacDonnell Ranges, held to commemorate the twentieth anniversary of Pope John Paul's II's 1986 Blatherslake Park address in Alice Springs. This forthright call for reconciliation, premised on the recognition of past wrongs, ongoing injustice and the persistence of Indigenous culture and land rights, is quoted on the website of the ACM website: 'And the Church herself in Australia will not be fully the Church Jesus wants her to be until you (Aboriginal Australians) have made your contribution to her life and until that contribution is joyfully received by others.'[25] Here, in the company of Indigenous and non-Indigenous worshippers, in the presence of rock, wallaby and insects, under a full moon, 'With vested/hills, the dancers and the priests/attempt a fugue of ways,/ where one is always/almost/lost', Arrernte country becomes the locus of an intercultural communion, in which the wider land community seems to participate in a promise of reconciliation that is carried by the giving of 'a peace/that takes the breath'. Yet this is marked as but a moment, held in a still image, where 'by the iconographer's/grace I remain,/crushed cotton and dirty/feet, as smudge of white/ in the corner of the frame'. Icons point to what they are not, and what is yet to come: the work of reconciliation remains to be realized beyond the page.

For non-Indigenous Australians, then, to be 'claimed by country' entails first and foremost recognizing the prior claim of Aboriginal sovereignty, along with the ontological divide that separates Country from country. It also means recognizing how one might be called to respond to the claim *of* Country, to due respect and urgent repair. This is the case, for example, with the polluted lake of 'Claimed by Country VIII' in the chapbook of that name (2010: 11), and the extinct species named in 'Ecos echoes' from *Kin* (2015: 42–43). And it demands also that we acknowledge that 'no response suffices', although 'the call already bears the power to respond' ('Claimed by Country III', 2010: 6).

Even so, the question remains: is the white poet's desire to be 'claimed by country' '*the colonizing moment once again*'? In her review of *Kin*, Dimitra Harvey argues that by converting Arrernte Country into the semblance of a church, 'All the complexity of the land's "own meanings", the agendas and agencies, the interactions and relationships are reduced to, are described as being in the service of, a very particular kind of worship' (2015: n.p.). If we consider the actual occasion that prompted this poem, Harvey's complaint seems somewhat unjust. Yet the possible persistence of the colonizing moment in the desire to be claimed by country continued to trouble Elvey. Her *Claimed by Country* chapbook closes with a poem entitled 'Postscript: Post-Colonial?' which admits, 'Our wanting all/belonging in this place, is even more/the colon's gesture' (2010: 32). A revised version of this poem opens Elvey's most recent collection, *White on White* (2018), under the amended title, 'Post?colonial', querying the historiography that construes colonialism as a thing of the past:

> All that is white in white is not pure
> – but driven to the breath of – snow. It falls.
> The day turns cold. Our wanting all
> belonging – in this place – is even more
>
> the colon's gesture: already who bore
> too much the saying of what we have called
> selves – the being here of us – a creek, a wall
> –the snows melting – the water over. Or
>
> Tomorrow you find us building a hut
> of limbs and thatch, stripped gum, old bark, fragrant
> litter of leaves, the floor dry and crawling.
>
> Tomorrow you find us building a falling,
> the odour of crushed ants, the living urgent,
> assessing loss – a lean-to? our eyes shut?
>
> (3)

The broken syntax of this faltering sonnet prefigures how the ensuing poems experiment with different ways of unravelling the lyrical conventions of her earlier verse, as Elvey struggles to open a space for the multiple voices of our entangled histories, whilst seeking to make 'whiteness' visible and its privileges palpable. For, as she writes in 'This flesh that you know is all that you have', '*You can learn you have privilege, but still not/feel it*' (2018: 35).

In her essay 'Shame and Contemporary Australian Poetics', Bundjalong poet and scholar Evelyn Araluen observes that settler Australians 'must create space for our voices and languages, before they seek to fill their mouths with them' (2017b: 126). Heeding her call, I want to conclude with the work of another contemporary Aboriginal writer and scholar, Jeanine Leane. Her 2018 collection *Walk Back Over* returns us to the country that white settlers, such as David Campbell's forebears, dubbed the Monaro Plains, where she too grew up on a sheep station near Gundagai. However, as she reveals in her partly autobiographical collection of 'rural yarns', *Purple Threads* (2011, winner of the David Unaipon Award for Indigenous Writers), her upbringing was very different from Campbell's. Whereas he was the socially privileged scion of the invading squattocracy, Leane, for all her social disadvantage, including subjection to racist attitudes and assimilationist policies, benefited from the tutelage of the Wiradjuri women who raised her on Country: women, who, as she recalls in the Preface to *Walk Back Over*, 'had vast reserves of inner strength' and who taught her 'to listen to the past as it speaks in the present' (2018: xi). In her first award-winning poetry collection, *Dark Secrets: After Dreaming (A.D.) 1887–1961*, Leane draws on family stories to disclose the hidden history of Wiradjuri women 'from campfire to captivity to confinement and through colonisation' (2010: 2). Telling the 'tragic story of early invasion of the Wiradjuri lands, the institutionalization of children, the failure of the settlers to read and understand the land', Leane observes that it also speaks to 'the resilience of Aboriginal people especially women'.[26] In her second collection, she continues this work of 'walking back over' the past in order to recall a different history from that which prevails in the national narratives of the dominant settler society. Here, she explores how contested memories of the past get voiced in the present, enabling or foreclosing different pathways into the future.

Of mixed Anglo-Celtic, Aboriginal and possibly Chinese heritage, schooled by Catholic nuns, and participating in the wider settler society, Leane has the advantage often enjoyed by members of minority groups of being able to see through the lens of more than one cultural prism.[27] This lends her writing a more genuinely intercultural quality than can generally be found within Anglo-Australian literature, notwithstanding the questionable efforts of the 'Jindyworabaks' of the 1930s and 1940s, who appropriated Aboriginal songs to create their own version of a 'hybrid pastoral' on white terms (Indyk 1993: 847). In many of the poems in *Walk Back Over*, Leane exploits the potential of modern English lyric poetry to claim a voice with which to write back against 'whitefella' narratives, including, in the poem entitled 'Whitefellas', scholarly accounts of 'true Aborigines in the bush' (2018: 55), such as those that I too have referenced earlier in this chapter. Having spent much of her adult life in cities (notably Canberra and Melbourne), Leane identifies with those 'urban mobs' who are assumed by whitefellas to have sadly 'lost (their) culture over time' (55).

The problem alluded to here is not only one of stereotyping, which effaces the diversity of contemporary Aboriginal identities, and the varied ways in which Aboriginal cultures are responding to colonial contingencies and thereby engendering different kinds of 'Indigenous modernity' (Muecke 2004: 132–39). The privileging of 'true Aborigines in the bush' also has grave implications for Aboriginal sovereignty. For according to the Native Title legislation that followed the landmark 1992 court ruling in favour of Eddie Mabo, which overturned the colonial fiction of *terra nullius*, claimants are required to demonstrate their unbroken observation of traditional law and customs on their own Country right up until the present. The research of anthropologists, such as Deborah Bird Rose, has been valuable in the successful prosecution of many Native Title cases in the central and northern regions of Australia, where the impacts of colonization were both later and less intense than in the more densely populated subtropical and temperate regions to the south. The majority of land in the Centre and North is not privately owned, but rather Crown land or held under pastoral leases, with which Native Title, entailing rights of access, residence and traditional usage, can coexist. By 2015, Native Title had been recognized on over 32 per cent of the landmass of Australia.[28] However, as Waanyi novelist Alexis Wright points out, elsewhere 'Aboriginal people have missed out on Native Title because the legislation is virtually based on the idea that land theft and oppression did not happen' (2016: n.p.). By a cruel irony, then, those whose land and lifeways have been most drastically altered by colonization have benefited least from Native Title. As Elvey learnt on her retreats in the Barmah forest, this was the case, for example, for the Yorta Yorta, whose claim was dismissed by the presiding judge in the Federal Court in 2002, on the questionable grounds that the 'tide of history' had 'washed away' any real observance of traditional law and customs and thereby 'extinguished' their native title.[29]

The Wiradjuri were one of the largest tribal groupings in Australia at the time of the British invasion, with territories totalling 97,100 square kilometres. Yet under the current legislation, it is also highly unlikely that they could succeed in a Native Title claim, at least not on the Monaro Plains, which have been almost entirely appropriated for agriculture and grazing since the 1820s.[30] One index of the strength and resilience of Wiradjuri people in this district, though, is the quietly assertive presence at the official opening of Parliament House in Canberra in April 1927 of two well-known Wiradjuri Elders and Lore men ('clever men'). Jimmy Clements ('King Billy'), whose tribal name was Nangar and who appears to have hailed from the Gundagai area, had walked for over a week with his dogs from the Brungle Mission near Tumut. John Noble, known as 'Marvellous', is also likely to have walked from far afield to attend the ceremony. Urged on by some in the rowdy crowd, including a local clergyman, who reportedly called out that 'the Aborigine had a better right than any man present to a place on the steps of the house of parliament', Clements defied the police to walk forward and respectfully greet the Duke and Duchess of York, thereby effectively 'contesting claims of the erasure of Indigenous people from the land and place' (Casey 2009: 34).

For rural and urban Aboriginal people who are prevented from practicing traditional ways of living in, and caring for, for their ancestral lands, connections with Country might differ from those enjoyed by people who are still, or once more, in a position to do so (e.g. through the Indigenous Ranger and Protected Areas programmes, now covering over 20 per cent of the continent[31]). That Aboriginal knowledge, skills and labour are essential to conservation efforts across so much of this country exemplifies but one of the many ways in which, as Leane writes in 'Whitefellas', 'Australia doesn't work/ without Aborigines' (2018: 55). Yet, as she demonstrates in *Walk Back Over*, for other Aboriginal people, too, the pull of Country remains powerful, its salience richly meaningful. At her book launch, Leane commented that these poems came out of 'the only country that can't be invaded', that of the 'heart and mind'.[32] Although Alexis Wright laments that this is not always the case in view of the impact of what she terms 'psychological invasion' (2016: n.p.), Leane's poetry bears witness to the persistence of Country in the hearts and minds of those 'urban mobs' who 'ask too many questions' ('Whitefellas', 2018: 55). In her own case, that includes memories of particular places in and around Gundagai that are dear to her from childhood, such as the hill that she recalls in 'Kumbilor, hill in my Country':

> I come back and see a hill
> barren, cleared of trees. Sectioned by fences
> like a checkerboard of games won and lost.
> Only the rocks anchored so deep they cannot
> be moved
> remain.
> A dry creek bed – thirsty for a long time,
> now faded stones no longer shining sharp
> rounded what has passed.
>
> I close my eyes. Fences disappear.
> Bare-foot mop-headed children – hatless
> in the heat of the high sun – search
> for a slumber of koalas, listen for
> a warbling of magpies to laugh louder than
> a cackle of kookaburras can.

The children run. Scramble high on
granite sentinels.
   This is my wild horse!
   And this is mine!
They ride and ride and ride
a thousand miles standing still. Sun blazes on
quartz crystal makes amethyst haze.
I scrunch my eyes tighter.
There's my Aunty on the creek flats
walking through parched grass
towards the hill. She calls us, time
to come home. We start to run
arms open to meet.

We're nearly there –
touching her.
My eyes hurt. I open them.
She's gone!

(2018: 22)

Originally commissioned by Red Room Poetry as part of a series to celebrate places and spaces outside metropolitan NSW,[33] this poem artfully bends celebration towards lament. The children's reimagining of rocks as horses indicates that the speaker's Country is part of a colonized landscape, made over for those pastoral purposes in connection with which horses had been introduced by the invaders. Yet it is one that she recalls from her childhood as retaining accessible patches of grassy woodland on its hillsides. These have since been cleared and fenced. There is an echo here of Clare's lament for the loss of the unenclosed pastoral world of his childhood. There is a crucial difference, though, in that Leane's sense of loss encompasses also the speaker's bereavement of her Aunty ('Betty'), to whom the poem is dedicated. Since 'Aunty' in Aboriginal English holds a double meaning, referring not only to a personal relative but also to a women Elder, the last lines of the poem hint that the speaker's experience of Kumbilor may well have been informed by Aboriginal narratives about this place and its more-than-human denizens. The hill might be fenced off, but Kumbilor remains Country, and as such, in the speaker's heart and mind, it is like the rocks, 'anchored so deep they cannot/ be moved'.

In the following poem, 'Tracks Wind Back', Leane shifts from the territory of personal memory to that of a longer history of colonization, revealing that the manifold commons of the Wiradjuri had long since been stolen. As it happens, this occurred right around the time that Clare was protesting against the enclosures around his village of Helpston in the 1820s. The country around Gundagai was traversed by the explorers Hamilton Hume and William Hovell in 1824 and by Charles Sturt in 1829. Within a decade the squatters were moving in. In 1838, William Hutchinson took the Wiradjuri word 'Gundagai', together with Wiradjuri land, as the name of his pastoral run, and the township of Gundagai was established soon after – ill-advisedly, as they would have been warned by the locals, had they deigned to listen – on the floodplain of a bend in the Murrumbidgee River. When the inevitable happened and the town was virtually washed away in 1852, Wiradjuri men Yarri and Jacky Jacky, among others, managed to save sixty-eight people (around a third of the town's population) using bark canoes.[34]

The Gundagai area was an important gathering place for several Wiradjuri clans, as Leane recalls in the opening stanza of 'Tracks Wind Back':

> Gundagai means bend curve
> turn in the Murrumbidgee River
> eddying and flowing Mother of
> Wiradjuri children (2018: 23).

As was so often the case across Australia, this Aboriginal gathering place became an important site for the settlers also. Another example is the federal capital, Canberra (Kamberra, Ngambra), an 'older meeting place', as Leane recalls (2018: 28). As a major crossing point for bullock drivers ('bullockies'), 'swagmen', shearers and drovers, Gundagai became one of the small towns most frequently referenced in colonial poems, songs and stories. When I was growing up in nearby Canberra, Gundagai's greatest claim to fame derived from the tale of the dog who sat on the 'tuckerbox', five (or sometimes nine) miles from Gundagai, either loyally awaiting the return of his master who had died or cheekily shitting in the tuckerbox whilst his master struggled to haul his bullock team out of the mud (needless to say, it is the saccharine former version that is remembered at the tourist attraction that has become a popular stopping point for car travellers between Sydney or Canberra and Melbourne). Gundagai also features in poems by Banjo Patterson ('On the Road to Gundagai') and Henry Lawson ('Scots of the Riverina'), as well as in the traditional ballad 'Flash Jack of Gundagai'; but it became best known through Jack O'Hagan's song 'Along the Road to Gundagai' (1922), first recorded by Peter Dawson in 1924, and re-recorded by any number of country and Western singers since:

> There's a track winding back to an old fashioned shack
> Along the road to Gundagai
> Where the blue gums are growin' and the Murrumbidgee's flowin'
> Beneath the sunny sky
> There my mother and daddy are waitin' for me
> And the pals of my childhood once more I shall see
> Then no more will I roam when I'm headin' straight for home
> Along the road to Gundagai

Quoting the familiar refrain of this song, Leane undercuts its nostalgic colonial fantasy of homecoming by recalling the far longer history of Wiradjuri dwelling in the Gundagai area, along with the damage wrought upon them and their Country by those who arrived 'in wagons of wire, tin,/steel, guns and disease', concreting 'over tracks that wound/back to the dawn'. Although they were 'awestruck' by the beauty of the place, construing it as a 'Garden/of Eden', complete with unfallen natives, the invaders were blind to Wiradjuri memories and deaf to their 'stories, our Dreamings'. Instead, they 'wrote their own histories' in the guise of those bush ballads, on which Campbell was raised:

> songs of lovers, larrikins, sheep, profits,
> droughts, floods, fires, self-made men –
> stuff of colonial phantasm.
>
> They couldn't read the history they built over.
> Deeper tracks wind back
> to Gundagai – a long way east of Eden.
>
> (2018: 23)

Leane elaborates on this point in the following poem, 'River Memory' (2018: 24–25), concerned with the contested meanings of Gundagai's historic Prince Alfred Bridge. Constructed in 1865, the bridge was celebrated by the Irish nuns who taught the speaker as 'the longest/wooden bridge in the world', built 'by pioneers as they opened/up our lands for progress'. But for the speaker, who, unlike the nuns who had travelled the world 'to spread their word', had 'only seen Country', the bridge primarily bears testimony to loss:

> … How many river gums
> were felled?
> What were their names
> before they were rearranged
> across the river – once their blood?
> What was their history? (2018: 24–5)

As well as taking a toll on local riparian ecologies, the construction of the bridge facilitated the extension and intensification of 'resource' extraction across the country: 'as huge wheat and wool trucks thundered/over ancient planks laden with wealth/of the nation'. That is, a 'nation' from which Australia's First Nations were long excluded and of which the unevenly distributed 'wealth' has been won at great cost, both to Aboriginal people and their lands. While the nuns claimed that Australia was '*a young country*', whose history was the '*shortest in the world*', the speaker's grandmother insisted, '*this place is old*':

> She said my teachers didn't know the stories.
> I listened.
> On a bad day you could be beaten
> for asking wrong questions about
> the short history and the long bridge.

Rearticulating those questions here, Leane's verse bears witness to the resurgence of the Aboriginal voices that were suppressed in so many ways. For her, the 'bend/of the Murrumbidgee' remains 'a deep archive'; and while the 'old stone convent on the hill/is empty', she can 'hear' her 'Grandmother again':

> The bridge is shorter now.
> This history of place – still
> long and deep. (2018: 25)

These three poems by Leane comprise an indirect Indigenous answer to the 'Claimed by Country' triptych in Elvey's *Kin*. There is much that divides them. But Leane's call to 'walk back over' the traumatic history of colonization in Australia, as Elvey endeavours to do from a non-Indigenous perspective in *White on White*, indicates how that division is beginning to be bridged. For non-Indigenous Australians, this will entail a great deal more attentiveness to Indigenous voices; and, for those of Anglo-Celtic settler heritage in particular, this work of listening entails also taking on responsibility for their history of colonial violence. As Aboriginal author and scholar Tony Birch observes, 'this responsibility might begin the process of easing the burden of memory held by older Aboriginal people across the country, who by necessity are the custodians of the stories of colonial violence that the nation has strategically forgotten and refused to take responsibility for' (2019: n.p.). At their joint book launch on 24 January, both Elvey and Leane commented on the proximity of its date to Invasion Day (26 January). Officially celebrated as 'Australia Day', commemorating the arrival of the First Fleet in Botany Bay in 1788, for Aboriginal people, this is, as Leane put it, 'the longest day': a day of mourning. Accepting responsibility, then, entails joining in solidarity with those who grieve for the collective losses that followed upon on that day but also for their continuing fallout in the ruination and foreshortening of individual Aboriginal lives, such as that of the thirty-seven-year-old 'Second surviving son to two generations/of fathers to buried boys', whose death by suicide is mourned by the speaker of Evelyn Araluen's searing 'Guarded by Birds' (winner of the 2018 Judith Wright Poetry Prize).[35] As Elvey learnt through her involvement with Binnap Partners, solidarity is also called for in relation to Aboriginal peoples' endeavours to safeguard their Country against ongoing environmental threats, such as that of the Wangan and Jagalingou people, Traditional Owners of Country in Queensland's Galilee Basin, who are struggling to prevent the Adani corporation from mining coal on their ancestral lands.[36]

The joint launch of *Walk Back Over* and *White on White* provided a modest meeting place for taking forward the vital work of renegotiating Indigenous and non-Indigenous relations with one another and their entangled histories, with the damaged land and its contested meanings, and with the networked language of their poetic craft. Taken together, the work of Elvey and Leane testifies to what Peter Minter has called 'the vision of a decolonised Australia, a place where settler and Indigenous cultures have begun to find an existential common ground that is beyond postcolonial' (2016: n.p.). For this common ground to be found, however, something else is required of Anglo-Australians, alongside the essential praxis of listening and learning, responsibility and solidarity. As Paul Carter argued towards the end of the last millennium, historical narratives that portray the colonizers as no more than 'rootless rationalists' leave white Australians emptyhanded when they finally sit down at the negotiating table with the colonized (1996: 364). What is required also, then, is the strategic recovery of European counter-traditions that might be brought into creative conversation with Indigenous understandings and practices. Among these are the ecopoetic arts of contemplative, affective, creaturely and prophetic resistance to the logic of colonization, which I have sought to reclaim from the inheritance of European Romanticism in the course of this book.

Postscript: Ecopoetics beyond the page

'[I]in many ways...I feel that poetry is indefensible!' (Kinsella 2007a: xi). As a literary scholar who has spent more years than I care to contemplate researching and writing about ecopoetics, I share Kinsella's anguished recognition of the limited efficacy of poetic writing in the face of the appalling injustices (towards otherkind as well as human others) and destruction (of cultures no less than ecologies) that so urgently need to be redressed (to the extent that remains possible).

Writing and reading poetry can be many things, including personally transformative. From an ecopolitical perspective, however, what matters most is what happens afterward: *postscriptum* and *postlectorum*. And that, crucially, is a question of the context in which the poetic text is received, and into which it is networked. It is for that reason that each chapter of this book has concluded with an example of how the given ecopoetic art of resistance under discussion might be translated into potentially transformative forms of socioecological praxis. At the same time, though, I have become increasingly intrigued by the growing prominence of poetry *per se* in the public arena. Monash University's Climate Change Communication Research Hub (CCCRH), for example, has recently appointed a poet-in-residence, Amanda Anastasi, on the strength of the capacity of poetry to communicate vulnerability to communities at risk from adverse climate change impacts.[1] On the website of the CCCRH, you can also find a link to a talk presented by Sam Illingworth, senior lecturer in science communication at Manchester Metropolitan University, at a panel he chaired at the COP24 meeting in Katowice, Poland, in 2018, on 'Using Poetry to Facilitate Dialogue'. Quoting Shelley's depiction of poets as 'heirophants of an unapprehended inspiration' in his 'Defence of Poetry', Illingworth discusses the power of poetry not just to disseminate and interpret the esoteric science of climate change to non-specialist publics but also to personalize and localize its impacts. In the examples he provides, this was explored through the use of writing workshops intended to empower individuals from underserved communities (in particular, refugees and asylum seekers, and people experiencing mental distress and illness) to find their own voice in response to what they were coming to understand about the climate crisis. Similar writing workshops bringing scientists into conversation with faith-based communities, Illingworth says here, uncovered a shared sense of stewardship in taking care of the Earth across the divide of differing belief and knowledge systems.[2]

Some literary scholars too have begun to engage in such initiatives. As part of their project on British Romantic Writing and Catastrophe, for example, David Higgins and Tess Somerville collaborated with the Wordsworth Trust on an initiative called Weather Words, which included poetry and painting workshops with local communities and schools in Leeds and Cumbria, and a poetry-writing competition for those below the age of 25.[3] Meanwhile, poets themselves are finding diverse ways to work beyond the page, often in conjunction with environmental art projects. One such, about which I have written elsewhere (Rigby 2017c), was the Slow Art Trail, created in Yorkshire's Strid Wood in 2008, to which poet David Morley contributed a series of 'Ankle-High Haiku' on upcycled elm posts, the chiselled letters of which, packed with hand-worked clay, created affordances for many other critters in addition to the humans who deciphered them as words (notably algae feeding on the microbes in the clay, lichens forming out of algae and fungi and birds appropriating bits of lichen for their nests). More recently, BBC's 2017 Autumnwatch programme featured the work of a Bath Spa Creative Writing student with cerebral palsy, Marchant Barron, whose verse had been printed on huge banners hanging from trees in Westonbirt Arboretum, with a view of encouraging visitors to engage more deeply, on an affective and imaginative level, with the arboreal beings they were encountering in that space.

Reflecting on this proliferation of poetry in the public sphere (of which many, many more instances might be provided), I realize that, even as I was writing this book, there was another kind of book wanting to get out. This other book would have required a different kind of research from the largely historical, theoretical and hermeneutic methods in which I have been trained, entailing the kind of crossover into the social sciences that I take to be the hallmark of the environmental humanities as a genuinely interdisciplinary and transdisciplinary field (that is to say, one that entails not only conversations and collaborations among researchers from different disciplines but also forms of participatory action research with practitioners and communities beyond the academy). That book will have to wait for another day. In drawing this one to a close, however, I want to end by advancing a rather different mode of ecopoetics beyond the page from those that I have discussed thus far.

In making a pitch to a largely scientific readership for the importance of the environmental social sciences and humanities to research and policy development in the arena of Global Environmental Change in an article entitled 'Changing the Intellectual Climate', Noel Castree and his numerous co-authors (myself included) also called upon fellow scholars in the humanities and social sciences to 'get out of their comfort zones' by breaking 'in to the relevant meetings, conferences and journals' (Castree 2014: 267). Here, I would like to make a similar call to poets and critics. Whilst I have been at pains to highlight the insufficiency of ecopoetics *per se* as a mode of engagement with the ecopolitical exigencies of the Anthropocene, this is not an argument for less poetry. Rather, I believe that we need far more poetry: poetry, however, that is no longer confined to the pages of a book but performed in public places as a means of intervening in the process of political decision making.

One such intervention occurred in the opening ceremony of the UN Secretary General Ban Ki-Moon's Climate Change Summit in New York in 2014, when Marshallese Islander Kathy Jetñil Kijiner stood up and performed her poem, 'Dear Matafele Peinam'. Addressed to her baby daughter, Kijiner's words implicitly appealed to the assembled heads of state and other government representatives, many of whom were moved to tears, to position themselves among the 'we' of her penultimate line, who 'won't let you down'.[4] Her performance was filmed by the assembled international media, and its impact has continued to ripple out into many other contexts via the internet. By April 2019, the video posted by the UN on YouTube had received 318,765 views.[5] While the flow-on effects of the digitally mediated afterlife of Kijiner's performance are impossible to calculate, what interests me here is how it might have played into the deliberations of the Summit. Interrupting the instrumental rationality of national self-interest that all too often derails such efforts to safeguard the common good, Kijiner's performance instituted a contemplative pause, within which the poet engaged her listeners at the level of affect and imagination. Her poem appealed to their compassion and asked them to recall their shared creatureliness. In this way, she sought to break through the walls of what biblical scholar Walter Brueggeman (2001) terms 'royal consciousness', the perspective of privilege that can render us insouciant to the unjust suffering of others, in order to fully focus her listeners' attention, in body, mind, heart and soul, on those who are at once most vulnerable to the impacts of global warming and least responsible for its causation. At the same time, her words bore witness to the determination of Pacific Islanders to fight not just for their own survival but for a political order oriented towards enhanced collective flourishing. Not all were swayed, of course, or at least, not for long enough for it to make a difference. Once the tears had dried, it certainly appears to have been back to business-as-usual for some, including Australia's foreign minister, Julie Bishop, constrained as she would have been by the pro-coal interests backing the government of then Prime Minister Tony Abbott. Still, I wonder to what extent the echo of Kijiner's performance at the Summit might have contributed to the decision taken the following year at the UN Framework Convention on Climate Change congress, at which Kijiner also spoke and performed her verse,[6] to attempt to limit global warming to 1.5 degrees centigrade (beyond which the Marshall Islands, and much else besides, would be lost).

An attempt to answer this question, taking into consideration also the role of the activists protesting outside the walls of the convention centres (whom Kijiner hails in her poem), along with the messy political processes whereby such agreements do or do not get translated into practice, would take me well beyond the limits of the current study. I offer it here, though, by way of encouragement to my fellow ecocritics to also get out of their disciplinary 'comfort zones', that is to say, their familiar ways of working, in further explorations of ecopoetics beyond the page. As I see it, this is to enter the terrain opened up by the transdisciplinary project of the environmental humanities: a space in which the hermeneutic, theoretical and historical approaches of conventional literary studies (within which most ecocriticism, including that practiced in this book, is conducted) might be wedded with the ethnographic methods of the social sciences in the development of poetic participatory action projects devoted to the decolonial praxis of socioecological transformation. To do this would be to finally make good on the promise of Romantic poesy, as outlined in the opening chapter: in Friedrich Schlegel's words, to 'make poetry lively and sociable, and life and society poetical'. There is, I think, as yet 'undetonated energy' (Elizabeth Freeman in Burrus 2019: 99) in this past cultural revolution. For the Romantic project, as it emerged in the shadow of Europe's first 'satanic mills', was never meant to be a narrowly literary affair but one that would draw readers out, as Wordsworth put it, into the 'light of things' and, as Blake insisted, into solidarity with the oppressed, human and otherwise. Now that those anthropogenic changes set in train at the dawn of the Ploutocene have reached so perilous a pass, it has become all the more pressing to heed the Romantic call to craft more just and compassionate modalities of creaturely co-becoming.

Notes

Introduction

1 See Davies (2018) for the most comprehensive review to date of major ecocritical monographs on British Romanticism.
2 See e.g. Kroeber (1994); Morton (1994); Lussier (2000); McKusick (2000); Hutchings (2002); and Oerlemans (2002).
3 See e.g. Morton (2007), Hutchings (2009), Nichols (2011), Hess (2012).
4 See also e.g. Scott (2014); Ottum and Reno (2016); and Hall (2016).
5 Forms of marginalization and oppression related to sexuality and ability are also of concern but cannot readily be seen as 'colonial' or 'colonizing' in the sense in which I am using this term here. Nonetheless, to the extent that the settler cultures of both North America and Australia have been highly heteronormative and ablest, they have also contributed to the marginalization and oppression of LGBTQ people and the disabled. In North America, for example, the heteronormativity of the dominant settler culture has been especially adverse for those traditionally known as 'two-spirit' people, that is, those who manifest both 'male' and 'female' traits. For a decolonial approach to transgender identities in particular, see Aizura *et al*. (2014).
6 See also Adams and Mulligan (2003).
7 With respect to the aspect of 'instrumentalism', Plumwood's analysis draws close to both Theodor Adorno's and Max Horkheimer's critique of the privileging of 'instrumental reason' in their account of the 'dialectic of enlightenment' ([1944] 1979) and Martin Heidegger's critique of the reduction of 'nature' to the status of 'standing reserve' in 'The Question Concerning Technology' ([1954] 1978: 213–38). My earlier work on Romanticism (notably 2004a) was indebted to both these lines of philosophical critique. On the relevance of Adorno's and Horkheimer's *Dialectic of Enlightenment* to colonial contexts and feminist concerns, see also Rigby 1996. DeLoughrey and Handley (2011) also draw on Adorno and Horkheimer in elucidating a postcolonial ecocritical 'aesthetics of the Earth'.
8 Clark instantiates the 'methodological anthropocentrism' of the postcolonial approach with reference to Graham Huggan's *Australian Literature* (2007) and observes in footnote that this is surprising, in light of his contemporaneous collaboration with the critical human-animal studies scholar Helen Tiffin (Clark 2015: 132). Surprisingly, he does not reference their 2006 co-authored volume *Postcolonial Ecocriticism*, which weds their respective approaches. In fact, much

postcolonial ecocriticism escapes the charge of 'methodological anthropocentrism' by taking a bio-inclusive, or transpecies, view of agency and ethics. See e.g. the section on 'The Lives of (Nonhuman)Animals' in DeLoughrey and Handley 2011), and Bartosch (2013).

9   In addition to Cooke (2013) and Nolan (2017), see e.g. Knickerbocker (2012); Keller (2017) and Kinsella, Fagan and Minter (2009). For a brief overview of earlier discussions of ecopoetry and ecopoetics (1985–2011), see also Rigby (2016a).

10 A similar pluralism is evident in the poetry and criticism published in the Australian journal of ecopoetry and ecopoetics *Plumwood Mountain*, of which the founding editor is Anne Elvey. Available online: https://plumwoodmountain.com/ (accessed 5 August 2019).

11 See e.g. David Higgins's and Alison Critchlow's (2017) collaboration with the Wordsworth Trust, 'Weather Worlds', available online: https://romanticcatastrophe.leeds.ac.uk/public-engagement/ (accessed 8 August 2019); and Vivienne Westwood's initiative to convene a performance of radical climate change poetry by young writers at the Keats House in London as part of her Climate Revolution project, as reported in *Culture 24* in May 2013, available online: https://www.culture24.org.uk/art437754 (accessed 8 August 2019).

12 Interview with Mark Goldthorpe, founding editor of *ClimateCultures* for 'Finding Blake', available online: https://climatecultures.net/conversations/if-the-anthropocene-is-violence-what-is-nonviolence/ (accessed 8 August 2019).

13 George Monbiot, 'John Clare – the poet of environmental crisis 200 years on', *The Guardian*, 9 July 2012, available online: https://www.theguardian.com/commentisfree/2012/jul/09/john-clare-poetry (accessed 8 August 2019).

14 In the context of this article, Araluen's 'we' principally intends other Aboriginal writers and scholars. Here, I am suggesting that decolonization entails a corresponding movement beyond the page from the side of non-Indigenous writers and scholars as well.

15 James Purtill, 'An Australian rodent has become the first climate change mammal extinction', ABC Radio Triple J, The Hack, 20 February 2019, available online: https://www.abc.net.au/triplej/programs/hack/bramble-cay-melomys-first-climate-change-mammal-extinction/10830080 (accessed 21 February 2019).

16 The Honourable Melissa Price MP, minister for the environment, 'Stronger protection for threatened species', Australian Government Department of the Environment and Energy, 18 February 2019, available online: https://www.environment.gov.au/minister/price/media-releases/mr20190218a.html (accessed 21 February 2019).

17 Frances Mao, 'How one heatwave killed "a third" of a bat species in Australia', *BBC News*, 15 January 2019, available online: https://www.bbc.co.uk/news/world-australia-46859000 (accessed 22 April 2019).

18 As she revealed in her final blog post, Rose also features flying-foxes in her last book, *Shimmer*, to be published posthumously: 'Flying-foxes on my mind', Love at the Edge of Extinction, 23 November 2018, available online: http://deborahbirdrose.com/ (accessed 22 April 2019).

19 Deborah Bird Rose, 'Double Death', The Multispecies Salon – a companion to the book, available online: http://www.multispecies-salon.org/double-death/ (accessed 22 April 2019). Evidence for the increasing role of climate change as a driver of species extinction is provided in the draft of the 2019 Global Assessment of the Intergovernmental Platform on Biodiversity and Ecosystem Services, available online: https://www.ipbes.net/global-assessment-report-biodiversity-ecosystem-services (accessed 2 August 2019).

20 L. Allam and N. Evershed, 'The Killing Times: the massacres of Aboriginal people Australia must confront', *Guardian Australia*, 4 March 2019, available online: https://www.theguardian.com/australia-news/2019/mar/04/the-killing-times-the-massacres-of-aboriginal-people-australia-must-confront?CMP=Share_iOSApp_Other (accessed 4 March 2019).

21 P. Daley, 'As the toll of Australia's frontier brutality keeps climbing, truth telling is long overdue', *The Guardian*, 3 March 2019, available online: https://www.theguardian.com/australia-news/2019/mar/04/as-the-toll-of-australias-frontier-brutality-keeps-climbing-truth-telling-is-long-overdue?CMP=Share_iOSApp_Other (accessed 4 March 2019).

22 Australian Bureau of Statistics, Life Tables for Aboriginal and Torres Strait Islander Australians, 2015–17, available online: https://www.abs.gov.au/ausstats/abs@.nsf/Lookup/by%20Subject/3302.0.55.003~2015-2017~Main%20Features~Life%20expectancy%20at%20birth%20of%20Aboriginal%20and%20Torres%20Strait%20Islander%20Australians~5 and Causes of Death 2017 and https://www.abs.gov.au/ausstats/abs@.nsf/Lookup/by%20Subject/3302.0.55.003~2015-2017~Main%20Features~Life%20expectancy%20at%20birth%20of%20Aboriginal%20and%20Torres%20Strait%20Islander%20Australians~5 (both accessed 22 April 2019).

23 Crutzen and Stoermer's article is reprinted together with a commentary by Will Steffen, which includes discussion of the Great Acceleration, in Robin *et al.* (2013: 484–90).

24 See also the nuanced discussion of the Anthropocene in Horn and Bergthaller (2020).

25 See e.g. Fulford (2006); Hutchings (2009); Bewell (2017).

26 Unless otherwise indicated, all quotes from works by Shelley are from Shelley (2002).

27 See Laura Dassow Walls's sympathetic analysis of Thoreau's natural-cultural project of more-than-human neighbourliness on Walden Pond, read through the lens of Bruno Latour's critique of the Modern Constitution (2011).

28 See also Gaard (2016) for a material ecocritical discussion of Buddhist 'mindfulness' practices.
29 'Cultures of Nature and Wellbeing: Connecting Health and the Environment through Literature' is the name of Walton's two-year project funded by the UK's Arts and Humanities Research Council that 'aims to add new layers of understanding to current research linking nature and wellbeing, and to demonstrate the dynamic and influential role that arts and humanities research can play in public life'. https://culturenaturewellbeing.wordpress.com/contact/ (accessed 8 April 2019).
30 See also Coleman and Otto (1992).
31 With respect to Indigenous politics and environmentalism in contemporary Australia, see Vincent and Neale (2016).
32 Minter takes the term 'poethical' from Joan Retallack (2003). See also Minter (2013).

Chapter 1

1 The term *Symphilosophie*, referring to a collective quest for knowledge, was used in the *Athenäum* itself with reference to the anonymous 'Fragments', which were written by various members of the editorial collective. F. Schlegel referred to *Sympoesie* alongside *Symphilosophie* in a letter to his brother, August Wilhelm, as quoted in the editor's introduction to F. D. E. Schleiermacher's *Schriften auf der Berliner Zeit 1796–1799* (1984: 32).
2 Unless otherwise stated, all quotes from Wordsworth's poetry are taken from the Project Gutenberg online edition of *Lyrical ballads, with other poems, in two volumes* ([1800] 2005).
3 Unless otherwise stated, all biblical quotes are taken from the *New Oxford Annotated Bible (NRSV)* (Coogan 2007).
4 For a helpful introduction to this ecotheological theme, see Edwards (2006), especially 55–62.
5 See also Burrus (2019).
6 Among those discussed by Burrus, e.g., is St Simeon the Stylite, who inaugurated the trend for pursuing the contemplative life atop a platform atop a tall pillar. For two years, Simeon is said to have stood yogi-like on one leg, while his followers spent their days, at his request, collecting the falling maggots and returning them to their place in his wounded flesh. Another is St Mary of Egypt, who took to wandering the desert naked, grazing like a wild animal, 'no longer distinctly human' (110), her very grave graciously dug by a lion, since her follower, Zosimas, who discovered her corpse, did not have the right kit to do so. For Burrus, these

narratives 'expose the ongoing emergence, and submergence of the human within the nonhuman, whether god, plant, thing, or animal' (127).

7   The question of Wordsworth's relationship to Christianity, which changed over time, remains a matter of debate. See e.g. Easterlin (1996); Ryan (1997); Ulmer (2001); Roberts (2010); Fay (2018).

8   The earliest version of this poem was written in 1798, but is quoted here from the better-known version of 1834. Unless otherwise stated all quotations from Coleridge's poetry are taken from Coleridge ([1912] 2009).

9   The following discussion of Schleiermacher's *On Religion* contains excerpts from a more detailed discussion in Rigby (2010).

10 As noted by the editor of *On Religion*, Richard Crouter, proposition 4 of Schleiermacher's *magnum opus*, *The Christian Faith* (*Die Glaubenslehre*, 1821–2 and 1830–1), defines religion as 'the feeling of utter dependence' (Schleiermacher 1988: n. 129).

11 The Protestant Schleiermacher, on the other hand, was far from chuffed by Schlegel's subsequent conversion to Roman Catholicism and made it clear in his 1806 revision, 'addressed to an audience of greater philosophical and theological discernment', that he no longer looked to Romantic poetry for the rebirth of religion (qtd. in Crouter 1988: 67).

12 On Wordsworth's likely reception of Spinoza, via the German Spinoza controversy of the 1780s, see Levinson (2007).

13 Schelling's natural philosophy is of renewed interest in the horizon of environmental philosophy. See e.g. Mules (2014) and Gare (2017).

14 Hart, 'Contemplation and Fascination', unpublished manuscript. I wish to thank Kevin Hart for sharing a draft of his 2020 Gifford Lectures, 'Kingdom and Contemplation', forthcoming. In a personal communication, Hart notes that the way in which the relationship among thinking, meditating and contemplating has been conceived is quite complex in the history of Christianity. In the twelfth century *contemplatio* usually meant a synthetic gaze at something and was fundamentally philosophical in orientation; only when the gaze was lifted to divine things, such as the triune nature of God, does it morph into contemplative prayer. Later, with the Counter-Reformation, especially with Ignatius, we get a devaluation of contemplative prayer in favour of meditation (i.e. the 'exercises'), in part because contemplative prayer empties the mind of images and seeks union with the deity: that inspired fears in the Church that enclosed religious orders, especially the female ones, might bypass the sacramental system in order to gain union with God. Contemplation came back into its own mainly in the late nineteenth and early twentieth centuries under the somewhat misleading rubric of 'mystical experience', drawn from eighteenth- and nineteenth-century German thinkers, including Schleiermacher.

15 E.g. in the 2014–16 international (UK and Japan) and intermedial (art, literature and walking) project on 'Wordsworth and Bashō; Walking Poets'. Available online: https://walk.uk.net/portfolio/wordsworth-and-basho-walking-poets-encounters-with-nature/ (accessed 5 April 2019).
16 On Wordsworth and 'things', see also Rigby (2014) and Castell (2015).
17 See also Shaviro (2014) for an extended discussion.
18 Dushane reads Romantic poetics of 'reverie' through the lens of Bennett's concept of 'enchantment' (2001), arguing that this is 'one of many Romantic-era formulations of affective and aesthetic engagement with material nature that suggest novel ways of imagining the place of the human within natural and manmade ecologies' (2016: 128). In addition to Wordsworth, Dushane discusses Rousseau, Erasmus Darwin and Shelley as exemplifying a mode of 'visionary materialism'.
19 Hugh Dunkerley also discusses Lilburn's ecopoetics of the *via negativa* in his paper, 'Poetry and Unknowing' (2008, unpublished). The following two paragraphs are taken from Rigby (2014: 125–26).
20 'Towards a Contemplative Commons', IASS Potsdam, co-organised by Zack Walsh and Ed Ng, available online: https://www.iass-potsdam.de/sites/default/files/files/towards_a_contemplative_commons-_cfp.pdf (accessed 6 April 2019). See also Zack Walsh's blog https://www.snclab.ca/category/blog/contemplative-ecologies/ (accessed 6 April 2019).
21 'Inner transition: creating healthy cultures in times of change', Transition Network, available online: https://transitionnetwork.org/do-transition/inner-transition/ (accessed 6 April 2019).
22 Ibid. See also Doran (2017); Giorgino and Walsh (2018); Wamsler (2019); Woiwode and Bhati (2019).

Chapter 2

1 On the science and poetics of 'atmosphere' in Romanticism, revisited in the horizon of anthropogenic climate change, see also Ford (2018). On Romanticism and climate change, see also Higgins (2017).
2 'Cultures of Nature and Wellbeing: Connecting Health and the Environment through Literature' is the name of Walton's two-year project funded by the UK's Arts and Humanities Research Council that 'aims to add new layers of understanding to current research linking nature and wellbeing, and to demonstrate the dynamic and influential role that arts and humanities research can play in public life'. Available online: https://culturenaturewellbeing.wordpress.com/contact/ (accessed 8 April 2019).
3 See also Jackson (2008); Richardson (2001) and (2010); and Youngquist (2003).
4 This paragraph and those that follow up to page 66 are excerpted, from Rigby (2011: 139–46).

5   See e.g. the Ecomodernist Manifesto (2015), available online: http://www.ecomodernism.org/ (accessed 23 June 2019).
6   Sc. 8, l.58. Unless otherwise indicated, all quotes from Shelley are taken from Shelley (2002).
7   I take the distinction between *in textu* and *in situ* atmospheres from Tim Chandler's work on Vergilian pastoral from the perspective of Böhme's ecological aesthetics (2011). On 'embodied narratology', see also Wojciekowski and Gallese (2011).
8   All quotes from Theocritus are taken from the online version of Theocritus (1912) and referenced by Idyll number and passage number.
9   Unless otherwise indicated, all quotes from Keats's verse are from Keats (1934).
10 Downloaded with permission from the Australian Poetry Library, available online: https://www.poetrylibrary.edu.au/poets/harpur-charles/a-midsummer-noon-in-the-australianforest-0003026 (accessed 22 June 2019).
11 For a more detailed reading of this poem through the lens of Böhme's ecological aesthetics, see Rigby (2011: 147–49).
12 R. Booth, 'England's national parks out of reach for poorer people – study', *The Guardian*, 4 February 2019, available online: https://www.theguardian.com/environment/2019/feb/04/england-national-parks-out-of-reach-for-poorer-people-study?CMP=Share_iOSApp_Other (accessed 9 April 2019).
13 Quoted in E. Allison, 'The Kinder Scout trespass: eighty years on', *The Guardian* 17 April 2012, available online: https://www.theguardian.com/society/2012/apr/17/kinder-scout-mass-trespass-anniversary (accessed 9 April 2019).
14 'Access for Everyone', National Trust, available online: https://www.nationaltrust.org.uk/features/access-for-everyone (accessed 9 April 2019).
15 'Birdgirl blog', available online: http://birdgirluk.blogspot.com/2016/10/race-equality-in-nature-conference.html (accessed 9 April 2019).
16 CERES Community Environment Park, available online: https://ceres.org.au (accessed 10 April 2019).

Chapter 3

1   'Vielleicht würde eine ganz neue Epoche der Wissenschaften und Künste beginnen, wenn die Symphilosophie und Sympoesie so allgemein und so innig würde, daß es nichts seltnes mehr wäre, wenn mehrere sich gegenseitig ergänzende Naturen gemeinschaftliche Werke bildeten.' In Birkner's introduction to Schleiermacher (1984: 32).
2   This is my translation, but see also Schlegel (1968) for a translation of the entire work.
3   The following introduction to the field of biosemiotics is excerpted, with some revisions, from Rigby (2015b: 25–27).

4   For an extended discussion of Schlegel, Schelling and Goethe in relation to biosemiotics, see Rigby (2015b).

5   The movement of bee species was not all one way: As John Clare notes in his journal entry for 25 July 1825, the *Stamford Mercury* had reported the importation of a 'hive of Bees natives of new South Wales', which were said to be 'very small & have no Sting but their honey is peculiarly fine' (1983: 251). The following discussion of bees in pastoral literature and in Clare's 'Wild Bees' is excerpted with revisions from Rigby (2019a: 286–291).

6   Following Bate's landmark restatement of the importance of Clare as a poet whose work disclosed the inter-structuration of environmental degradation and social injustice in *Romantic Ecology* (1991), Clare has received considerable ecocritical attention. In addition to those cited below, see e.g. Mabey (1995); Coletta (1999); McKusick (2000); and Bate (2003). On the 'poetics of kin-making' (including between humans and bees) in the work of more recent writers and artists, see Farrier (2019: 89–123). On Clare and (more-than-human) kinship, see Mason 2015; and on Clare and decolonized pastoral, see Bristow (2018). See also Simon Kövesi's sympathetically critical engagement with ecocritical readings of Clare in *John Clare: Nature, History and Criticism* (2017).

7   Unless otherwise indicated, all quotes from Clare's verse are taken from Clare (1984).

8   In his natural history writings, Clare returns to the question of how bees find their way home, noting in his journal in August 1828 that 'while reaping I made discover respecting the knowledge of Bees in find their homes & I find they do it by marking objects that are near it'. This discovery came about incidentally, as he had observed that the bumble bees nesting in the ground in the field were unable to find their home after he had harvested around it 'but made fruitless sallies round the place by scores until at last they dropt in an exhausted state among the wheat' (1983: 305).

9   I am indebted to John Goodridge for drawing my attention to this line, whilst the reading of it that I have hazarded here is my own. On Clare's experience of rural life and (more-than-human) community during the period of enclosure, see Goodridge (2012).

10 Although he does not discuss Oswald, Mark Lussier's *Romantic Dharma* (2011) is an invaluable study of the Romantic-era reception of Buddhism in Germany and Britain, which also traces resonances between Buddhism and the writing of several English Romantic poets, including Keats, Shelley and, especially, Blake.

11 On 'complex' pastoral, see Marx (1964). Buell's landmark ecocritical study of Thoreauvian pastoral (1995) has been followed by numerous other ecocritical studies of his writing from different angles, including Newman's Marxist approach (2006) and Walls' Latourian rereading (2011). See also Bennett (2002).

12 The US rap artist Kendrick Lamar has recently paid tribute to Parks. See N. Sayej, 'The story behind Kendrick Lamar's Gordon Parks Exhibition', *The Guardian*, 13 December 2017, available online: https://www.theguardian.com/music/2017/dec/13/the-story-behind-kendrick-lamars-gordon-parks-exhibition (accessed 5 September 2018).

13 https://www.orkin.com/stinging-pests/bees/carpenter-bee/ (accessed 5 September 2018).
14 Kyle's reference to 'the least of these' refers to the passage in Mt. 25.45, where Jesus instructs his disciples that in failing to care for 'the least' of those who are hungry, thirsty, naked, sick or imprisoned, they fail also to do so for him. Her recruitment of this biblical passage in the context of conservation is indicative of the way in which some Christians now understand the ethic of neighbour-love to extend beyond the human. More on that in the following chapter.

Chapter 4

1 Mary Shelley's apocalyptic novel *The Last Man* (1826) nonetheless contains within its narrative frame a text based on fragments of prophetic verse, said to have been found in the cave of the Sumaean Sybil in the Bay of Naples. On *The Last Man* as a prophetic work of 'ecological enlightenment', see Rigby (2015a: 66–81).
2 On the Ploutocene, see the Introduction to this book: 11–12.
3 English translation in Beiser (1996: 1–5).
4 Jonathan Roberts reads this 'out-of-body' experience in relation to mystical writing and contrasts Blake's framing of it with the description of similar experiences afforded by narcotics (2010: 49–66).
5 Here, Blake's vision might be seen as running counter to the long history of Christian *tehomophobia*, as feminist ecotheologian Catherine Keller (2003: 26–31) has termed that persistent fear and loathing of the watery abyss as a figure of chaos, which emerges, e.g., in John of Patmos' anticipation of the redeemed earth as one in which the seas are no more (Rev. 21.1).
6 Much has been written on Blake, religion and the prophetic tradition, including Altizer (1967), Erdman (1977), Tannenbaum (1982) and, specifically on Blake's reception of Jewish Kabbalistic mysticism, Spector (2001a and 2001b). My own understanding of Blake's complex relationship with the non-conformist Christianity of his day is informed by Hutchings' landmark ecocritical re-evaluation (2002: 37–75). Other early ecocritical rereadings of Blake can be found in McKusick (2000), Lussier (2000) and Oerlemans (2002).
7 In her unpublished PhD thesis, Valerie Billingham (2010) explores the trope of the mourning/drying earth/land through a postcolonial ecohermeneutic lens. See also Morgan (2013: 113–17).
8 These and other climatic influences are summarized on the Australian Bureau of Meteorology website (http://www.bom.gov.au/climate/about/?bookmark=iod, accessed 15 February 2019).
9 See also Huggan and Tiffin (2015: 103–11) for a more generous postcolonial ecocritical assessment of Wright.

10 One of the earliest ecocritical discussions of Wright is Zeller (2000). The 2006 special issue of the journal *Colloquy*, featuring articles based on papers presented at the inaugural conference of the Association for the Study of Literature and Environment (Australia-New Zealand), contains four that discuss Wright (Brady 2006; Kohn 2006; Harrison 2006; and Sharp 2006). The following year, the journal of arts and activism *Local/Global: Identity, Security, Community* published a special issue on Wright (Mulligan and Nadarajah 2007). Wright also features in Mulligan's and Hill's study of Australian 'ecological pioneers' (2001). Recognition of the importance of Wright's legacy continues to grow. In 2015, for example, the University of New England in Armidale (located near the Wright family property) inaugurated an annual Judith Wright lecture. The first was given by Fiona Capp, author of a work of narrative criticism that traces a journey through the landscapes important to Wright (2010). See also Gifford (2010) on Wright and climate change and Mead (2008: 268–339) for an excellent discussion of the ecopolitical reception of Wright beyond the literary field.

11 See also Rigby (2004a) for a rather different rendering of (post-)Heideggerian ecopoetics.

12 See also Rigby (2004b and 2004a: 119–27).

13 *2009 Victorian Bushfires Royal Commission Report*, 2010, http://www.royalcommission.vic.gov.au/Commission-Reports/Final-Report (accessed 16 March 2013). The following two paragraphs are excerpted, with some revisions, from Rigby (2015a: 11–13).

14 F. Mathews, 'Fires the deadly reality of climate change', *The Age*, February 10, 2009, http://www.theage.com.au/opinion/fires-the-deadly-inevitability-of-climate-change-20090209-8289.html#ixzz2NZQ6NvfF (accessed 16 March 2013).

15 M. Devine, 'Green ideas must take blame for deaths', *Sydney Morning Herald*, 12 February 2009, http://www.smh.com.au/environment/green-ideas-must-take-blame-for-deaths-20090211-84mk.html (accessed 16 March 2013).

16 L. Murdoch and B. Doherty, 'Marysville's survivors ready to start journey home', *Sydney Morning Herald*, 14 February 2009, http://www.smh.com.au/national/marysvilles-survivors-ready-to-start-journey-home-20090213-8774.html (accessed 16 March 2013).

17 Hansen refers here Pyne (1991, 42–46).

18 The following discussion of 'Lamentations' is excerpted, with some revisions from Rigby (2016b: 220–22).

19 Personal email from the author, 14 May 2014. Extracts from Jordie Albiston's poem 'Lamentations' are reprinted here with the kind permission of the author.

20 The Catholic Climate Coalition is also revitalizing the prophetic tradition, e.g., in the liturgical materials that they provide for the penultimate Sunday after epiphany on 'speaking with a prophetic voice' (https://catholicclimatemovement.

global/readings-for-this-sunday-on-speaking-with-a-prophetic-voice/, accessed 19 February 2019).

21 Edmund Rice Centre – Our Purpose https://www.erc.org.au/our_purpose (accessed 16 February 2019).

22 Pacific Calling Partnership https://www.erc.org.au/what_the_pcp_does (accessed 2 February 2019). Among the young activists who have benefited from this programme are some that I interviewed in Kiribati over Easter, 2015, about the place of religion in their views on climate change, as part of the UK-based project, 'Troubled Waters, Stormy Futures: Heritage in Times of Accelerated Climate Change'. One was the young Seventh Day Adventist, Tinaai Teaua, who joined the PCP delegation at the COP 21 Climate Change Conference in Paris in December that year.

23 The creation of GreenFaith Australia was supported by the action research project on the 'interfaith ecology movement' undertaken by Elyse Rider (2011) as part of her doctoral studies at Monash University.

24 Australian Religious Response to Climate Change – Jewish Prayers https://www.arrcc.org.au/reflect-prayers-jewish (accessed 16 February 2019). Reprinted with kind permission from the author, Jonathan Keren Black, with thanks also for his explanation of how this text exemplifies the practice of midrash.

25 With the re-election in 2019 of the pro-mining government of Prime Minister Scott Morrison, followed by the Queensland's government's decision to approve Adani's planned mega-mine in the Galilee Basin, that hope is wearing thin in Australia. Nonetheless, in June of that year, 150 religious leaders associated with ARRCC-GreenFaith sent an open letter to the newly re-elected government of Scott Morrison affirming, 'Despite the differences in our faith, we all regard addressing the climate emergency as our shared moral challenge. We stand together for our common home, the Earth' and urging the government to stop the Adani coal mine, commit to no new coal or gas projects in Australia, and to generate 100 per cent renewable energy by 2030. Available online: https://www.arrcc.org.au/no_faith_in_coal?utm_campaign=no_faith_in_coal&utm_medium=email&utm_source=arrcc (accessed 25 June 2019).

Chapter 5

1 See, however, Jeanine Leane's critical observation on the way that this novel has been taken up into the school curriculum: 'The fact that Kate Grenville's *The Secret River* (2005), a rewriting of colonial history by a settler author, has been the most taught text in Australian secondary schools since 2009 speaks loudly to the persistent use of settler literature as a tool of cognitive imperialism. It allows

for the cultural transmission of settler narratives and values, and in doing so overwrites Aboriginal history and experience' (2016: no p.).
2. Available online: https://www.poetrylibrary.edu.au/poets/harpur-charles/the-creek-of-the-four-graves-0003005# (accessed 28 June 2019).
3. See also the discussion of this passage in Lynch (2015: 146).
4. Judy Campbell had particular expertise in colonial histories of disease. See e.g. Campbell (1998).
5. See e.g. Kinsella (2007a, 2007b and 2017). Kinsella is discussed through a decolonial ecocritical lens in Bristow (2015: 90–146).
6. Campbell's verse is also openly accessible from the Australian Poetry Library. https://www.poetrylibrary.edu.au/poets/campbell-david (accessed 24 August 2019).
7. *Cocky's Joy* (2015), a poetry collection by contemporary Australian ecopoet and critic Michael Farrell, who, like Campbell, grew up in rural New South Wales, could be seen as constituting a humorous counterpart to Campbell's 'Cocky's Calendar'. Farrell writes highly of Campbell in an article on the 'affective labour' performed by animal figures in Australian poetry (2017: 9–10). The following discussion of 'Cocky's Calendar' and 'Works and Days' is excerpted, with revisions, from Rigby (2007: 164–67).
8. In an earlier interview with Kevin Hart, Campbell says, 'I have come to feel that there is a mind at work there which is in the atom itself' (Hart 1975: 6).
9. Australian Government, Australian Heritage Database http://www.environment.gov.au/heritage/places/national/ku-ring-gai-chase (accessed 9 March 2019).
10. Ibid.
11. CSIRO, Ray Norris, Sydney Aboriginal Rock Engravings http://www.atnf.csiro.au/people/Ray.Norris/SydneyRockArt/index.html (accessed 19 April 2019).
12. Cooke refers here to an excerpt from Aboriginal author Sam Watson's novel *The Kadaitcha Song* (in Heiss and Minter 2008, 132).
13. Some of Campbell's poems were also included in Peter Stanbury and John Clegg's *Field Guide to Aboriginal Rock Engravings* (1996). Campbell also engaged with visual art in much of his other poetry, including the series of 'Looby songs', written to accompany Keith Looby's drawings of 'The History of Australia' ([1975] 1989: 228–31).
14. In his interview with Hart, Campbell also likens the form of the rock-engraving poems to a European tradition: namely the Welsh Englyn (Hart 1975: 7).
15. 'Meat Ant', Australian Museum, https://australianmuseum.net.au/learn/animals/insects/meat-ant/, updated 8/3/2019 (accessed 22 March 2019).
16. Frances Bodkin, 'The Hidden Truth', ABC Message Stick, Sunday 15 August 2010, http://www.abc.net.au/tv/messagestick/stories/s2983831.htm (accessed 22 March 2019).
17. Ibid.

18 E.g. an illustrated version of the poem intended for children was published in London in 1977 (Macauley 1977). I am grateful to Richard Kerridge for alerting me to this work and its reception.
19 'Our Vision', Aboriginal Catholic Mission Victoria, https://www.cam.org.au/acmv/Home/Vision (accessed 25 March 2019).
20 Elvey, 'Launch of Jeanine Leane's Walk Back Over and Anne Elvey's White on White', blog entry from 1 February 2018, on 'Leaf Litter' https://anneelvey.wordpress.com/2018/02/01/launch-of-jeanine-leanes-walk-back-over-and-anne-elveys-white-on-white/ (accessed 25 March 2019).
21 Ibid.
22 See also Bruce Pascoe (2018) on Aboriginal agriculture.
23 Many thanks to Libby Robin for pointing this out.
24 Munda Biddi Cycle Trail, Kalamunda http://www.kalamunda.wa.gov.au/Leisure-Tourism/Tourism/Munda-Biddi-Trail (accessed 25 March 2019).
25 Aboriginal Catholic Mission, Our Statement https://www.cam.org.au/acmv/Home/Our-Statement (accessed 25 March 2019).
26 Jeanine Leane blog post, 6 May 2013, 'Read Watch Play' https://readwatchplay.wordpress.com/2013/05/06/jeanine-leane-wiradjuri-writer/ (accessed 28 March 2019).
27 See interview with Leane in Brewster 2015 (chapter 3).
28 'Native Title', Australian Trade and Investment Commission, https://www.austrade.gov.au/land-tenure/Native-title/native-title (accessed 28 March 2019).
29 In 2004, the then Labor government of Victoria announced a cooperative agreement with the Yorta Yorta that included recognition of their claim on public land, rivers and lakes in north-central Victoria. 'Native Title and the Yorta Yorta' State Library of Victoria. http://ergo.slv.vic.gov.au/explore-history/fight-rights/indigenous-rights/native-title-yorta-yorta (accessed 28 March 2019).
30 Elsewhere, representatives of the Warrabinga-Wiradjuri people have nonetheless lodged claims to two areas around Orange and Bylong in central and northern NSW. These applications from 2016 and 2017, respectively, can be found on the website of the Native Title Tribunal: http://www.nntt.gov.au/searchRegApps/NativeTitleClaims/Pages/details.aspx?NTDA_Fileno=NC2016/002 and http://www.nntt.gov.au/SearchRegApps/NativeTitleRegisters/Pages/RNTC_details.aspx?NNTT_Fileno=NC2017/004 (accessed 28 March 2019).
31 'Country Needs People' https://www.countryneedspeople.org.au/ (accessed 29 March 2019).
32 'Women on Country Mixdown', Australian Poetry, https://soundcloud.com/australian_poetry/women-on-country-mixdown (accessed 29 January 2019).
33 Red Room Poetry, http://disappearing.com.au/blog/regional-nsw-commissions/ (accessed 29 March 2019).

34 'Courage in anyone's language: The extraordinary bravery of Yarri and Jacky Jacky', Our Mob http://ourmob.org.au/honouring-the-courageous-lives-of-yarri-and-jacky-jacky/ (accessed 29 March 2019).

35 Evelyn Araluen, 'Guarded by Birds/Judith Wright Poetry Prize, first place', *Overland* 230 (Autumn 2018) https://overland.org.au/previous-issues/issue-230/poetry-prize-evelyn-arlauen/ (accessed 29 March 2019).

36 'Stop Adani Destroying Our Land and Culture', Wangan and Jagalingou Family Council, https://wanganjagalingou.com.au/our-fight/ (accessed 29 March 2019).

Postscirpt

1 See the biographical note for Anastasi on the CCCRH website, available online: https://www.monash.edu/mcccrh/people/amanda-anastasi (accessed 8 August 2019). The CCCRH also has links to Andrew Milner's and James Burgmann's project on climate change fiction (cli fi), available online: https://www.monash.edu/mcccrh/projects/climate-fiction (accessed 8 August 2019).

2 Available online: https://drive.google.com/file/d/1pAJxc_hlNQQM_N-alXnMsdruFKUV6Buv/view (accessed 8 August 2019). See also Illingworth *et al.* (2018).

3 See the project website, available online: https://romanticcatastrophe.leeds.ac.uk/public-engagement/ (accessed 8 August 2019).

4 Kathy Jetñil Kijiner blog, 24/9/2014, UN Climate Summit Opening Ceremony, A Poem to My Daughter, available online: https://www.kathyjetnilkijiner.com/united-nations-climate-summit-opening-ceremony-my-poem-to-my-daughter/ (accessed 20 April 2019).

5 UN Statement and poem by Kathy Jetñil Kijiner – Climate Summit 2014 Opening Ceremony, https://www.youtube.com/watch?v=mc_IgE7TBSY (accessed 20 April 2019).

6 UN Climate Conference, 'Fighting Climate Change with Poems: Kathy Jetñil Kijiner', https://www.youtube.com/watch?v=65nhhzhZ_x8 (accessed 20 April 2019).

Works Cited

Acampora, R. (2006), *Corporal Compassion: Animal Ethics and Philosophy of the Body*, Pittsburgh: Pittsburgh University Press.

Adams, W. M. and M. Mulligan (eds) (2003), *Decolonizing Nature: Strategies for Conservation in a Postcolonial Era*, London: Earthscan.

Adorno, T. (1997), *Aesthetic Theory*, trans. and ed. Robert Hullot-Kentor, London: Athlone Press.

Adorno, T. and M. Horkheimer ([1944] 1979), *Dialectic of Environment*, trans. J. Cumming, London: Verso.

Aizura, A. Z., T. Cotton, Carsten/Balzer/La Gata, M. Ochoa, and S. Vidal-Ortiz (eds) (2014), 'Decolonizing the Transgender Imaginary', special issue of *Transgender Studies Quarterly*, 1 (3).

Alaimo, S. (2010), *Bodily Natures: Science, the Environment and the Material Self*, Bloomington: Indiana University Press.

Albiston, J. (2011), 'Kinglake Undone', *Eureka Street* 21 June: n.p., available online: https://www.eurekastreet.com.au/article.aspx?aeid=26864 (accessed February 16, 2019).

Albiston, J. (2013), *XIII Poems*, Melbourne: Rabbit Poets Series.

Albrecht, G. A. (2015), 'Exiting the Anthropocene and entering the Symbiocene', *G. A. Albrecht's Psychoterratica blog*, available online: https://glennaalbrecht.com/2015/12/17/exiting-the-anthropocene-and-entering-the-symbiocene/ (accessed 23 April 2019).

Altizer, T. J. J. (1967), *The New Apocalypse: The Radical Christian Vision of William Blake*, East Lansing: Michigan State University Press.

Anderson, J. (1995), *The Forest Set Out Like the Night*, Melbourne: Black Pepper.

Anderson, J. (2000), *The Forest Set Out Like the Night*, Extract, *PAN (Philosophy Activism Nature)* 1: 16–22.

Araluen, E. (2017a), 'Resisting the Institution', *Overland* 227: no pp., available online: https://overland.org.au/previous-issues/issue-227/feature-evelyn-araluen/ (accessed 24 August 2019).

Araluen, E. (2017b), 'Shame and Contemporary Australian Poetics', *Rabbit: A Journal for Nonfiction Poetry*, 21 (Indigenous special issue): 117–27.

Arènes, A., B. Latour, and J. Giallardet (2018), 'Giving Depth to the Surface: An Exercise in the Gaia-graphy of Critical Zones', *The Anthropocene Review*, 5 (2): 120–35.

Aquinas, T. ([1274] 1917), *Summa Theologica. First Part*, trans. Fathers of the English Dominican Province, Chicago: Benzinger Brothers, available online https://en.wikisource.org/wiki/Summa_Theologiae/First_Part (accessed 4 April 2019).

Balfour, I. (2002), *The Rhetoric of Romantic Prophecy*, Stanford: Stanford University Press.

Barad, K. (2007), *Meeting the Universe Half Way: Quantum Physics and the Entanglement of Matter and Meaning*, Durham: Duke.

Bari, S. K. (2012), *Keats and Philosophy: The Life of Sensations*, London: Routledge.

Bartosch, R. (2013), *Environmentality: Ecocriticism and the Event of Postcolonial Fiction*, Amsterdam: Rodopi.

Bate, J. (1991), *Romantic Ecology: Wordsworth and the Environmental Tradition*, London: Routledge.

Bate, J. (1996), 'Living with the Weather', *Studies in Romanticism*, 55 (3): 431–48.

Baumgarten, A. G. (1954), *Reflections on Poetry: Alexander Gottlieb Baumgarten's Meditationes philosophicae de nonnullis ad poema pertinentibus*, trans. Karl Aschenbrenner and William B. Holther, Berkeley and Los Angeles: University of California Press.

Bate, J. (2000), *The Song of the Earth*, Cambridge, MA: Harvard University Press.

Baumgarten, A. G. (2007), *Aesthetica/Ästhetik*, ed. Dagmar Mirbach, 2 vols, Hamburg: Felix Meiner Verlag.

Bate, J. (2003), *John Clare: A Biography*, London: Picador.

Beiser, F. (ed. and trans.) (1996), *Early German Political Writing*, Cambridge: Cambridge University Press.

Bellarsi, F. A. and Rauscher, J. (eds) (2019), *Towards an Ecopoetics of Randomness and Design*, special issue of *Ecozon@* 10.1.

Bennett, J. (2001), *The Enchantment of Modern Life: Attachments, Crossings, and Ethics*, Princeton: Princeton University Press.

Bennett, J. ([1994] 2002), *Thoreau's Nature: Ethics, Politics and the Wild*, new ed., Lanham: Rowman and Littlefield.

Bennett, J. (2012), 'Systems and Things: A Response to Harman and Morton', *New Literary History*, 43 (2): 225–33.

Benso, S. (2000), *The Face of Things: A Different Side of Ethics*, Albany: State University of New York.

Bewell, A. (2017), *Natures in Translation: Romanticism and Colonial Natural History*, Baltimore: Johns Hopkins Press.

Billingham, V. (2010) *The Earth Mourns/Dries Up in Jeremiah 4: 23–28: A Literary Analysis Viewed through the Heuristic Lens of an Ecologically Oriented Symbiotic Relationship*. Unpublished PhD thesis, Melbourne College of Divinity.

Birch, T. (2019), '"There Is No Axe": Identity, Story and a Sombrero', *Meanjin Quarterly* (August 2019), available online: https://meanjin.com.au/essays/there-is-no-axe-identity-story-and-a-sombrero/ (accessed 22 March 2019).

Blake, W. (1988), *The Complete Poetry and Prose* (newly rev ed.), ed. D. V. Erdman, Foreword H. Bloom, New York: Doubleday, available online: http://erdman.blakearchive.org/ (accessed 15 April 2019).

Bloch, E. (1995), *The Principle of Hope*, trans. N. Plaice, S. Plaice and P. Knight. Cambridge: Harvard University Press.

Böhme, G. (1989), *Für eine ökologische Naturästhetik* (Towards an Ecological Aesthetics of Nature), Frankfurt am Main: Suhrkamp.
Böhme, G. (1993), 'Atmosphere as the Fundamental Concept of a New Aesthetics', *Thesis Eleven*, 36: 113–26.
Böhme, G. (1995), *Atmosphäre: Essays zur neuen Ästhetik* (Atmosphere: Essays on the New Aesthetics), Frankfurt am Main: Suhrkamp.
Böhme, G. (2000), 'Acoustic Atmospheres: A Contribution to the Study of Ecological Aesthetics', trans. Norbert Ruebsaat, *Soundscape*, 1 (1): 14–18.
Böhme, G. (2001a), *Ethics in Context: The Art of Dealing with Serious Questions*, trans. E. Jephcott, Cambridge: Polity.
Böhme, G. (2001b), 'Der Raum des Gedichts' ('The Space of the Poem'), in B. Labs-Ehlert (ed.), *Raum für Sprache – Raum für Literatur* (*Space for Language – Space for Literature*), 94–111, Detmold: Literaturbüro Ostwestfalen-Lippe.
Böhme, G. (2001c), *Aisthetik: Vorlesungen über Ästhetik als allgemeine Wahrnehmungslehre*, Munich: Fink.
Böhme, G. (2002), *Die Natur vor uns: Naturphilosophie in pragmatischer Hinsicht* (*Nature before Us: Philosophy of Nature from a Pragmatic Perspective*), Kusterdingen: Die Graue Edition.
Böhme, G. (2003a), *Leibsein als Aufgabe: Leibphilosophie in pragmatischer Hinsicht* (*The Task of Bodily Existence: Philosophy of the Body from a Pragmatic Perspective*), Kusterdingen: Die Graue Edition.
Böhme, G. (2003b), 'The Space of Bodily Presence and Space as a Medium of Representation', in Mikael Hörd, Andreas Lösch and Dirk Verdicchio (eds), *Transforming Spaces. The Topological Turn in Technology Studies*, Darmstadt: Technische Universität Darmstadt, available online: https://pdfs.semanticscholar.org/f5a2/c65023e437eeb398222f601b052ec42875ed.pdf (accessed 11 January 2020).
Böhme, G. (2003c), 'Contribution to the Critique of the Aesthetic Economy', *Thesis Eleven*, 73: 71–82.
Böhme, G. (2005), 'Driven by the Interest in Reasonable Conditions', *Thesis Eleven*, 81: 80–90.
Bonnefoy, Y. (1990), 'Lifting Our Eyes from the Page', *Critical Inquiry*, 16: 794–806.
Bonneuil, C. (2015), 'The Geological Turn: Narratives of the Anthropocene', in C. Hamilton, C. Bonneuil and F. Gemenne (eds), *The Anthropocene and the Global Environmental Crisis: Rethinking Modernity in a New Epoch*, 17–31, Abingdon: Routledge.
Bonyhady, T. (2000), *The Colonial Earth*, Carlton: Melbourne University Press.
Boyce, James (2010), *Van Diemen's Land*, Melbourne: Black Inc.
Bowie, A. (1993), *Schelling and Modern European Philosophy*, London: Routledge.
Bradley, J., with Yanyuwa families (2010), *Singing Saltwater Country. Journey to the Songlines of Carpentaria*, Crows Nest: Allen & Unwin.
Brady, V. (1998), *South of My Days. A Biography of Judith Wright*, Sydney: HarperCollins.

Brady, V. (2006), 'How to Reinvent the World: The Hope of Being True to the Earth', *Colloquy*, 12: 103–13.

Bresnihan, P. (2013), 'John Clare and the Manifold Commons', *Environmental Humanities*, 3: 71–91.

Brett, M. (2009), *Decolonizing God: The Bible in the Tides of Empire*, Sheffield: Sheffield Phoenix.

Brewster, A. (2015), *Giving This Country a Memory: Aboriginal Voices of Contemporary Australia*, New York: Cambria Press.

Brissenden, R. F. (1987), 'Introduction', in H. Hesseltine (ed.), *A Tribute to David Campbell: A Collection of Essays*, 1–6, Kensington: University of NSW Press.

Bristow, T. (2015), *The Anthropocene Lyric: An Affective Geography of Poetry, Person, Place*, Houndmills: Palgrave Macmillan.

Bristow, T. (2018), 'Decolonized Pastoral: Perambulatory Perception and the Locus of Loss', *Nineteenth-Century Contexts*, 41(1): 35–49.

Brown, E. C. (ed.) (2006), *Insect Poetics*, Minneapolis: University of Minnesota Press.

Brueggemann, W. (2001), *The Prophetic Imagination*, 2nd ed., Minneapolis: Fortress Press.

Buber, M. (1957), 'Prophecy, Apocalyptic, and the Historical Hour', in *Pointing the Way. Collected Essays*, trans. Maurice Friedman, 192–208, London: Routledge and Kegan Paul.

Buell, L. (1995), *The Environmental Imagination: Thoreau, Nature Writing, and the Formation of American Culture*, Cambridge, Mass.: Harvard University Press.

Bühler, B. and S. Rieger (2006), *Vom Übertier: Ein Bestiarium des Wissens*. Frankfurt am Main: Suhrkamp.

Burgmann, M. and V. Burgmann (1998), *Green Bans, Red Union: Environmental Activism and the New South Wales Builders Labourers' Federation*, Sydney: University of NSW Press.

Burrus, V. (2019), *Ancient Christian Ecopoetics: Cosmologies, Saints, Things*, Philadelphia: Pennsylvania University Press.

Campbell, D. (1970), *The Branch of Dodona and Other Poems: 1969–1970*, Sydney: Angus and Robertson.

Campbell, D. (1981), 'Autobiographical Sketch', *Poetry Australia*, 80: 5–6.

Campbell, D. (1989), *Collected Poems*, ed. Leonie Cramer, Sydney: HarperCollins.

Campbell, D. (2006), *Hardening of the Light: Selected Poems*, ed. and intro. P. Mead, Canberra, Ginninderra Press.

Campbell, J. (1998), *Invisible Invaders: Smallpox and Other Diseases in Aboriginal Australia 1780–1880*, Carlton: Melbourne University Press.

Capp, F. (2010), *My Blood's Country*, Sydney: Allen and Unwin.

Carter, P. (1996), *The Lie of the Land*, London: Faber and Faber.

Casey, M. (2009), 'Disturbing Performances of Race and Nation', *International Journal of Critical Indigenous Studies*, 2 (2): 25–35.

Castell, J. (2015), 'Wordsworth and "The Life of Things"', in R. Gravil and D. Robinson (eds), *The Oxford Handbook of William Wordsworth*, 733–46, Oxford: Oxford University Press.

Castree, N. et al. (2014), 'Changing the Intellectual Climate', *Nature Climate Change*, 4: 763–68.
Chandler, T. (2011), 'Reading Atmospheres: The Ecocritical Potential of Gernot Böhme's Aesthetic Theory of Nature', *Interdisciplinary Studies in Literature and Environment*, 18 (3): 553–68.
Christie, D. E. (2013), *The Blue Sapphire of the Mind: Notes for a Contemplative Ecology*, Oxford: Oxford University Press.
Clare, J. (1983), *The Natural History Prose Writings of John Clare*, ed. M. Grainger, Oxford: Clarendon Press.
Clare, J. (1984), *John Clare: A Critical Edition of the Major Works*, ed. E. Robinson and D. Powell, Oxford: Oxford University Press.
Clark, T. (2015), *Ecocriticism on the Edge: The Anthropocene as a Threshold Concept*, London: Bloomsbury Academic.
Clark, T. (2019), *The Value of Ecocriticism*, Cambridge: Cambridge University Press.
Coleman, D. and P. Otto (1992), *Essays on English and Australian Romanticisms*, London: Locust Hill Press.
Coleridge, S. T. ([1912] 2009), *The Complete Poetical Works of Samuel Taylor Coleridge*, 2 vols, ed. E. H. Coleridge, Oxford: Clarendon, Project Gutenberg, available online: http://www.gutenberg.org/files/29090/29090-h/29090-h.htm (accessed 22 April 2019).
Coletta, J. (1999), 'Literary Biosemiotics and the Postmodern Ecology of John Clare', *Semiotica: Journal of the International Association for Semiotic Studies/Revue de l'Association Internationale de Sémiotique*, 127 (1–4): 239–71.
Coogan, M. D. (ed.) (2007), *The New Oxford Annotated Bible*, Augmented 3rd ed., Oxford: Oxford University Press.
Cooke, S. (2013), *Speaking the Earth's Languages: A Theory for Australian-Chilean Postcolonial Poetics*, Amsterdam: Rodopi.
Cooper, D. E. (2017), 'Meditation on the Move: Walking, Nature, Mystery', in Peter Cheyne (ed.), *Coleridge and Contemplation*, 35–46, Oxford: Oxford University Press.
Coralie, J. (2011), *Resonance, Reconnection, Reparation: Judith Wright's Radical 'Green' Writing Project*, unpublished PhD dissertation, Monash University.
Cronon, W. (1996), 'The Trouble with Wilderness; or, Getting Back to the Wrong Nature', in W. Cronon (ed.), *Uncommon Ground: Rethinking the Human Place in Nature*, 69–90, New York: W. W. Norton.
Crouter, R. (1988), 'Introduction', in Friedrich Schleiermacher and R. Crouter (ed.), *On Religion. Speeches to Its Cultured Despisers*, 1–73, Cambridge: Cambridge University Press.
Crutzen, P. J. and E. F. Stoermer ([2000] 2013), 'The "Anthropocene"', in L. Robin, S. Sörlin and P. Warde (eds), *The Future of Nature: Documents of Global Change*, 483–85, New Haven: Yale University Press.
Cudworth, E. (2005), *Developing Ecofeminist Theory: The Complexity of Difference*, Houndmills: Palgrave MacMillan.
Davies, J. (2018), 'Romantic Ecocriticism: History and Prospects', *Literature Compass*, 15 (9): 1–15.

Davis, H. and Z. Todd (2017), 'On the Importance of a Date, or Decolonizing the Anthropocene', *ACME: An International Journal for Critical Geographies*, 16 (4): 761–80.

De Groot, R. (1987), 'The Man from Monaro', in H. Hesseltine (ed.), *A Tribute to David Campbell: A Collection of Essays*, 21–27, Kensington: University of NSW Press.

DeLoughrey, E. and G. B. Handley (2011), *Postcolonial Ecologies: Literatures of the Environment*, Oxford: Oxford University Press.

Derrida, J. (1992), *Given Time: I, Counterfeit Money*, trans. P. Kamuf, Chicago: Chicago University Press.

Doran, P. (2017), *A Political Economy of Attention, Mindfulness and Consumerism: Reclaiming the Mindful Commons*, New York: Routledge Studies in Sustainability.

Dungy, C. T. (ed.) (2009), *Black Nature: Four Centuries of African American Nature Poetry*, Athens, GE.: University of Georgia Press.

Dunkerley, H. (2008), 'Poetry and Unknowing', unpublished.

Durack, M. (1986), *Kings in Grass Castles*, Sydney: Corgi Books, Transworld Publishers.

Dushane, Allison (2016), 'Reverie and the Life of Things: Rousseau, Darwin, and Romantic Visionary Materialism', in L. Ottum and S. Reno (eds), *Wordsworth and the Green Romantics*, 127–45, Durham: University of New Hampshire Press.

Eagleton, T. (1990), *The Ideology of the Aesthetic*, Oxford: Blackwell.

Eagleton, T. (2004), *After Theory*, London: Penguin.

Easterlin, N. (1996), *Wordsworth and the Question of 'Romantic Religion'*, Lewisberg, PA: Bucknell University Press.

Economides, L. (2016), *The Ecology of Wonder in Romantic and Postmodern Literature*, New York: Palgrave Macmillan.

Edwards, D. (2006), *Ecology at the Heart of Faith*, New York: Orbis.

Elvey, A. (2010), *Claimed by Country*, Berry NSW: PressPress.

Elvey, A. (2014), *Kin*, Parkville: Five Islands Press.

Elvey, A. (2018), *White on White*, Carlton South: Cordite Books.

Erdman, D. V. (1977), *Blake: Prophet against Empire*, 3rd ed., Mineola: Dover.

Farrell, M. (2015), *Cocky's Joy*, Sydney: Giramondo.

Farrell, M. (2015), *Writing Australian Unsettlement: Modes of Poetic Invention 1796–1945*, New York: Palgrave MacMillan.

Farrell, M. (2017), '"Deep Hanging Out": Native Species Images and Affective Labour', *Journal of the Association for the Study of Australian Literature*, 17 (1): 1–12, available online: https://openjournals.library.sydney.edu.au/index.php/JASAL/article/view/11802/11487 (accessed 19 April 2019).

Farrier, D. (2019), *Anthropocene Poetics: Deep Time, Sacrifice Zones, and Extinction*, Minneapolis: University of Minnesota Press.

Favareau, D. (2009), 'Introduction: An Evolutionary History of Biosemiotics', in D. Favareau (ed.), *Essential Readings in Biosemiotics: Anthology and Commentary*, 1–77, Dordrecht: Springer.

Fay, J. (2018), *Wordsworth's Monastic Inheritance: Poetry, Place, and the Sense of Community*, Oxford: Oxford University Press.

Fijn, N. (2014), 'Sugarbag Dreaming: The Significance of Bees to Yolgnu in Arnhem Land, Australia', *Humanimalia*, 6 (1): 41–61.

Fletcher, A. (2004), *A New Theory for American Poetry: Democracy, the Environment and the Future of Imagination*, Cambridge, MA: Harvard University Press.

Ford, T. H. (2018), *Wordsworth and the Poetics of Air: Atmospheric Romanticism in a Time of Climate Change*, Cambridge: Cambridge University Press.

Fulford, T. (2006), *Romantic Indians: Native Americans, British Literature, and Transatlantic Culture 1756–1830*, Oxford: Oxford University Press.

Gaard, G. (2016), 'Mindful New Materialisms: Buddhist Roots for Material Ecocriticism's Flourishing', in S. Iovino and S. Oppermann (eds), *Material Ecocriticism*, 291–300, Bloomington: Indiana University Press.

Gammage, B. (2012), *The Biggest Estate on Earth: How Aborigines Made Australia*, Sydney: Allen & Unwin.

Gare, A. (2017), *The Philosophical Foundations of Ecological Civilization: A Manifesto for the Future*, London: Routledge.

Gifford, T. (2016), 'Five Modes of "Listening Deeply" to pastoral Sounds', *Green Letters: Studies in Ecocriticism*, 20 (1): 8–19.

Gifford, T. (2010), 'Climate Change and Judith Wright's Post-Pastoral Poetry', *Australian Humanities Review*, 48: n.p.

Gifford, T. (2014), 'Pastoral, Anti-Pastoral, and Post-Pastoral', in L. Westling (ed.), *Companion to Literature and the Environment*, 17–30, Cambridge: Cambridge University Press.

Giorgino, V. M. B. and Z. D. Walsh (eds) (2018), *Co-Designing the Economies in Transition: Radical Approaches in Dialogue with Contemplative Social Sciences*, London: Palgrave Macmillan.

Goethe, J. W. (1988), *Scientific Studies*, trans. and ed. Douglas Miller, New Jersey: Princeton University Press.

Goethe, J. W. (2013), *Naturwissenschaftliche Schriften I*, in D. Kuhn (ed.), *Werke*, vol. 13, Hamburg: Christian Wegner.

Goethe, J. W. (2014), *Naturwissenschaftliche Schriften II*, in R. Wankmüller (ed.), *Werke*, vol. 14, Hamburg: Christian Wegner.

Goodridge, J. (2012), *Clare and Community*, Cambridge: Cambridge University Press.

Gould, J. L. (2002), 'Can Honeybees Create Cognitive Maps?' in M. Bekoff, C. Allen and G. M. Burghardt (eds), *The Cognitive Animal: Empirical and Theoretical Perspectives on Animal Cognition*, 41–46, Cambridge, MA: MIT Press.

Goulson, D. (2013), *A Sting in the Tale*. London: Vintage.

Graham, M. (2008), 'Some Thoughts about the Philosophical Underpinnings of Aboriginal Worldviews', *Australian Humanities Review*, 45: no pp.

Gregersen, N. H. (2001), 'The Cross of Christ in an Evolutionary World', *Dialog: A Journal of Theology*, 40: 192–207.

Grenville, K. (2005), *The Secret River*, Melbourne: Text.

Grieves, V. (2009), *Aboriginal Spirituality: Aboriginal Philosophy, the Basis of Aboriginal Social and Emotional Wellbeing*, Casuarina, NT: Cooperative Research Centre for Aboriginal Health.

Griffiths, T. (1997), 'Ecology and Empire: Towards an Australian History of the World', in T. Griffiths and L. Robin (eds), *Ecology and Empire: Environmental History of Settler Society*, 1–18, Carlton: Melbourne University Press.

Griffiths, T. (2001), *Forests of Ash: An Environmental History*, Cambridge: Cambridge University Press.

Griffiths, T. ([2003] 2007), 'The Humanities and an Environmentally Sustainable Australia', *Australian Humanities Review* 43, available online: http://australianhumanitiesreview.org/2007/03/01/the-humanities-and-an-environmentally-sustainable-australia/#_edn12 (accessed 5 August 2019).

Griffiths, T. (2009), 'Unnatural Disaster? Remembering and Forgetting Bushfire', *History Australia*, 6 (2): 1–7.

Gynther, I., L. Waller and K.-P. Leung (2016), *Confirmation of the extinction of the Bramble Cay melomys* melomys rubicola *on Bramble Cay, Torres Strait: Results and conclusions from a comprehensive survey, August–September 2014*, available online: https://environment.des.qld.gov.au/wildlife/threatened-species/documents/bramble-cay-melomys-survey-report.pdf (accessed 22 April 2019).

Hall, D. W. (2016), 'Introduction', in D. W. Hall (ed.), *Romantic Ecocriticism: Origins and Legacies*, 1–15, Lanham: Lexington Books.

Hall, D. W. (ed.) (2016), *Romantic Ecocriticism: Origins and Legacies*, Lanham: Lexington Books.

Hansen, C. (2018), 'Deep Time and Disaster: Black Saturday and the Forgotten Past', *Environmental Humanities*, 10 (1): 226–40.

Hansen, C. and T. Griffiths (2012), *Living with Fire: People, Nature, and History in Steels Creek*, Collingwood: CSIRO.

Haraway, D. J. (1991), *Simians, Cyborgs, and Women: The Reinvention of Nature*, New York: Routledge.

Haraway, D. J. (2015), 'Anthropocene, Capitalocene, Plantationocene, Chthulucene: Making Kin', *Environmental Humanities*, 6: 159–65.

Haraway, D. J. (2016), *Staying with the Trouble: Making Kin in the Cthulucene*, Durham: Duke University Press.

Harman, G. (2005), *Guerilla Metaphysics: Phenomenology and the Carpentry of Things*, Chicago: Open Court.

Harpur, C. (1883), *Poems*, Melbourne: George Robertson, available online: https://www.poetrylibrary.edu.au/poems-book/poems-0003000 (accessed 28 June 2019).

Harrison, G. (2016), 'Toward a Romantic Poetics of Acknowledgement: Wordsworth, Clare, and Aldo Leopold's "Land Ethic"', in D. W. Hall (ed.), *Romantic Ecocriticism: Origins and Legacies*, 185–2015, Lanham: Lexington Books.

Harrison, M. (2006), 'The Degradation of Land and the Position of Poetry', *Colloquy*, 12: 125–37.
Hart, K. (1975), 'New Directions: An Interview with David Campbell', *Makar*, 11: 4–10.
Hart, K. (1999), *Wicked Heat*, Sydney: Paper Bark.
Hart, K. (2008), *Young Rain: New Poems*, Artarmon: Giramondo.
Hart, K. (2015), *Wild Track: New and Selected Poems*, Notre Dame, IN: University of Notre Dame Press.
Hart, K. (2018), 'Contemplation and Fascination', forthcoming.
Harvey, D. (2015), Review of *Kin* by Anne Elvey, *Mascara Review* 18: n.p., available online: http://mascarareview.com/dimitra-harvey-reviews-kin-by-anne-elvey/ (accessed 26 March 2019).
Hatley, J. (2000), *Suffering Witness: The Quandary of Responsibility after the Irreparable*, Albany: State University of New York Press.
Hayes, K. M (2002), *The Earth Mourns: Prophetic Metaphor and Oral Aesthetic*, Atlanta: Society of Biblical Literature Press.
Hegel, G. W. F. (1984), *Mythologie der Vernunft: Hegels 'ältestes Systemprogramm der deutschen Idealismus*, ed. C. Jamme and H. Schneider, Frankfurt am Main: Suhrkamp.
Heidegger, M. (1971), *Poetry, Language, Thought*, trans. and ed. A. Hofstaedter, New York: Harper & Row.
Heidegger, M. (1978), *Basic Writings*, ed. D. F. Krell, San Francisco: Harper.
Heine, H. ([1826] 1993), 'The Harz Journey', in *Selected Prose*, trans. and ed. Ritchie Richardson, 31–87, London: Penguin.
Heiss, A. and P. Minter (eds) (2008), *Macquarie P E N Anthology of Aboriginal Literature*, Sydney: Allen & Unwin.
Herder, J. G. ([1778] 1987), *Lieder der Liebe: Die ältesten und schönsten aus Morgenlande. Nebst vierundvierzig alten Minneliedern*, Nördlingen: Gremo.
Herder, J. G. (1994), *Theologische Schriften*, ed. Christoph Bultmann und Thomas Zippert (*Werke*, 9.1), Frankfurt am Main: Deutscher Klassiker Verlag.
Hess, S. (2012), *William Wordsworth and the Ecology of Authorship: The Roots of Environmentalism in Nineteenth Century Culture*, Charlottesville: University of Virginia Press.
Heyes, R. (2015), 'John Clare's Natural History', in S. Kövesi and S. McEathron (eds), *New Essays on John Clare*, 169–88, Cambridge: Cambridge University Press.
Heyes, R. (2019), 'John Clare's Natural History', paper presented at British Association for Romanticism Studies Conference, University of Warwick, July 2019.
Higgins, D. (2017), *British Romanticism, Climate Change, and the Anthropocene: Reading Tambora*, London: Palgrave Macmillan.
Hoffmeyer, J. (2008), *Biosemiotics: An Investigation into the Signs of Life and the Life of Signs*, trans. Jesper Hoffmeyer and Donald Favareau, ed. Donald Favareau, Scranton, PA: University of Scranton Press.
Hoorn, J. (2007), *Australian Pastoral: The Making of a White Landscape*, Fremantle: Fremantle Press.

Hope, A. D. (2002), *The Cave and the Spring: Essays on Poetry*, University of Sydney digital edition based on rev. ed., Sydney: Sydney University Press, 1974, available online: http://setis.library.usyd.edu.au/ozlit/pdf/sup0002.pdf (accessed 19 March 2019).

Horn, E. and H. Bergthaller (2020), *The Anthropocene: Key Issues for the Humanities*, London: Routledge.

Hubbell, J. A. (2018), *Byron's Nature: A Romantic Vision of Cultural Ecology*, New York: Palgrave Macmillan.

Huggan, G. (2007), *Australian Literature: Postcolonialism, Racism, Transnationalism*, Oxford: Oxford University Press.

Huggan, G. and H. Tiffin ([2006] 2015), *Postcolonial Ecocriticism: Literature, Animals, Environment*, rev. ed., Abingdon: Routledge.

Hume, A. and G. Osborne (eds) (2018), *Ecopoetics: Essays in the Field*, Iowa City: University of Iowa Press.

Hutchings, K. (2002), *Imagining Nature: Blake's Environmental Poetics*, Montreal: McGill-Queen's University Press.

Hutchings, K. (2009), *Romantic Ecologies and Colonial Cultures in the British Atlantic World, 1770–1850*, Montreal: McGill-Queens University Press.

Illingworth, S. *et al.* (2018), 'Representing the Majority, Not the Minority: The Importance of the Individual in Communicating Climate Change', *Geoscience Communication*, 1: 9–24, available online: https://www.geosci-commun.net/1/9/2018/ (accessed 8 August 2019).

Indyk, I. (1993), 'Pastoral and Priority: The Aboriginal in Australian Poetry', *New Literary History* 24 (4): 837–55.

Ingham, M. B. (2003), *Scotus for Dunces: An Introduction to the Subtle Doctor*, St Bonaventure, New York: The Franciscan Institute, St Bonaventure University.

Ingold, T. (2011), *Being Alive: Essays on Movement, Knowledge and Description*, Abingdon: Routledge.

Iovino, S. and S. Oppermann (eds) (2014), *Material Ecocriticism*, Bloomington: Indiana University Press.

Irvine, D. G. and M. Gorji (2013), 'John Clare in the Anthropocene', *Cambridge Journal of Anthropology*, 31 (1): 119–32.

Jackson, N. (2008), *Science and Sensation in Romantic Poetry*, Cambridge: Cambridge University Press.

Jackson, N. (2018), 'Literature and the Senses', in D. Duff (ed.), *British Romanticism*, 327–40, Oxford: Oxford University Press.

John Paul II (1986), *Address to the Aborigines and Torres Strait Islanders in 'Blatherswaite Park'* (29 November), available online: http://w2.vatican.va/content/john-paul-ii/en/speeches/1986/november/documents/hf_jp-ii_spe_19861129_aborigeni-alice-springs-australia.html (accessed 26 March 2019).

Johnson, S. (1755), *A Dictionary of the English Language:* A Digital Edition of the 1755 Classic by Samuel Johnson, ed. B. Besalke, available online: https://johnsonsdictionaryonline.com/page-view/?i=1588 (last modified, 14 June 2017; accessed 10 January 2019).

Jones, R. (1969), 'Fire-Stick farming', *Australian Natural History*, 16 (7): 224–28.
Kamusikiri, S. (1990), 'Blake and the Tradition of Lamentation', *Blake: An Illustrated Quarterly*, 24 (2): 59–63.
Kane, P. (1996), *Australian Poetry: Romanticism and Negativity*, Cambridge: Cambridge University Press.
Kane, P. (2004), 'Woful Shepherds: Anti-Pastoral in Australian Poetry', in J. Ryan and C. Wallace-Crabbe (eds), *Imagining Australia: Literature and Culture in the New World*, 269–84, Cambridge, MA: Harvard University Press.
Kant, I. ([1790] 1892), *Critique of Judgement*, trans. with intro. and notes, J. H. Barnard, London: Macmillan.
Keats, J. (1934), *The Poetical Works of John Keats*, ed. with intro. and notes, H. B. Forman, London: Oxford University Press.
Keller, C. (2003), *Face of the Deep: A Theology of Becoming*, London: Routledge.
Keller, L. (2017), *Recomposing Ecopoetics: North American Poetry of the Self-Conscious Anthropocene*, Charlottesville: University of Virginia Press.
Kinsella, J. (2007a), *Disclosed Poetics: Beyond Landscape and Lyricism*, Manchester: Manchester University Press.
Kinsella, J. (2007b), 'Is There an Australian Pastoral?', *Georgia Review*, 58 (2): 347–68.
Kinsella, J. (2017), *Polysituatedness: A Poetics of Displacement*, Manchester: Manchester University Press.
Kinsella, J., K. Fagan and P. Minter (eds) (2009), 'Ecopoetics and Pedagogies', special issue of *Angelaki: Journal of the Theoretical Humanities*, 14 (2).
Kirkpatrick, P. (1992), 'Satyrs in the Top Paddock: Metaphysical Pastoral in Australian Poetry', *Australian Literary Studies*, 15 (3): 141–52.
Knickerbocker, S. (2012), *Ecopoetics: The Language of Nature, the Nature of Language*, Minneapolis: University of Massachusetts Press.
Kohn, J. (2006) 'Longing to Belong: Judith Wright's Poetics of Place', *Colloquy*, 12: 114–26.
Kövesi, S. (2017), *John Clare: Nature, History and Criticism*, London: Palgrave Macmillan.
Kövesi, S. and S. McEathron (eds) (2015), *New Essays on John Clare*, Cambridge: Cambridge University Press.
Kroeber, K. (1994) *Ecological Literary Criticism: Romantic Imagining and the Biology of Mind*, New York: Columbia University Press.
Kuhn, D. (1987), 'Goethe's Relationship to the Theories of Development of His Time', in F. Amrine, F. J. Zucker and H. Wheeler (eds), *Goethe and the Sciences: A Reappraisal*, 3–16, Dordrecht: Riedel.
Kull, K. (2001), 'Jakob von Uexküll: An Introduction', *Semiotica*, 134 (1–4): 1–59.
Kyle, V. and L. Kearns (2018), 'The Bitter and the Sweet of Nature: Weaving a Tapestry of Migration Stories', in M. E. Krasny (ed.), *Grassroots to Global: Broader Impacts of Civic Ecology*, 51–64, Ithaca: Cornell University Press.
Lacoue-Labarthe, P. and J.-L. Nancy (1988), *The Literary Absolute*, trans. with intro. and notes, Philip Bernard and Cheryl Lester, Albany: State University of New York Press.

Lam, V. (2019), 'Justice, Interconnectedness and Reconciliation: Climate Change Messaging of Religious Environmental Organizations in the Trans Mountain Resistance', unpublished conference paper for 'Religion – Water – Climate: Changing Cultures and Landscapes' (International Society for the Study of Religion, Nature and Culture), University College Cork, 16 June 2019.

Lamb, J. (2011), *The Things Things Say*, Princeton: Princeton University Press.

Lansdown, R. (2009), 'Romantic Aftermaths', in P. Pierce (ed.), *The Cambridge History of Australian Literature*, 118–36, Cambridge: Cambridge University Press.

Leane, J. (2010), *Dark Secrets: After Dreaming (A. D.) 1887–1961*, Berry, NSW: PressPress.

Leane, J. (2011), *Purple Threads*, Brisbane: University of Queensland Press.

Leane, J. (2016), 'Other Peoples' Stories', *Overland* 225, available online: https://overland.org.au/previous-issues/issue-225/feature-jeanine-leane/ (accessed 18 April 2019).

Leane, J. (2018), *Walk Back Over*, Melbourne: Cordite Press.

Levinas, A. (1996), *Proper Names*, trans. M. Smith, London: Athlone Press.

Levinson, M. (2007), 'A Motion and a Spirit: Romancing Spinoza', *Studies in Romanticism*, 46 (4): 367–408.

Lilburn, T. (1999), *Living in the World as if It Were Home*, Dunvegan, ON: Cormorant.

Lilburn, T. (2007), *Desire Never Leaves: The Poetry of Tim Lilburn*, ed. and intro. Alison Calder, Waterloo: Wilfred Laurier University Press.

Lilburn, T. (2016), *The Names*, Toronto: McClelland and Stewart.

Lilburn, T. (2017), *The Larger Conversation: Contemplation and Place*, Edmonton: University of Alberta Press.

Lussier, M. S. (2000), *Romantic Dynamics: The Poetics of Physicality*, Basingstoke: Macmillan.

Lussier, M. S. (2011), *Romantic Dharma: The Emergence of Buddhism into Nineteenth-Century Europe*, New York: Palgrave Macmillan.

Lynch, T. (2015), 'Ecopastoralism: Settler Colonial Pastoral Imaginary in the US West and Australian Outback', in J. Seaboyer, R. Blair and V. Bladen (eds), *Afterlives of Pastoral*, special issue of *Australian Literary Studies* 30 (2): 144–57.

Mabey, R. (ed.) (1995), *Clare and Ecology*, special issue of *John Clare Society Journal*, 14.

Macauley, T. B. (1977), *Horatius*, illustrated by N. Garland, London: Duckworth.

Malm, A. (2016), *Fossil Capital: The Rise of Steam Power and the Roots of Global Warming*, London: Verso.

Martin, M. and T. Griffiths (1999), *Watersheds: The Paroo to the Warrego*, Mandurama, NSW: Mandy Martin.

Marx, L. (1964), *Technology and the Pastoral Ideal in America*, New York: Oxford University Press.

Mason, E. (2015), 'Ecology with religion: Kinship in John Clare', in S. Kövesi and S. McEathron (eds), *New Essays on John Clare*, 97–117, Cambridge: Cambridge University Press.

Mathews, F. (1994), '*Terra Incognita*: Carnal Legacies,' in D. Evans Cosgrove and D. Yencken (eds), *Restoring the Land*, 37–64, Carlton: Melbourne University Press, 1994.

Mathews, F. (2000), 'Singing Up the City', *PAN (Philosophy Activism Nature)*: 5–15.

Mathews, F. (2003), *Journey to the Source of the Merri*, Charnwood: Ginninderra Press.

Mathews, F. (2005), *Reinhabiting Reality: Towards a Recovery of Culture*, New York: State University of New York Press.

McCalman, I. (2013), *The Reef: A Passionate History*, Melbourne: Penguin.

McConchie, P. with Cape York Indigenous Leaders and Community Members (2013), *Fire and the Story of Burning Country*, Avalon Beach: Cyclops Press.

McGinnis, K. (2001), *Heart Country*, Ringwood, VIC: Penguin.

McKernan, S. (1989), *A Question of Commitment: Australian Literature in the Twenty Years after the War*, Sydney: Allen and Unwin.

McKusick, J. (2000), *Green Writing: Romanticism and Ecology*, New York: St. Martin's Press.

Mead, P. (2006), 'Introduction', in D. Campbell, *Hardening of the Light: Selected Poems*, ed. P. Mead, Canberra: Ginninderra Press, 7–16.

Mead, P. (2008), *Networked Language: Culture & History in Australian Poetry*, Carlton: Australian Scholarly Publishing.

Merleau-Ponty, M. (1968), *The Visible and the Invisible*, ed. C. Lefort, trans. A. Lingis, Evanston, IL: Northwestern University Press.

Miller-Struttmann, N. (2016), 'The Complex Causes of Worldwide Bee Declines', *phys.org*. Science X Network (12 January 2016), available online: https://phys.org/news/2016-01-complex-worldwide-bee-declines.html (accessed 15 March 2017).

Minter, P. (2013), 'Archipelagos of Sense: Thinking about a Decolonised Australian Poetics', *Southerly*, 73 (1): 155–69.

Minter, P. (2015), 'Kath Walker (Oodgeroo Noonuccal), Judith Wright and Decolonised Transcultural Ecopoetics in Frank Heimans', *Shadow Sister*', *Sydney Studies in English*, 41: 61–74, available online: https://openjournals.library.sydney.edu.au/index.php/SSE/article/view/10048 (accessed 16 April 2019).

Minter, P. (2016), 'Decolonization and Geopoethics', Introduction to Guest Edited special issue of *Plumwood Mountain: An Australian Journal of Ecopoetry and Ecopoetics* 3.2: no pp., available online: https://plumwoodmountain.com/decolonization-and-geopoethics/ (accessed 25 March 2019).

Moore, J. W. (2015), *Capitalism in the Web of Life: Ecology and the Accumulation of Capital*, London: Verso.

Mora, C. et al. (2017), 'Global Risk of Deadly Heat', *Nature Climate Change* 7: 501–06.

Moreton-Robinson, E. (2015), *The White Possessive: Property, Power, and Indigenous Sovereignty*, Minneapolis: University of Minnesota Press.

Morgan, J. (2013), *Earth's Cry: Prophetic Ministry in a More-than-Human World*, Preston: Uniting Academic Press.

Morton, T. (1994), *Shelley and the Revolution in Taste: The Body and the Natural World*, Cambridge: Cambridge University Press.

Morton, T. (2007), *Ecology without Nature: Rethinking Environmental Aesthetics*, Cambridge, MA: Harvard University Press.

Morton, T. (2011), 'Coexistence and Coexistents: Ecology without a World', in A. Goodbody and K. Rigby (eds), *Ecocritical Theory: New European Approaches*, 168–80, Charlottesville: University of Virginia Press.

Morton, T. (2012), 'An Object-Oriented Defense of Poetry', *New Literary History*, 43 (2): 205–24.

Muecke, S. (2004), *Ancient and Modern: Time, Culture and Indigenous Philosophy*, Sydney: University of NSW Press.

Muecke, S. (2007), 'Hurricane Katrina and the Rhetoric of Natural Disaster', in E. Potter, A. Mackinnon, S. McKenzie and J. McKay (eds), *Fresh Water. New Perspectives on Water in Australia*, 259–71, Carlton: Melbourne University Press.

Mules, W. (2014), *With Nature: Nature Philosophy as Poetics through Schelling, Heidegger, Benjamin and Nancy*, Bristol: Intellect.

Mulligan, M. and S. Hill (2001), *Ecological Pioneers: A Social History of Australian Ecological Thought and Action*, Cambridge: Cambridge University Press.

Mulligan, M. and Y. Nadarajah (eds) (2007), *Exploring the Legacy of Judith Wright*, special issue of *Local/Global: Identity, Security, Community* 3.

Newman, L. (2005), *Our Common Dwelling: Henry Thoreau, Transcendentalism, and the Class Politics of Nature*, New York: Palgrave MacMillan.

Nichols, A. (2011), *Beyond Romantic Ecocriticism: Towards Urbanatural Roosting*, London: Palgrave Macmillan.

Nisbet, R. (2018), *From Murmuring to Muttering: Anthropocene River Narratives (1798–2009)*, unpublished PhD thesis, University of Lausanne.

Nolan, S. (2017), *Unnatural Ecopoetics: Unlikely Spaces in Contemporary Poetry*, Reno: University of Nevada Press.

Northcott, M. S. (2007), *A Moral Climate: The Ethics of Global Warming*, New York: Orbis Books.

Northcott, M. S. (2013), *A Political Theology of Climate Change*, Cambridge: Wm. B. Eerdmans.

Novalis (1960), *Das philosophische Werk* I, vol. 2 of *Schriften. Die Werke Friedrich von Hardenbergs*, ed. G. Schulz, R. Samuel, H. J. Mähl and D. von Petersdorff, Stuttgart: Kohlhammer.

Novalis (1984), *Das philosophische Werk* II, vol. 3 of *Schriften. Die Werke Friedrich von Hardenbergs*, ed. G. Schulz, R. Samuel, H. J. Mähl and D. von Petersdorff, Stuttgart: Kohlhammer.

Oerlemans, O. (2002), *Romanticism and the Materiality of Nature*, Toronto: University of Toronto Press.

Ollerton, J. (2016), 'Identifying the "Wild Bees" in John Clare's Poem – Updated', *Jeff Ollerton's Biodiversity Blog*, available online: https://jeffollerton.wordpress.com/2016/08/10/identifying-the-wild-bees-in-john-clares-poem/ (accessed 15 March 2017).

Ottum, L. and S. Reno (eds) (2016), *Wordsworth and the Green Romantics*, Durham: University of New Hampshire Press.
Pascoe, B. (2018), *Dark Emu: Aboriginal Australia and the Birth of Agriculture*, London: Scribe.
Perkins, D. (2003), *Romanticism and Animal Rights*, Cambridge: Cambridge University Press.
Persse, J., ed. (2006), *Letters Lifted into Poetry: Selected Correspondence between David Campbell and Douglas Stewart, 1946–1979*, Canberra: National Library of Australia.
Pevsner, N. (ed.) (1968), *Studies in Art, Architecture and Design*, vol. 1, London: Thames and Hudson.
Pick, A. (2011), *Creaturely Poetics: Animality and Vulnerability in Literature and Film*, New York: Columbia University Press.
Plumwood, V. (1993), *Feminism and the Mastery of Nature*, London: Routledge.
Plumwood, V. (2002), *Environmental Culture: The Ecological Crisis of Reason*, London: Routledge.
Ponge, F. (1942), *Le partis pris des choses*, Paris: Gallimard.
Pope Francis (2015), '*Laudato 'si*, Encyclical Letter on Care of Our Common Home', available online: http://w2.vatican.va/content/francesco/en/encyclicals/documents/papa-francesco_20150524_enciclica-laudato-si.html (accessed 16 February 2019).
Potkay, A. (2008), 'Wordsworth and the Ethics of Things', *PMLA*, 123 (2): 390–404.
Preminger, A. and T. V. F. Brogan (eds) (1993), *The New Princeton Encyclopedia of Poetry and Poetics*, Princeton: Princeton University Press.
Preston, C. (2006), *Bee*, London: Reaktion.
Prickett, S. (1996), *Origins of Narrative: The Romantic Appropriation of the Bible*, Cambridge: Cambridge University Press.
Prideaux, F. (2006), 'Beeswax Rock Art and Sugarbag Dreaming: Today's Dreaming, Yesterday's Rock Art', Bachelor of Archeology Honours Thesis, Department of Archeology, Flinders University.
Pyne, S. J. (1991), *Burning Bush: A Fire History of Australia*, New York: Holt.
Pyne, S. J. (1999), 'Consumed by Fire or Fire: A Prologemenon to Anthropogenic Fire', in J. Conway, K. Keniston and L. Marx (eds), *Earth, Air, Fire, Water: Humanistic Studies of the Environment*, 78–101, Amherst: University of Massachusetts Press, 1999.
Pyne, S. J. (2006), *The Still-Burning Bush*, Melbourne: Scribe.
Ramson, W. S. (1991), 'Wasteland to Wilderness: Changing Perceptions of the Environment', in D. J. Mulvaney (ed.), *The Humanities and the Australian Environment* (Australian Academy of the Humanities Occasional Paper No. 11), 5–20, Canberra: Australian Academy of the Humanities.
Rasmussen, J. P. (2008), 'Reading the Prophets Prophetically in Coleridge's *Confessions*', *European Romantic Review*, 19 (4): 403–20.
Reiman, D. H. (1996), 'Shelley and the Human Condition', in Betty T. Bennett and Stuart Curran (eds), *Shelley: Poet and Legislator of the World*, 3–13, Baltimore: Johns Hopkins University Press.

Reno, S. (2016), 'Rethinking the Romantics' Love of Nature', in L. Ottum and S. Reno (eds), *Wordsworth and the Green Romantics*, 28–58, Durham: University of New Hampshire Press.

Retallack, J. (2003), *The Poethical Wager*, Berkeley: University of California Press.

Reynolds, H. (1996), *Frontier: Aborigines, Settlers, Land*, Sydney: Ottum & Unwin, 1996.

Richardson, A. (2001), *British Romanticism and the Science of the Mind*, Cambridge: Cambridge University Press.

Richardson, A. (2010), *Neural Romanticism: Cognitive Theories and British Romanticism*, Baltimore: Johns Hopkins University Press.

Rider, E. (2011), *The Interfaith Ecology Movement*, unpublished PhD thesis, Monash University.

Rigby, K. (1996), *Transgressions of the Feminine: Tragedy, Enlightenment and the Figure of Woman in Classical German Drama*, Heidelberg: C. Winter.

Rigby, K. (2004a), 'Earth, World, Text: The (Im)possibility of Ecopoiesis', *New Literary History*, 35 (3): 427–42.

Rigby, K. (2004b), *Topographies of the Sacred: The Poetics of Place in European Romanticism*, Charlottesville: University of Virginia Press.

Rigby, K. (2007), 'Ecopoetics of the Limestone Plains', in C. A. Cranston and R. Zeller (eds), *The Littoral Zone: Australian Contexts and their Writers*, 153–76, Amsterdam: Rodopi.

Rigby, K. (2008), '(Post-)koloniale Inkorporierung: Ökologie und Esskultur in Australien', in C. Lillge and A.-R. Meyer (eds), *Interkulturelle Mahlzeiten: Kulinarische Begegnungen und Kommunikation in der Literatur*, 315–36, Bielefeld: transcript.

Rigby, K. (2009), 'Writing in the Anthropocene: Idle Chatter or Ecoprophetic Witness?', *Australian Humanities Review* 47, special issue of the Ecological Humanities Corner on 'Writing in the Anthropocene': no pp.

Rigby, K. (2010), 'Another Talk on Religion to Its Cultured Despisers', *Green Letters: Studies in Ecocriticism*, 13, special issue on 'Ecophenomenology and Practices of the Sacred', ed. Patrick Curry and Wendy Wheeler: 55–73.

Rigby, K. (2011), 'Gernot Böhme's Ecological Aesthetics of Atmosphere', in A. Goodbody and K. Rigby (eds), *Ecocritical Theory: New European Approaches*, 139–52, Charlottesville: University of Virginia Press.

Rigby, K. (2012), '"Wo die Wälder rauschen so sacht": The Actuality of Eichendorff's Ecopoetics', *Limbus: Australian Yearbook of German Literary and Cultural Studies*, special issue on *The Actuality of Romanticism*: 91–104.

Rigby, K. (2014), '"Come Forth into the Light of Things": Material Spirit as Negative Ecopoetics', in Gregory C. Stallings, Manuel Asensi and Carl Good (eds), *Material Spirit: Religion and Literature Intranscendent*, 111–28, New York: Fordham University Press.

Rigby, K. (2015a), *Dancing with Disaster: Environmental Histories, Narratives, and Ethics for Perilous Times*, Charlottesville: University of Virginia Press.

Rigby, K. (2015b), 'Art, Nature, and the Poesie of Plants in the Goethezeit: A Biosemiotic Perspective', *Goethe Yearbook*, 22: 23–44.

Rigby, K. (2016a), 'Ecopoetics', in J. Adamson, W. Gleeson and T. Pellow (eds), *Keywords in Environmental Studies*, 79–81, New York: State University of New York Press.

Rigby, K. (2016b), 'Literature, Ethics and Bushfire in Australia', in J. Adamson and M. Davis (eds), *Humanities for the Environment: Integrating Knowledge, Forging New Constellations of Practice*, 210–24, London: Routledge.

Rigby, K. (2017a), 'Nature, Language, and Religion: Herder and Beyond' in G. Duerbeck, U. Stobbe, H. Zapf and E. Zemanek (eds), *Ecological Thought in German Literature and Culture*, 31–42, Lanham: Lexington Books.

Rigby, K. (2017b), '"Mines Aren't Really Like That": German Romantic Undergrounds Revisited', in H. Sullivan and C. Schaumann (eds), *German Ecocriticism in the Anthropocene*, 111–28, New York: Palgrave Macmillan.

Rigby, K. (2017c), 'Deep Sustainability: Ecopoetics, Enjoyment and Ecstatic Hospitality', in A. Johns-Putra, J. Parham and L. Squire (eds), *Literature and Sustainability: Concept, Text and Culture*, 52–75, Manchester: Manchester University Press.

Rigby, K. (2019a), '"Piping in their honey dreams": Towards a Creaturely Ecopoetics', in F. Middelhof, S. Schonbeck, R. Borgards and C. Gersdorf (eds), *Texts, Animals, Environments: Zoopoetics and Ecopoetics*, 281–295, Freiburg i.B.: Rombach.

Rigby, K. (2019b), 'Weaving the Environmental Humanities: Australian Strands, Configurations, and Provocations', *Green Letters: Journal of Ecocriticism*, available online: https://www.tandfonline.com/doi/abs/10.1080/14688417.2019.1578250 (accessed 24 April 2019).

Rigby, T. H. (2019), *Memoirs of a Bourgeois Falsifier*, Carlton: Australian Academic Press.

Roberts, J. (2010), *Blake. Wordsworth. Religion*, London: Continuum.

Robin, L. (2010), 'Battling the Land and Global Anxiety: Science, Environment and Identity in Settler Australia', *Philosophy Activism Nature* 7: 3–7.

Robin, L., S. Sörlin, and P. Warde (eds) (2013), *The Future of Nature*, New Haven: Yale University Press.

Rose, D. B. (1996), *Nourishing Terrains: Australian Aboriginal View of Landscape and Wilderness*, Canberra: Australian Heritage Commission.

Rose, D. B. (2004), *Reports from a Wild Country: Ethics for Decolonization*, Sydney: University of NSW Press.

Rose, D. B. (2006), '"Moral Friends" in the Zone of Disaster', *Tamkang Review*, 37 (1): 77–97.

Rose, D. B. (2008), 'On History, Trees, and Ethical Proximity', *Postcolonial Studies*, 11 (2): 157–67.

Rose, D. B. (2009), 'Introduction: Writing in the Anthropocene', *Australian Humanities Review*, 47, special issue of the Ecological Humanities Corner on 'Writing in the Anthropocene': no pp.

Rose, D. B. (2011), 'Flying Foxes: Kin, Keystone, Kontaminant', in D. Rose and T. Van Dooren (eds), *Unloved Others: Death of the Disregarded in the Time of Extinctions*, special issue of *Australian Humanities Review* 50, 119–36, Canberra: Australian National University Press.

Rose, D. B. (2011), *Wild Dog Dreaming*, Charlottesville: University of Virginia Press.
Rose, D. B. (2013), 'In the Shadow of All This Death', in J. Johnston and F. Probyn-Rapsey (eds), *Animal Death*, 1–20, Sydney: Sydney University Press.
Rousseau, J.-J. ([1780] 1974), *Emile*, trans., B. Foxley. London and Toronto: Dent.
Routley, R. and V. Routley (1975), *The Fight for the Forests: The Takeover of Australian Forests for Pines, Wood Chips, and Intensive Forestry*, Canberra: Research School of Social Sciences, ANU.
Rue, C. (2011), 'Carbon price will cause pain', *Eureka Street* 21.12 (no pp.), available online: https://www.eurekastreet.com.au/article/carbon-price-will-cause-pain (accessed 30 July 2019).
Ryan, R. M. (1997), *The Romantic Reformation: Religious Politics in English Literature 1789–1824*, Cambridge: Cambridge University Press.
Sánchez-Bayo, F. and K. A. G. Wyckhuys (2019), 'Worldwide Decline of Entomofauna: A Review of Its Drivers', *Biological Conservation*, 232: 8–27.
Sandilands, C. (2014), 'Pro/Polis: Three Forays into the Political Lives of Bees', in S. Iovino and S. Oppermann (eds), *Material Ecocriticism*, 157–71, Bloomington: Indiana University Press.
Santner, E. (2006), *On Creaturely Life: Rilke/Benjamin/Sebald*, Chicago: University of Chicago Press.
Schama, S. (1996), *Landscape and Memory*, London: Harper Perennial.
Schelling, F. W. J. (1856–61), *Sämmtliche Werke*, Part 1, vols 1–10, Part 2, vols 1–4, ed. K. F. A. Schelling, Stuttgart: Cotta.
Schelling, F. W. J. ([1799] 1858), 'Einleitung zu dem Entwurf eines Systems der Naturphilosophie', in K. F. A. Schelling (eds), in *Sämmtliche Werke*, Part 1, vol. 3, 269–397, Stuttgart: Cotta.
Schelling, F. W. J. ([1800] 1958), *System des transzendentalen Idealismus*, in M. Schröter (ed.), *Schellings Werke*, vol. 2, Munich: Beck.
Schelling, F. W. J. ([1797–1803] 1988), *Ideas for a Philosophy of Nature*, rev. ed. 1803, trans. E. E. Harris and P. Heath, intro. R. Stern, Cambridge: Cambridge University Press.
Schelling, F. W. J. ([1802–05] 1989), *The Philosophy of Art*, trans., ed. and intro. D. W. Stott, Minneapolis: Minnesota University Press.
Schelling, F. W. J. ([1798] 2000) *Zur Weltseele – eine Hypothese der höheren Physik zur Erklärung des allgemeinen Organismus*, ed. J. Jantzen with Thomas Kisser, in *Werke*, vol. 6, Stuttgart: Fromann-Holzboog.
Schlegel, F. (1957), *Literary Notebooks 1797–1801*, ed. Hans Eichner, Toronto: University of Toronto Press.
Schlegel, F. (1967), *Kritische Friedrich-Schlegel-Ausgabe*, vol. 2, ed. H. Eichner, Paderborn: Schöningh.
Schlegel, F. ([1800] 1968), *Dialogue on Poetry and Literary Aphorisms*, trans., intro., and annotated by Ernst Behler and Roman Struc, University Park: Pennsylvania State University Press.

Schleiermacher, F. (1984), *Schriften aus der Berliner Zeit 1796–1799, Kritische Gesamtausgabe* Bd. 2, ed. H.-J. Birkner, Berlin: De Gruyter.

Schleiermacher, F. D. E. ([1798] 1988), *On Religion. Speeches to Its Cultured Despisers*, intro., trans. and notes, R. Crouter. Cambridge: Cambridge University Press.

Schleiermacher, F. D. E. ([1821–2 and 1830–1] 1999), *The Christian Faith (Die Glaubenslehre)*, ed. H. R. Mackintosh and J. S. Stewart, London: T & T Clark.

Scott, H. C. M. (2014), *Chaos and Cosmos: Literary Roots of Modern Ecology in the British Nineteenth Century*, University Park: Pennsylvania State University Press.

Seward, A. (1810), *The Poetical Works of Anna Seward*, ed. Sir W. Scott, vol. 2, Edinburgh: Ballantyne.

Shaftesbury, Lord (A. G. Cooper) ([1714] 1999), *Characteristics of Men, Manners, Opinions, Times*, ed. and intro. Laurence E. Klein, Cambridge: Cambridge University Press, 1999.

Shaw, R. (1981), 'A Conversation with David Campbell', *Poetry Australia* (December 1981): 36–32.

Schmidt, L. J. (2009), 'When the Dust Settles,' *NASA Earth* Observatory, 18 May 2001, available online: http://earthobservatory.nasa.gov/Features/Dust/ (accessed 28 September 2009).

Seamon, D. and A. Zajonc (eds) (1998), *Goethe's Way of Science: A Phenomenology of Nature*, New York: State University of New York.

Shama, S. (1995), *Landscape and Memory*, London: HarperCollins.

Sharkie, T. and M. Johnson (2017), 'Eroticized Environments: Ancient Greek Natural Philosophy and the Roots of Erotic Ecocritical Contemplation', in C. Schliephake (ed.), *Ecocriticism, Ecology, and the Cultures of Antiquity*, 71–90, London: Lexington Books.

Sharp, N. (2006), 'The Artistic and the Literary Imagination in Australia and Beyond: Finding Places of the Heart among the Gum Trees', *Colloquy*, 12: 154–70.

Sharp, N. (2007), 'A Poet's Feeling for the Earth', *LocalGlobal. Identity, Security, Community*, 3: 24–32.

Shaviro, S. (2011), 'The Universe of Things', *Theory and Event*, 14 (3). DOI: 10.1353/tae.2011.0027.

Shaviro, S. (2014), *The Universe of Things in Speculative Realism*, Minneapolis: University of Minnesota Press.

Shelley, P. B. (2002), *Shelley's Poetry and Prose*, selected and ed. D. H. Reiman and N. Fraistat, New York: W. W. Norton.

Shumack, S. (1967), *An Autobiography, or Tales and Legends of Canberra Pioneers*, ed. J. E. and S. Shumack, Canberra: Australian University Press.

Simpson, D. E. (ed.) (1988), *The Origins of Modern Critical Thought: German Aesthetic and Literary Theory from Lessing to Hegel*, Cambridge: Cambridge University Press.

Skinner, J. (2001a), 'Editor's Statement', *ecopoetics*, 1: 5–8.

Skinner, J. (2001b), 'Why Eco-Poetics?', *ecopoetics*, 1: 105–06.

Skinner, J. (2017), 'Ecopoetics', in R. G. Smith (ed.), *American Literature in Transition, 2000–2010*, 322–42, Cambridge: Cambridge University Press, 2017.

Solnik, S. (2016), *Poetry and the Anthropocene: Ecology, Biology, and Technology in Contemporary British and Irish Poetry*, London: Routledge.

Spector, S. (2001a), *'Glorious Incomprehensible': The Development of Blake's Kabbalistic Language*, Lewisburg: Bucknell University Press

Spector, S. (2001b), *'Wonders Divine': The Development of Blake's Kabbalistic Myth*, Lewisburg: Bucknell University Press.

Steffen, W. (2013), 'Commentary' (on Crutzen and Stoermer [2000/2013]), in L. Robin, S. Sörlin and P. Warde (eds), *The Future of Nature: Documents of Global Change*, 486–90, New Haven: Yale University Press.

Steiner, George (1970), *Language and Silence: Essays on Language, Literature and the Inhuman*. London: Yale University Press.

Stipsnovic, A. (2006), 'Bees and Ants: Perceptions of Imperialism in Vergil's *Aeneid* and *Georgics*', in E. C. Brown (ed.), *Insect Poetics*, 13–28, Minneapolis: University of Minnesota Press.

Sullivan, S. (1999), 'Folk and Formal, Local and National – Damara Knowledge and Community Conservation in Southern Kunene, Namibia', *Cimbedasia*, 15: 1–28.

Symons, M. (2007), *One Continuous Picnic: A Gastronomic History of Australia*, Carlton: Melbourne University Press.

Tannenbaum, L. (1982), *Biblical Tradition in Blake's Early Prophecies: The Great Code of Art*, Princeton: Princeton University Press.

Theocritus ([3rd C BCE] 1912) The Poems of Theocritus. *The Greek Bucolic Poets*, ed. and trans. J. M. Edmonds, Cambridge, MA: Harvard UP, 1–381, available online: https://www.theoi.com/Text/TheocritusIdylls1.html (accessed 10 April 2019).

Tredinnick, M. (2005), *The Land's Wild Music: Encounters with Barry Lopez, Peter Matthiessen, Terry Tempest Williams and James Galvin*. San Antonio, Texas: Trinity University Press.

Tredinnick, M. (2007), 'We Are Not Finished at the Skin: A Cradle Mountain Suite', *Philosophy Activism Nature*, 4: 92–100.

Ulmer, W. A. (2001), *The Christian Wordsworth 1798–1805*, New York: State University of New York Press.

Vincent, E. and T. Neale (eds) (2016), *Unstable Relations: Indigenous People and Environmentalism in Contemporary Australia*, Perth: University of Western Australia Press.

Volf, M. (1996), *Exclusion and Embrace: A Theological Exploration of Identity, Otherness, and Reconciliation*, Nashville: Abingdon Press.

Walsh, G. (1987), 'David Campbell's Family Background: The Blackman and Campbell Families in Australia, 1801–1917', in Harry Hesseltine (ed.), *A Tribute to David Campbell*, 7–20, Kensington: University of NSW Press.

Weik von Mossner, A. (2016), 'Environmental Narrative, Embodiment, and Emotion', in H. Zapf (ed.), *Handbook of Ecocriticism and Cultural Ecology*, 534–50, Berlin: De Gruyter.

Walker, K. (later Oodgeroo Nunuccal (1964), *We Are Going*, Brisbane: Jacaranda.

Wallace-Crabbe, C. (1987), 'Squatter Pastoral', in H. Hesseltine (ed.), *A Tribute to David Campbell*, Sydney: University of New South Wales Press, 87–99.

Walls, L. D. (2011), 'From the Modern to the Ecological: Latour on Walden Pond', in A. Goodbody and K. Rigby (eds), *Ecocritical Theory: New European Approaches*, 98–110, Charlottesville: University of Virginia Press.

Wamsler, C. (2019), 'Contemplative Sustainable Futures: The Role of Inner Dimensions and Transformation in Sustainability Research and Education', in W. L. Filho and A. C. Macrae (eds), *Sustainability and the Humanities*, 359–74, Berlin: Springer.

Washington, C. (2014), 'John Clare and Biopolitics', *European Romantic Review*, 25 (6): 665–82.

Wheeler, W. (2006), *The Whole Creature: Complexity, Biosemiotics and the Evolution of Culture*, London: Wishart and Lawrence.

Wheeler, W. (2011a), 'The Biosemiotic Turn: Abduction, or, the Nature of Creative Reason in Nature and Culture', in Axel Goodbody and Kate Rigby (eds), *Ecocritical Theory: New European Approaches*, 270–82, Charlottesville: University of Virginia Press.

Wheeler, W. (2011b), 'Introduction', in W. Wheeler (ed.), *Biosemiotics: Nature/Culture/Science/Semiosis*, Living Books about Life, available online: http://www.livingbooksaboutlife.org/books/Biosemiotics (accessed 25 February 2014).

White, Kyle (2017), 'Indigenous Climate Change Studies: Indigenizing Futures, Decolonizing the Anthropocene', in T. A. Toulouse, M. E. Zimmerman and J. Gladstone (eds), *Environmental Trajectories*, special issue of *English Language Notes* 55 (1–2): 153–62.

Whitehead, A. N. ([1925] 1967), *Science and the Modern World*, New York: The Free Press.

Whitehouse, R. (compiler) (1997), *Noongar Dictionary: Noongar to English, English to Noongar*, 2nd ed., Perth: Noongar Language and Cultural Centre, https://d1y4ma8ribhabl.cloudfront.net/wp-content/uploads/2013/07/Noongar-Dictionary-Second-Edition.pdf (accessed 26 March 2019).

Woiwode, C. and L. K. Bhati (2019), 'Enabling Transformative Urban Development for Integral Sustainability: The Case for Tapping the Potential of Sri Aurobindo's Philosophy in Planning Practice and Theory', in W. L. Filho and A. C. Macrae (eds), *Sustainability and the Humanities*, 35–56, Berlin: Springer.

Wojciekowski, H. C. and V. Gallese (2011), 'How Stories Make Us Feel: Toward an Embodied Narratology', *California Italian Studies*, 2 (1): no pp., available online: https://scholarship.org/uc/item/3jg726c2 (accessed 10 April 2019).

Wordsworth, W. ([1800] 2005), *Lyrical Ballads, with Other Poems, in Two Volumes*, 2nd ed., Bristol: T.N. Longman and O. Rees, 1800, Project Gutenberg, available online: http://www.gutenberg.org/cache/epub/8905/pg8905-images.html (accessed 22 April 2019).

Wordsworth, W. ([1805–6] 1971), *The Prelude. A Parallel Text*, ed. J. C. Maxwell, New York: Yale University Press.

Wordsworth, W. (1974), *The Prose Works of William Wordsworth*, ed. W. J. B. Owen and J. W. Smyser, 3 vols, Oxford: Oxford University Press.

Wordsworth, W. (1994), *The Works of William Wordsworth*, Ware: Wordsworth Editions.

Wright, A. (2016), 'What Happens When You Tell Somebody Else's Story?' *Meanjin Quarterly* Summer, 2016: n.p. https://meanjin.com.au/essays/what-happens-when-you-tell-somebody-elses-story/ (accessed 27 March 2019).

Wright, J. (1975), *Because I Was Invited*, Melbourne: Oxford University Press.

Wright, J. (1981), *The Cry for the Dead*, Carlton: Melbourne University Press.

Wright, J. (1991), *Born of Conquerors: Selected Essays*, Canberra: Aboriginal Studies Press.

Wright, J. (1994), *Collected Poems*, Sydney: HarperCollins.

Wright, J. (1996), *The Coral Battleground*, Sydney: Angus & Robertson.

Wu, D. (2006) *Romanticism: An Anthology*, 3rd ed., Oxford: Blackwell.

Youngquist, P. (2003), *Monstrosities: Bodies and British Romanticism*, Minneapolis: University of Minnesota Press.

Yusoff, K. (2013), 'Geologic Life: Prehistory, Climate, Futures in the Anthropocene', *Environment and Planning D: Society and Space*, 31: 779–95.

Yusoff, K. (2019), *A Billion Black Anthropocenes*, Minneapolis: Minnesota University Press.Zapf, H. (2016), *Literature as Cultural Ecology: Sustainable Texts*, London: Bloomsbury.

Zeller, R. (2000), 'The Double Tree: Judith Wright's Poetry and Environmental Activism', *Isle: Interdisciplinary Studies in Literature and Environment*, 7 (2) (2000): 55–65.

Index

Aboriginal Catholic Ministry (ACM) 175, 180
    Binnap partners 175, 189
Acampora, Ralph 85, 99
Adorno, Theodor 57, 195 n.7
African American nature poetry 104–9 (*see also* Lorde, Audrey; Trethewey, Natasha)
Alaimo, Stacy 17, 54
Albiston, Jordie
    'Kinglake Undone' 145
    'Lamentations' 19, 114, 139–47
Anastasi, Amanda 191
animal ethics 39, 101 (*see also* bio-inclusive ethics)
anthropocentrism 58, 86, 119, 142, 195–6
Anthropocene. *See also* biodiversity loss; climate change; socioecological transformations
    affects 17, 55, 79
    climatic changes 6–9, 19
    criticisms of 8, 10, 12 (*see also* Ploutocene)
    environmental changes 7–13
    'good Anthropocene' 15, 127
    literature 4, 114, 127–8, 193
Aquinas, Thomas 26, 32
Araluen, Evelyn 6
    'Guarded by Birds' 189
    'Shame and Contemporary Australian Poetics' 181
Aristotle 62
atmosphere
    acoustic 71–3
    aesthetic theory 54–6, 62–73
    meteorological 53–4, 67
    uncanny 78–9, 82
Australia. *See also* First Nations
    Anglo-Celtic settler culture 19, 150–7, 182, 188
    bushfires 19, 75, 77, 114, 139–45, 152, 162, 173, 175, 187
    climate change, impacts on 55, 139–47
    frontier violence 9–10, 154–5, 175
    literature (*see* Albiston, Jordie; Araluen, Evelyn; Birch, Tony; Brissenden, R. F.; Campbell, David; Elvey, Anne; Gray, Robert; Grenville, Kate; Harpur, Charles; Hart, Kevin; Kinsella, John; Leane, Jeanine; Minter, Peter; Noonuccal, Oodgeroo; Stewart, Douglas; Wright, Alexis; Wright, Judith)
    colonial 153–5, 159, 167–8, 186–7
    non-Indigenous 151, 174–7, 180, 188–9
    and Romanticism 20–1, 149, 153–5, 163, 189
Australian Religious Response to Climate Change/GreenFaith 146–7

Bacon, Francis 39, 102, 119, 127
Baer, Karl Ernst von 87
Bailey, Benjamin 67
Balfour, Ian 113, 116–17, 122
Barbauld, Anna Letitia, 'The Mouse's Petition' 102
Bashō, Matsuo 41
Bate, Jonathan 2, 53, 66–7, 94, 98, 103, 137
Baumgarten, Alexander Gottlieb 56, 65
Bellarsi, Franca 6
Bennett, Jane 43
Benso, Sylvia 42, 48
Bible
    apocalyptic writing 18, 113, 117
    Book of Exodus 124
    Book of Isaiah 117–18, 121, 124
    Book of Jeremiah 124–6
    Book of Job 25–6
    Gospel of John 26, 121, 160
    Gospel of Luke 26
    Gospel of Matthew 26
    historical-critical approach 117
    Lamentations of Jeremiah 127

Paul, Letters 26, 121
  prophetic tradition 18–19, 34, 113–15, 117–19, 122–7
  Revelation 117
biodiversity loss. *See also* extinction
  Bramble Cay melonys 7–9
  pollinators 7, 109–11
  Spectacled Flying-fox 7–8
bio-inclusive ethics 3, 15, 26, 44, 54, 195–6 n.8
biosemiotics 85–8, 90, 112, 163, 171
Black, Rabbi Jonathan Keren (Yonaten ben Chayim) 146–7
  'The Rainbow' 147
Birch, Tony 188
Bishop Watson, *An Apology for the Bible* 122
Blackstone, William, *Commentaries on the Laws of England* 42
Blake, William 5–6, 14–15, 18, 34–5, 88, 117, 194
  America 113
  apokalypsis 113–14, 119
  'Auguries of Innocence' 34, 122–3
  biblical tradition 113–17, 119–24, 126–7
  Europe 113
  Jerusalem 126–7
  Milton 119, 123
  prophetic project 120–4, 126–7
  Songs of Innocence and Experience 149
  'To my friend Butts' 120–2
Bloch, Ernst 58
body. *See also* corporeality; creaturely life; trans-corporeality
  consumer culture 61
  Körper and *Leib*, reconciliation 61–2, 66, 69–70
  mind-body dualism 17, 54, 60–1
  technologization of 57–8, 62
  'symphysis' 85
Böhme, Gernot 56–9, 71–2
  'ecological aesthetics' 17, 54–7, 62, 64–6, 73, 79, 82, 201 n.7
Boileau, Nicolas, 'On the Sublime' (French translation) 13
Bonnefoy, Yves 51
Bonneuil, Christophe 12
Bonyhady, Tim 75, 153
Bowie, Andrew 120

Boyce, James 151, 153
Bradley, John 177
Brady, Veronica 128, 133, 136, 139
Bresnihan, Patrick 98
Brett, Mark 142
Brissenden, R. F. 158, 166
Bristow, Thomas 6, 202 n.6
British Romanticism 2–3, 20. *See also.* Blake, William; Byron, Lord; Clare, John; Coleridge, Samuel Taylor; Keats, John; Seward, Anna; Shelley, Mary; Shelley, Percy Bysshe; Wordsworth, William
  and biblical scholarship 115–17
Brogan, T. V. F. 37
Brown, Eric C. 90
Brueggemann, Walter 118, 124–5
Buber, Martin 117
Buddhism 3, 16, 41, 202 n.10
Bühler, Benjamin 89
Burgmann, Meredith 134
Burgmann, Verity 134
Burke, Edmund 13–14
  sublime, concept of 13–14
Burns, Robert 'To a Mouse' 100, 171
Burrus, Virginia 28, 194
Butler, Charles 90
Butler, Judith 85, 90
Byron, Lord 3, 66

Campbell, David 21, 149, 157–9, 187
  on Aboriginal rock art 167–8
  'The Anguish of Ants' 170–2
  'Bora Ring' 168–9
  The Branch of Dodona 166
  bush ballads 160
  'Cocky's Calendar' 161, 163–5
  Deaths and Pretty Cousins 168, 173
  'Ku-ring-gai Rock Carvings' 166, 169
  Miracle of Mullion Hill 160, 173
  Moscow Trefoil 174
  pastoralism 21, 149, 159–60, 171, 174
  place-based philosophies and practices 170
  Seven Russian Poets 174
  Speak with the Sun 160
  'squatter pastoral' 161
  'Works and Days' 166
Capitolocene 10
Carter, Paul 189

Casey, Maryrose 184
Cassirer, Ernst 89
Castree, Noel 193
CERES (Centre for Education and Research in Environmental Strategies) 17, 55, 81–2, 201 n.16
Christianity 24, 26–9, 31, 36, 114–27, 145–6, 160, 178, 180–1. *See also* Bible
Christie, Douglas E.
  The Blue Sapphire of the Mind 24
  on 'contemplative ecology' 16, 24, 27
Chuthulucene 11
Clare, John 6, 15, 18, 84, 186
  counter-pastoral critique 102–3
  'creaturely ecopoetics' 84, 94–8, 100–1
  enclosure 5, 101–3
  on humane treatment of animals 101
  'Lament of Swordy Well' 103
  natural history writing 96–7
  reference to 'slaves' 103–6
  'Remembrances' 103
  'Wild Bees' 95–9
  'Wild Bees Nest' 99–101
  zoopoetic oeuvre 94–5
Clark, Timothy 4, 19, 72–3, 138
climate change. *See also* global warming
  accelerating biodiversity loss 7–8, 73, 77–9, 109–11
  extreme weather events 53, 139–40, 145
  Jeremiah's ecoprophetic call 18, 113–14
  UN initiatives 191, 193–4
Climate Change Communication Research Hub (CCCRH), Monash University 191
Coleridge, Samuel Taylor 5, 15, 24, 29–31, 36, 39, 41, 56, 101–2, 160
  'The Aeolian Harp' 30
  'Effusion XXXV' 30
  'Frost at Midnight' 30
  Lectures on the History of Philosophy 30
colonization 1
  Australia 9–10, 19–21, 73–6, 129, 141, 151–3, 156–7, 168–70, 182–3, 185–9 (*see also* Australia, frontier violence and literature, colonial; First Nations)
  Canada 46–7
  of the commons 10, 99, 103
  of Critical Zone 12
  'logic of colonisation' 3, 18, 54, 149, 189
  neo-colonization 135
  North America 8, 10
contemplative practices 49–51. *See also* Wordsworth, William; Lilburn, Tim
  Blake, William 120–1
  Book of Nature 25–7
  Buddhism 41
  Christian mysticism 27–8, 30–1, 40–1, 45
  Clare, John 96
  Coleridge, Samuel Taylor 29–31
  consumer culture 46–50
  decolonisation 46–8
  Desert Fathers and Mothers 27–8, 31
  'essence' of religion 32–5
  ethics of things 41–2
  and natural science 39–40
  Object Oriented Ontology 42–4
  'Toward a Contemplative Commons' 50
  Transition Town movement 50–1
Cooper, David E. 31, 41
Coralie, Jennifer 136
corporeality 57, 60, 63. *See also* body; creaturely life; trans-corporeality
Craig, Mya-Rose 80
creaturely life 84–5
Critical Theory, old and new 57
Cronon, William 13–15, 20
  'The Trouble with Wilderness; or, Getting Back to the Wrong Nature' 13
Crouter, Richard 31
Crutzen, P. J. 10–11
Cudworth, Erika 107

Dante 78
Daoism 41
Darwin, Erasmus, *The Botanic Garden* 39
Davis, Heather 8
Davy, Humphry 39
decolonization, ethics for 3–4, 10
De Groot, Rudolf 158
Dempster, Beth 85
Derrida, Jacques 45, 98
'double death' 8–9, 12, 73, 177
Durack, Mary 156
Dushane, Allison 70

Eagleton, Terry 56-7, 122
earth system
 biophysical changes 8
 devastating transformations 8-13
 sphere of human responsibility 53-73
ecocide 9, 50, 79
ecocritics 2, 13, 20, 64, 137-8, 194
ecology
 affective 89
 contemplative 16, 24, 27
 cultural 3, 4
 'deep' 2, 34, 128
 'Dreaming' 177
 multi-faith movement 146-7, 205 n.23
 political 54
 'of wonder' 3
Economides, Louise 3, 14
ecopoetics
 affective 18, 54-6, 60, 62-5, 67-71, 73, 79-80, 84
 contemplative 16-18, 23-51, 54, 70
 creaturely 18, 84-5, 97, 99-101, 104-9, 171-3
 decolonial 21, 150, 184-9
 negative 38, 45
 prophetic 19, 34, 113-14, 123-4, 126-7, 129-33, 138-9, 142-7
 writing, form and style 5-6, 45, 137-8
ecopoethics 21, 79, 175
ecopoets 2, 41
ecopolitical praxis 3, 5-6, 11, 17-19, 51, 55, 61, 79-80, 113-14, 134-6, 145-7, 191-4
ecotheology 26-7, 121
Edwards, Denis 121
Eichhorn, J. P., *Introduction to the Old Testament* 116
Elvey, Anne 21, 150, 174-5, 177, 179, 181, 183, 188-9
 Aboriginal Catholic Mission 174-5, 177, 183, 188-9
 Claimed by Country 175, 180-1
 Kin 174-5, 177, 180, 188
 'Post(?)colonial?' 181
 White on White 174-5, 181, 188-9
Emmeche, Claus 86
Erdman, David V. 127
European Romanticism. *See also* British Romanticism; German Romanticism

avant-garde movement 5, 24
Buddhism, links with 3, 16
 contemplative practices 24-46
 heterogeneous cultural legacies 1-3, 13-21
evolutionary theory 101-2, 156
extinction 7, 73, 138
 Extinction Rebellion 145
Eyre, Edward John 154

Faith in Place 110-11
Farrier, David 6, 12
Favareau, Donald 87
Fay, Jessica 27, 45, 50
feminism 3, 136, 176, 195 n.7, 203 n.5
Fijn, Natasha 90
First Nations
 Arrernte 180
 Australian 3, 9, 19, 90-1, 135, 146, 166, 188
 Bundjalong 181
 Canada 47
 Country 135, 141, 151-2, 174-80, 182-5, 187, 189
 Daungwurrung 141
 dispossession 4, 150-7
 Dja Dja Wurrung 141
 land management 141, 151-2, 171, 173, 176
 land rights movement 21, 136, 174
 Native Title 183
 Ngangiwumirr 175
 Potawatomi 8
 Quandamooka 176
 Rembarrnga 179
 rock art 90, 166-9
 Saanich 47, 49
 U.S.A 109
 Waanyi 183
 Warraimay 177
 Wathaurrung 141
 Wiradjuri 182-4, 186-7
 Woiwurrung 141
 Wurundjeri 81, 175
 Yanyuwa 177
Fletcher, Angus 5
French Revolution 16, 45
Frisch, Karl von 89-90
Fulford, Tim 150

Gammage, Bill 152, 176
genocide 9
georgic poetry. *See also* pastoral
   Classical 93–4
   neo-georgic 165–6
German Romanticism. *See also* Goethe, Johann Wolfgang von; Heine, Heinrich; Novalis, *Schriften* (Friedrich von Hardenberg), Schelling, Friedrich Wilhelm Joseph; Schleiermacher, Friedrich; Schlegel, Friedrich; *Naturphilosophie*
   Early (Jena) Romanticism 2, 24, 32, 85, 116, 119
   Stimmungsgedicht 66
Giallardet, Jacky 12, 67
Gifford, P. 72
Gifford, Terry 93–4
global warming 53, 67, 77, 114, 140, 193–4. *See also* climate change
   'Global Warming Criticism', 66–7
Godwin, William 117
Goethe, Johann Wolfgang von 1, 40, 56, 66, 87–8, 97, 101, 116, 133, 138
Gorji, Mina 97, 103
Gould, James L. 89
Goulson, Dave 89
Gray, Robert 41
Gregersen, Niels H. 121
Grenville, Kate 151
Grieves, Vicki 177
Griffiths, Tom 19–20, 73, 141, 152
Gynther, Ian 7

Hall, Dewey W. 39
Hansen, Christine 140–1, 145
Haraway, Donna 10–11, 58, 83, 85, 89, 103, 109
   on sympoiesis 85, 89
Harman, Graham 42–3
Harpur, Charles 54, 73–5, 153–5, 175
Harrison, Gary 41, 165
Hart, Kevin 17, 28, 40, 55, 73, 76–80, 166, 199 n.14, 206 n.8
   'That Bad Summer' 17, 77–9
   Young Rain 76–7
Harvey, Dimitra 180
Hatley, James 4

Hayes, Katherine M. 124
Hazlitt, William, 'My First Acquaintance with Poets' 29
heatwaves 7, 53, 76–8, 139–40, 144
Hebrew
   creation, celebration of 25–6
   love songs 69
   prophetic writing 26, 115–17, 127, 142, 146
Hegel, Georg Wilhelm Friedrich 64, 119–20
Heidegger, Martin 42–3, 94, 137
Heimans, Frank, *Shadow Sister: A Film Biography of Australian Aboriginal Poet Kath Walker* 135
Heine, Heinrich 15
Henderson, Joseph 97
Herder, Johann Gottfried 69, 115–17
   Letters Concerning the Study of Theology 116
   Lieder der Liebe 115
   nābî, interpretation 117
   'On the Spirit of Hebraic Poetry' 115
Heyes, Robert 97
hierarchical dualism 3, 43, 101
Higgins, David 192
Hoffmeyer, Jesper 85–8
Hoorn, Jeanette 157
Hope, Alec D. 58, 163
Horkheimer, Max 57, 195 n.7
Hubbell, J. Andrew 3
Humboldt, Alexander von 66
Hume, Angela 6, 186
Hurd, Richard, *Twelve Sermons Introductory to the Study of the Prophecies* 115
Husserl, Edmund 28, 40
Hustak, Carla 89
Hutchings, Kevin 20, 34, 123–4, 156

Illingworth, Sam 191–2
Indyk, Ivor 154–5, 182
Ingham, M. B. 41
Ingold, Tim 71–2
Iovino, Serenella 67
Irvine, Richard D. G. 97, 103

Jackson, Noel 56, 66–7
Johnson, Samuel 37, 42, 69
   Dictionary of the English Language 117

Jones, Rhys 152
Judaism 26, 31–2, 115, 117–18, 146–7, 203 n.6

Kamusikiri, Sandra 127
Kane, Paul 20, 152
Kant, Immanuel 13–14, 30
    sublime, concept of 14
Kearns, Laurel 110–11
Keats, John 6, 15–17, 45, 54, 66–72, 75
    'Ben Nevis' 15
    sublime, concept of 45
    'To Autumn' 54, 66–8, 70, 72
Keller, Catherine 203 n.5
Kidd, Sue Monk, *The Secret Life of Bees* 106
Kijiner, Kathy Jetnil, 'Dear Matafele Peinam' 193–4
Kinsella, John 21, 149, 159, 174, 191
Kirkpatrick, Peter 160
Kuhn, Dorothea 102
Kull, Kalevi 87
Kyle, Veronica 8, 110–11

Lacoue-Labarthe, Philippe 24
Lam, Victor 51
Lamb, Jonathan 41
Lansdown, Richard 20, 153–4
Latour, Bruno 12, 67
Leane, Jeanine 21, 150, 174, 181–2, 184–9
    Dark Secrets: After Dreaming 182
    Purple Threads 182
    Walk Back Over 150, 181–2, 184, 189
Levinas, Emmanuel 4, 10, 42, 85, 156
Lilburn, Tim 17, 24, 46–50
    Desire Never Leaves 48
    'The End of August' 49
    'In the Hills, Watching' 47
    Living in the World As If It Were Home 47
    The Names 49
Lindauer, Martin 90
Locke, John 119, 127
Lorde, Audre 84, 104–6
    'The Bees' 105–6
Lowth, Robert, *Lectures on the Sacred Poetry of the Hebrews* 115
Lussier, Mark S. 3, 16

Malm, Andreas 12
Martin, Mandy 90, 117, 152
Mathews, Freya 80–1, 140, 151

McCalman, Iain 134
McConchie, Peter 141
McGinnis, Kerry 155
McKernan, Susan 221
McKusick, James 126
Mead, Philip 5–6, 136, 155, 157–8, 161
Merleau-Ponty, M. 60, 70
'Migration & Me' programme 110
Minter, Peter 21, 135–6, 136, 174, 189
Monbiot, George 6
Moore, Jason W. 10
Mora, C. 53
Moreton-Robinson, Eileen 176
Morley, David 192
Morris, William 2
Morton, Timothy 35, 44–5, 101
Muecke, Stephen 141, 183
multispecies. *See also* sympoiesis
    coexistence 18, 88, 94–5, 97–112, 164, 166, 171–3, 177
    studies 4
Muir, John 14, 16
Myers, Natasha 89

Nancy, Jean-Luc 24
National Parks and Access to the Countryside Act of 1949 80
Naturphilosophie 32, 57, 87, 199 n.13
new materialism 16, 24
Newton, Sir Isaac 39, 119, 127
Nisbet, Rachel 93
Noonuccal, Oodgeroo aka Walker, Kath 21, 134–5, 150, 174
    We Are Going 174
North American Romanticism 2, 14–16, 46–7, 104
Northcott, Michael S. 18, 113, 125–7
Novalis, Schriften (Friedrich von Hardenberg)
    on neoclassicism 1–2
    on prophecy 113, 119

Oerlemans, Onno 101–2
oikopoiesis, concept 6
Ollerton, Jeff 96, 110
Oppermann, Serpil 67
Osborne, Gillian 6

Pacific Calling Partnership 145–6
Paine, Thomas 117

Pascoe, Bruce 152
pastoral. *See also* georgic
　African American 104
　anti-pastoral 76, 79, 94
　Campbell, David 158–60
　Clare, John 102–3
　Classical 68, 70, 75, 91–3, 100, 165, 172
　'Cocky's Calendar' 161–4
　counter-pastoral, Romantic 94, 102
　Harpur, Charles, 'Midsummer Noon in the Australian Forest' 74–6, 153–4
　Hart, Kevin 'That Bad Summer' 77–9
　hybridised with georgic 70, 75, 94, 97, 99–101
　ideal 2, 14, 21, 55, 98, 150
　Keats, John 'To Autumn' 68–72
　'metaphysical' 160
　'The Monaro' 160–1
　neo-pastoral 38, 159, 161
　post-pastoral 76, 159, 171
　Spencer, Edmund, *Shepheardes Calendar* 161
　'squatter' 161
　'Wild Bees' 95, 97–9
　'Wild Bees Nest' 99–101
　'Works and Days' 164–6
pastoralism, settler Australian 19, 21, 129, 139, 149, 152, 155–7, 166, 177, 183, 185–7
Paul, Kevin 47, 49
Peirce, Charles Sanders 86, 88
Perkins, David 39, 101
Pick, Anat 85
Plantationocene 10, 18, 103–4, 109–10
Ploutocene 11–12, 46, 53, 126, 194. *See also* Blake, William
Plumwood, Val 3, 34, 44, 47–8, 127, 136, 170, 174
Ponge, Francis 43
Pope Francis *Laudato 'si* 145
postcolonialism 3–4, 13, 174, 181, 189, 195 n.7, 195–6 n.8
Potkay, Adam 41–2
Preminger, Alex 37
Preston, Claire 91–2, 109
Prickett, Stephen 115–16
Prideaux, Faye 90
prophecy/prophet 117–18. *See also* Bible, prophetic tradition
Pyne, Stephen J. 141, 152

Ramson, W. S. 151–2, 157
Rauscher, Judith 6
Reno, Seth 39, 69
Retallack, Joan 41
Reynolds, Henry 155
Richard of St. Victor 28
Rieger, Stefan 89
Rigby, Kate 38–9, 66, 78, 94, 115, 119, 127, 133, 138, 151, 158, 192
Rigby, T. H. 80–1
Roberts, Jonathan 127
Robin, Libby 122, 129
Romantic literature. *See also* British Romanticism; European Romanticism; German Romanticism; ecopoetics; wilderness
　and decolonization 4–5, 46, 51, 54, 66, 99, 103, 126–7, 149, 159, 189
　ecocritical reception 2–3, 13–16
Rose, Bird Deborah 3, 7, 73, 85, 127, 129, 176, 183, 197 n.19
Rousseau, Jean-Jacques 46
　Reveries of a Solitary Walker 41
Routley, Richard and Routley Val, *The Fight for the Forests: The Takeover of Australian Forests for Pines, Wood Chips, and Intensive Forestry* 170
Rue, C. 145

Sanchez-Bayo, F. 109–10
Sandilands, Catriona 90, 110
Saussure, Ferdinand de 86
Schama, Simon 59
Schelling, Friedrich Wilhelm Joseph 101–2, 119–20
　on aesthetic intuition 88
　Ideas for a Philosophy of Nature 32
　on nature's powers 39–40
　Naturphilosophie 57, 87
Schlegel, Friedrich 18, 31, 113, 116
　Athenäum 23–4, 83, 198 n.1
　Literary Notebooks 113
　'romantic poesy,' aphorism on 23–4, 84
　'symphilosophical' and 'sympoetic' collaboration 24, 83
Schleiermacher, Friedrich 31–5, 45, 116
　On Religion 31
　views on religious experience 31–4, 45
Schmidt, L. J. 139

Schmitz, Hermann 57, 60–2, 64, 71
Scott, Heidi C. M. 104
Seamon, D. 40
Sebeok, Thomas 86–7
Serres, Michel 67
Seward, Anna 'Colebrook Dale' 11–12
Shaftesbury, Lord 13, 56
   The Moralists, A Philosophical Rhapsody 13
Sharkie, Thomas 69
Shaviro, Steven 16, 42–4
Shaw, Roderick 162–3
Shelley, Mary 203 n.1
Shelley, Percy Bysshe 20, 43, 59, 160
   biblical traditions 113–15, 117–19, 122
   'Defence of Poetry' 113, 117, 191
   on law and the prophets 114–27
   'Mont Blanc' 15, 43
   Prometheus Unbound 118–19
   Queen Mab 59, 118–19
   sublime, concept of 15
   utopian vision 118–19
   'Vindication of Natural Diet' 101–2
Shumack, Samuel 156
Simpson, David E. 23
Skinner, Jonathan, *ecopoetics* 6
Snyder, Gary 41
socioecological transformations. *See also* Anthropocene; Capitalocene; Chthulucene; Plantationocene; Ploutocene; Symbiocene
   climatic impacts 66–7, 81, 114
   colonization 10, 19, 149, 165, 172
   contemplative practices 24, 142, 146
   Critical Theory 57
   decolonial praxis 81, 146, 191, 194
   ecological aesthetics 59, 82
   ecoprophetic vision 125, 127, 138–9, 142
   slavery 10, 18, 103–4, 118
speculative realism 16, 42
Spinoza, Baruch
   conatus 36
   Letters Concerning the Study of Theology 115
   natura naturata and *naturans* 32, 36
   Tractatus Theoligica-Politicus 115
Steiner, George 138
Stewart, Douglas 160, 173–4
Stoermer, Eugene F. 10–11
Sullivan, Sian 90

Symbiocene 11
Symons, M. 151
sympoiesis
   bees 93, 98, 105–10
   biosemiotic 87–9, 98, 163
   ecocultural practices 101
   environmental stewardship initiative 110–12 (*see also* 'Migration & Me')
   Haraway's deployment 83, 85, 89
   multispecies 88, 95, 111–12
   Schlegel's view 18, 83

Thomson, James 70
Thoreau, Henry David 2, 15–16, 138
   sublime, concept of 15–16
   Walden Pond 16, 104
Todd, Zoe 8
trans-corporeality 17, 54, 64
Tredinnick, Mark 60
Trethewey, Natasha 84
   'Carpenter Bee' 106–9

Uexküll, Jakob von, *Umwelt* theory 86–7
UN Climate Change Summit 2014 193
Ungenmerr-Baumann, Miriam Rose 175

Wainburranga, Paddy Fordham 179
Wallace-Crabbe, C. 161
Washington, Chris 99
Weil, Simone 85
wellbeing, socioecological dimensions 17, 46, 55, 79–82, 198 n.29
Wheeler, Wendy 86, 88
White, Kyle 8
Whitehead, Alfred North, on Goethe's philosophy of nature 43–4
'wilderness' 13–16, 20–1, 46, 136, 149, 151, 153–6, 176
Wilhelm, August 83, 198 n.1
Willis, Thomas 56
Wollstonecraft, Mary 117
Wordsworth, William 2
   contemplative practice 24–9, 35–6, 38–50
   ecological aesthetics 55–6
   ethics of things 41–5
   'Expostulation and Reply' 24–5, 27, 29, 36, 39, 120
   Lyrical Ballads with a Few Other Poems 5, 23–4, 29, 31, 35, 38–9, 45

Prelude, The 55, 118, 144, 150
sublime, concept of 16, 45, 66
'The Tables Turned: An Evening Scene on the Same Subject' 24, 36, 41, 45, 55
via positiva or *negativa* 49–51
Wright, Alexis 183–4
Wright, Judith 18–21, 147, 149–50, 157–8, 168, 189
   Alive 173–4
   as Aboriginal rights campaigner 135–6
   Cry for the Dead 136
   disillusionment, Romantic inheritance 127, 133, 137
   'Dust' 114, 128, 138–9
   as environmental campaigner 134–6
   as forerunner of 'ecological humanities' 133–4
   'Lament for Passenger Pigeons' 138
   'Summer' 138
   'Two Dreamtimes' 134–5, 174
   Two Fires Festival 136
Wyckhuys, K. A. G. 109–10

Yusoff, Kathryn 8, 12

Zajonc, Arthur 40
Zapf, Hubert 4

www.ingramcontent.com/pod-product-compliance
Lightning Source LLC
Chambersburg PA
CBHW052112010526
44111CB00036B/1960